Founder Editor
Clifford Leech 1958–71

General Editors
E. A. J. Honigmann, J. R. Mulryne, D. Bevington
and E. M. Waith

THE REVENGER'S TRAGEDY

THE
REVENGERS
TRAGÆDIE.

*As it hath beene sundry times Acted,
by the Kings Maiesties
Seruants.*

AT LONDON
Printed by G. E ɪ ᴅ, and are to be sold at his
house in Fleete-lane at the signe of the
Printers-Presse.
1607.

THE REVENGER'S TRAGEDY

CYRIL TOURNEUR

Edited by
R. A. Foakes

MANCHESTER
UNIVERSITY PRESS

© R. A. Foakes 1966

This edition first published by Methuen & Co. Ltd. 1966
First paperback edition 1975

Reprinted 1980, 1986, 1988, 1990 by
Manchester University Press
Oxford Road, Manchester M13 9PL, U.K.
Distributed exclusively in the U.S.A. and Canada by
St. Martin's Press, Inc.,
175 Fifth Avenue, New York, N.Y. 10010, U.S.A.

ISBN 0 7190 1612 6

Printed in Great Britain by BPCC Wheatons Ltd, Exeter

For

ALLARDYCE NICOLL

General Editors' Preface

The series known as the Revels Plays was conceived by Clifford Leech. The idea for the series emerged in his mind, as he explained in his preface to the first of the Revels Plays in 1958, from the success of the New Arden Shakespeare. The aim of the new group of texts was 'to apply to Shakespeare's predecessors, contemporaries and successors the methods that are now used in Shakespeare editing'. The plays chosen were to include well known works from the early Tudor period to about 1700, as well as others less familiar but of literary and theatrical merit: 'the plays included,' Leech wrote, 'should be such as to deserve and indeed demand performance.' We owe it to Clifford Leech that the idea became reality. He set the high standards of the series, ensuring that editors of individual volumes produced work of lasting merit, equally useful for teachers and students, theatre directors and actors. Clifford Leech remained General Editor until 1971, supervising the first seventeen volumes to be published.

The Revels Plays are now under the direction of four General Editors, E. A. J. Honigmann, J. R. Mulryne, David Bevington and E. M. Waith. The publishers, originally Methuen, are now Manchester University Press. Despite these changes, the format and essential character of the series will continue, and it is hoped that its editorial standards will be maintained. Except for some work in progress, the General Editors intend, in expanding the series, to concentrate for the immediate future on plays from the period 1558–1642, and may include a small number of non-dramatic works of interest to students of drama. Some slight changes have been forced by considerations of cost. For example, in editions from 1978, notes to the introduction are placed together at the end, not at the foot of the page. Collation and commentary notes will continue, however, to appear on the relevant pages.

The text of each Revels play, in accordance with established practice in the series, is edited afresh from the original text of best authority (in a few instances, texts), but spelling and punctuation are modernised and speech headings are silently made consistent. Elisions in the original are also silently regularised, except where metre would be affected by the change; since 1968 the '-ed' form is used for non-syllabic terminations in past tenses and past participles ('-'d' earlier), and '-èd' for syllabic ('-ed' earlier). The editor emends, as distinct from modernises, his original only in instances where error is patent, or at least very probable, and correction persuasive. Act divisions are given only if they appear in the original or if the structure of the play clearly points to them. Those act and scene divisions not found in the original are provided unobtrusively in small type and in square brackets. Square brackets are also used for any other additions to or changes in the stage directions of the original.

Revels Plays do not provide a variorum collation, but only those variants which require the critical attention of serious textual students. All departures of substance from 'copy-text' are listed, including any relineation and those changes in punctuation which involve to any degree a decision between alternative interpretations; but not such accidentals as turned letters, nor necessarily additions to stage directions whose editorial nature is already made clear by the use of brackets. Press corrections in the 'copy-text' are likewise included. Of later emendations of the text, only those are given which as alternative readings still deserve attention.

One of the hallmarks of the Revels Plays is the thoroughness of their annotations. Besides explaining the meaning of difficult words and passages, the editor provides comments on customs or usage, text or stage-business – indeed, on anything he judges pertinent and helpful. Each volume contains a Glossarial Index to the Commentary, in which particular attention is drawn to meanings for words not listed in *O.E.D.*

The Introduction to a Revels play assesses the authority of the 'copy-text' on which it is based, and discusses the editorial methods employed in dealing with it; the editor also considers his play's date and (where relevant) sources, together with its place in the work of the author and in the theatre of its time. Stage history is offered, and in the case of a play by an author not previously represented in the series a brief biography is given.

It is our hope that plays edited in this fashion will promote further scholarly and theatrical investigation of one of the richest periods in theatrical history.

E. A. J. HONIGMANN
J. R. MULRYNE
DAVID BEVINGTON
EUGENE M. WAITH

Contents

Preface

The Revenger's Tragedy has attracted a great deal of critical commentary in recent years, and many scholars have exhausted themselves, and some of their readers, in controversy about its authorship, yet there is no modern edition which deals adequately with the lineation of the text, or which provides more than the barest annotation to explain its many complexities of language. The two scholarly editions of the last forty years, those by Allardyce Nicoll and Henri Fluchère, both preserve the haphazard lineation and stage-directions of the Quarto. In the present edition I have tried to work out afresh the lineation of the text, to provide adequate stage-directions, and to supply a helpful, but not overbearing, commentary on the text.

In the Introduction, I have sought to provide a useful summary of the developing critical arguments about the play, and to take these further by defining more closely its moral atmosphere, and its limitations as a tragedy. The other sections of the Introduction attempt to do justice to the problems involved in discussing authorship, text, and sources, without giving any of these matters undue prominence.

I am grateful to many people who have answered queries or supplied information, and especially to Mr John Crow, Mr Peter Murray, Professor G. R. Price, Mr L. G. Salingar, and Mr W. S. Wright. My work towards the edition was aided by a grant from the Research Fund of Durham University. My greatest debt is to the General Editor, who has contributed much to the detailed shaping of the edition, and has saved me from many errors and inconsistencies.

Canterbury, 1964   R. A. FOAKES

Abbreviations and Usages

1. *Some editions of* The Revenger's Tragedy *are cited frequently, especially in the collation, and these are given abbreviated references, as follows:*

Collins
: *The Plays and Poems of Cyril Tourneur*, edited by J. Churton Collins, 2 vols. (1878), Vol. I.

Dodsley 1
: *A Select Collection of Old English Plays*, published by Robert Dodsley, 12 vols. (1744), Vol. IV.

Dodsley 2
: Second edition, by I. Reed, 12 vols. (1780), Vol. IV.

Dodsley 3
: New edition, by J. P. Collier, 12 vols. (1825-7), Vol. IV.

Dodsley 4
: Fourth edition, by W. C. Hazlitt, 15 vols. (1874-6), Vol. X.

Fluchère
: *La Tragédie du Vengeur*, edited by Henri Fluchère (Collection Bilingue des Classiques Etrangers, 1958).

Harrier
: *Jacobean Drama*, edited by Richard C. Harrier, 2 vols. (1963), Vol. II.

Harrison
: *The Revenger's Tragedy*, edited by G. B. Harrison (The Temple Dramatists, 1934).

Nicoll
: *The Works of Cyril Tourneur*, edited by Allardyce Nicoll (n.d. [1930]).

Oliphant
: *Shakespeare and his Fellow Dramatists*, edited by E. H. C. Oliphant, 2 vols. (1929), Vol. I.

Scott
: *The Ancient British Drama*, edited by Sir Walter Scott, 3 vols. (1810), Vol. II.

Symonds
: *The Best Plays of Webster and Tourneur*, edited by J. A. Symonds (Mermaid Series, 1888).

Thorndike   *Webster and Tourneur,* edited by A. H. Thorn-
                   dike (Masterpieces of the English Drama,
                   1912).

2. *General abbreviations*

Abbott   E. A. Abbott, *A Shakespearian Grammar*
                   (1869).

Chambers, *E.S.*   E. K. Chambers, *The Elizabethan Stage,* 4 vols.
                   (1923).

E.L.H.   *Journal of English Literary History.*

Grosart   Thomas Dekker, *Non-Dramatic Works,* edited
                   by A. B. Grosart, 5 vols. (1884–6).

J.E.G.P.   *Journal of English and Germanic Philology.*

Kökeritz   Helge Kökeritz, *Shakespeare's Pronunciation*
                   (1953).

Middleton, *Works* *The Works of Thomas Middleton,* edited by
                   A. H. Bullen, 8 vols. (1885).

M.L.N.   *Modern Language Notes.*

M.L.Q.   *Modern Language Quarterly.*

M.L.R.   *Modern Language Review.*

M.S.R.   Malone Society Reprints.

Nashe, *Works*   *The Works of Thomas Nashe,* edited by R. B.
                   McKerrow, 5 vols. (1904–10).

O.E.D.   *A New English Dictionary,* edited by J. A.
                   Murray, H. Bradley, W. A. Craigie, and C. T.
                   Onions. 13 vols (1888–1933).

P.M.L.A.   *Publications of the Modern Language Associa-
                   tion of America.*

P.Q.   *Philological Quarterly.*

R.E.S.   *Review of English Studies.*

Sh. England   *Shakespeare's England,* 2 vols. (1916).

Sugden   E. H. Sugden, *A Topographical Dictionary to
                   the Works of Shakespeare and his Fellow-
                   Dramatists* (1925).

Tilley   M. P. Tilley, *A Dictionary of Proverbs in England in the Sixteenth and Seventeenth Centuries* (1950).

T.L.S.   *Times Literary Supplement.*

3. *Usages in this edition*

The text is printed from that of the Quarto, with the spelling modernized, except for one or two forms such as 'corse' (corpse) at I. ii. 36, which are kept either because of the demands of rhyme or because there is no real modern equivalent. The punctuation of the original is also modernized, but I have tried to retain the phrasing of the Quarto text as far as possible, and to preserve something of its light pointing. This pointing may, however, reflect the habits of a compositor or scribe as overlaying those of the author. Some lines in the Quarto are marked off as *sententiae* or gnomic phrases, either by being placed in inverted commas or by being italicized; in this edition all such lines are printed in italics. The stage-directions of the Quarto are reprinted with the abbreviations expanded; they are supplemented by additional material and by new directions, which are placed in square brackets. The first four acts are marked in the Quarto, and although the heading for Act v was omitted, all the act-headings are printed within the text in this edition, that for Act v being placed within square brackets. The Quarto has no division into scenes, which are here noted in brackets at the left of the page.

Quotations in the introduction, commentary, and appendices from sixteenth- and seventeenth-century authors are modernized, as are proper names and titles of books. Quotations from plays by Shakespeare, and line-references to these, are taken from the one-volume 'Tudor' edition by Peter Alexander (1951). The titles of Shakespeare's plays are abbreviated in accordance with the usage of C. T. Onions in his *A Shakespeare Glossary* (1911; revised 1946).

In the collation I have noted some unusual spellings found in the Quarto. The word 'so' before an editor's name indicates an arrangement of text first adopted by that editor, and not a substantive change from the text of the Quarto.

Introduction

I. *THE REVENGER'S TRAGEDY*

Modern interest in the play has grown out of the enthusiasm of some nineteenth-century critics for it. Their praise of it, notably for the 'fiery jet' of its 'molten verse', and its sustained intensity,[1] was rarely separated from an attempt to characterize the author, who was often imagined as possessing the qualities of his own chief characters. Practically nothing was known about Cyril Tourneur, then generally accepted as the author, and criticism tended to merge into evocations of a mysterious, bitter, horror-loving man, whose work was an expression of a disgust with life:

> Sin and misery, lust and cynicism, fixed their fangs deep in his splendid genius, marring and defacing his art, poisoning and paralysing the artist.[2]

This kind of response to the play was summed up memorably in T. S. Eliot's essay, originally printed in 1930 as a review of Allardyce Nicoll's edition of Tourneur. Here he wrote:

> The cynicism, the loathing and disgust of humanity expressed consummately in *The Revenger's Tragedy*, are immature in the respect that they exceed the object. Their objective equivalents are characters practising the grossest vices; characters which seem merely to be spectres projected from the poet's inner world of nightmare, some horror beyond words. So the play is a document on humanity chiefly because it is a document on one human being, Tourneur;

---

[1] The quoted phrases are from A. C. Swinburne's essay on Tourneur in *The Age of Shakespeare* (1887; edition cited 1908), p. 277; see also the introduction by J. Churton Collins to his edition (1878).

[2] Collins, I. lvi. The vivid response of Henri Fluchère to the play is in the tradition of such writing, although in his emphasis on Vindice's 'degré peu commun de morbidité mentale et de masochisme sexuel', he is careful to avoid identifying the character with the author of the play; see the introduction to his edition (1958), especially pp. 63–5.

its motive is truly the death motive, for it is the loathing and horror of life itself.[1]

The intensity of the play, its poetic force, and its lack of characters conceived realistically, or with the common virtues and affections, helped to lend authority to such a view, in which the consciousness of the author in his 'unique and horrible vision of life'[2] swallows up the consciousness of the characters he created; and the play has often been regarded as an expression of cynicism or disillusion, a revelation of a world-order of evil power, an image of horror.[3]

Accounts of the play confining it within the author's 'inner world of nightmare' inevitably provoked a reaction from those who could not explain its power and impact in such terms. Among the earliest and most influential of the essays marking a new response was that by L. G. Salingar, in which he pointed to its conventional nature as strongly influenced by the morality play, and to its satirical force as a comment on the commercialization of the gentry in the reign of James I; his attempt was to show that the author was not disgusted with life itself, but that

> The 'object' of his disgust is not the behaviour of his characters, singly or together, so much as the process they represent, the disintegration of a whole social order. It is this theme, particularized and brought to life by the verse, that shapes the pattern of the play; and it is developed with the coherence, the precise articulation, of a dramatist assured that his symbols are significant for his audience as much as for himself.[4]

Much of the more recent commentary on the play has accepted Salingar's main point, that it cannot be understood unless it is seen as a coherent work by an artist writing in a tradition, and reacting to his age and society. There have been three notable lines of approach; one has been concerned to show the play's relationship to

---

[1] *Selected Essays* (1951 edn), pp. 189–90.   [2] *Ibid.*, p. 189.

[3] As by U. M. Ellis-Fermor, *Jacobean Drama* (1936), pp. 153 ff.; Muriel Bradbrook, *Themes and Conventions of Elizabethan Tragedy* (1935), pp. 167, 172; Schoenbaum, *Middleton's Tragedies* (1955), pp. 30–5; Robert Ornstein, 'The Ethical Design of *The Revenger's Tragedy*', *E.L.H.*, xxi (1954), 82.

[4] '*The Revenger's Tragedy* and the Morality Tradition', *Scrutiny*, vi (1937–8), 402–3; Salingar was much influenced by L. C. Knights, *Drama and Society in the Age of Jonson* (1937).

other works of the period, and its cultural background; another has sought to determine exactly what positive standards are implied in the play, and where these are located; and the third has been concerned with the language, especially poetic imagery and puns.

The degree to which *The Revenger's Tragedy* belongs within the developing pattern of revenge tragedy has been pretty fully explored. The play's indebtedness to Marston for a number of its characteristics has been noted; Vindice owes something to the malcontent, to Marston's Malevole, as the son of one who died of 'discontent, the nobleman's consumption' (I. i. 127); there are more general analogies in the frequent use of disguise, the device of a masque to bring about the catastrophe, suggested probably by *Antonio's Revenge*, the elaborations of intrigue, the portents, and appeals to heaven, in the self-conscious allusions by characters to the rhetorical effectiveness of their speech in phrases like 'You flow well', and in the sudden reversals. One name for a character, Dondolo, was borrowed from *The Fawn*, and it seems evident that the author of *The Revenger's Tragedy* was familiar with several of Marston's plays; indeed, it has seemed to one critic at least that 'in mental and moral quality and bent, Tourneur and Marston are more alike than any two other dramatists of the Elizabethan age'.[1] The play has analogies also with Henry Chettle's *Hoffman*, though this in turn appears to owe to Marston some of the features it has in common with *The Revenger's Tragedy*. There is perhaps some connection between the opening scenes, where Hoffman speaks over the dead body of his father, and Vindice over the skull of his dead mistress; and the torture of Otho in Hoffman's 'cave' resembles the torture of the Duke by Vindice in an 'unsunned lodge' (III. v. 18). In both plays an assignation is made for lovers to meet in seclusion in a chapel 'porch' (*Hoffman*, l. 704) or a 'lodge', where one of the lovers is murdered; but this idea can be traced back to the famous killing of Horatio in the arbour in *The Spanish Tragedy* by Thomas Kyd.[2] *The Revenger's Tragedy* also owes much to *Ham-*

---

[1] E. E. Stoll, *John Webster* (1905), p. 106.

[2] F. T. Bowers, *Elizabethan Revenge Tragedy* (1940), pp. 132 ff., notes some of these connections, and finds other links between *The Revenger's Tragedy* and, firstly, *Soliman and Perseda* (in the idea of the poisoned lips, instrument of the Duke's death), secondly, Marlowe's *Jew of Malta* (in the

let, perhaps most notably in the arraignment of their mother, Gratiana, by Vindice and Hippolito (IV. iv), which has a general analogy and some verbal parallels with Hamlet's denunciation of Gertrude; both mothers suppose they are to be murdered, pretend ignorance of any misdeed on their own part, then admit their guilt and resolve to live a better life.[1]

If the play is indebted to the formulae and devices of contemporary tragedies of revenge, it can also be connected with older traditions and forms. So, for instance, it has links with the Morality plays, which survived in various more or less sophisticated forms into the late sixteenth century. The characters in Morality plays are personified abstractions, or type-figures, whose primary function lies less in their individuality than in their representative nature within an allegorical scheme.[2] The names of many of the characters in the play are equivalents in Italian of the type-names of the Moralities: for example, Lussurioso representing lust, Ambitioso representing ambition, Castiza representing chastity;[3] and the play has been seen as organized by 'the idea of the *exemplum horrendum*', displaying vice in order to denounce it.[4] The play's emphasis on death has also suggested analogies with one particular kind of moral emblem, perhaps one of the most powerful and pervasive of all in medieval and renaissance art, the Dance of Death, a 'timeless parable of man's wickedness and God's punishment for sin'.[5] Vin-

---

stabbing of a body thought to be alive). For the connections with *Hoffman*, see Harold Jenkins, 'Cyril Tourneur', *R.E.S.*, XVII (1941).

[1] See D. J. McGinn, *Shakespeare's Influence on the Drama of his Age Studied in Hamlet* (1938), pp. 102, 114.

[2] The first to stress this connection with Morality plays seems to have been L. G. Salingar, whose interpretation of *The Revenger's Tragedy* is based on the view that 'Tourneur could not have written successful drama except by means of their example' ('*The Revenger's Tragedy* and the Morality Tradition', p. 414).

[3] I discussed this in an essay 'On the Authorship of *The Revenger's Tragedy*', *M.L.R.*, XLVIII (1953), 134–5; see also below, p. 2.

[4] Inga-Stina Ewbank (Ekeblad), 'An Approach to Tourneur's Imagery', *M.L.R.*, LIV (1959), 489.

[5] Samuel Schoenbaum, '*The Revenger's Tragedy:* Jacobean Dance of Death', *M.L.Q.*, XV (1954), 201–7; the quotation is from p. 207; see also his *Middleton's Tragedies*, pp. 27–32. The general relations of the Dance of Death theme to Elizabethan tragedy were first examined by Theodore Spencer in his *Death and Elizabethan Tragedy* (1936).

dice can be seen as both participant in and moralizer on the 'pleasure of the palace' (II. i. 199), which turns the thoughts of the characters from that death which may strike at any moment, and the action culminates in dances in which masquers strike and are struck down at the height of their revels. It is in line with this that Vindice's most famous speeches, especially his apostrophes to the skull of his dead mistress, have been linked with other forms that have a medieval origin, the complaint and homily; for as these commented on man's nature as subject to corruption, or inveighed against his wickedness and neglect of God, so Vindice's words may be seen as intended to 'fright the sinner' (III. v. 92).[1]

The recognition that the play has roots not merely in the genre of revenge tragedy, but in the Morality play, and in other modes of moralistic art like the complaint, has no doubt helped to foster discussion of its attitudes, and the attempt to identify what positive values it upholds. For in so far as Vindice moralizes, attacking folly, vice, and the world's vanities, and in so far as the play's ironies suggest a satirical attitude to the corrupt characters in it, in something of Ben Jonson's vein,[2] *The Revenger's Tragedy* reflects something much more positive than that 'loathing and horror of life itself' found in it by T. S. Eliot. One of the first to reject this view of the play, L. G. Salingar, gave full weight to the alert and controlled attack on corruption in it, but yet felt that the downfall of Vindice, the main agent of this attack, undermines the establishment of positive values, that 'there is nothing in the play, in its scheme of moral and social values, to compensate for Vindice's fall'.[3] Perhaps he felt too strongly the extent to which Vindice himself shares the corruption of the court, and is a party to the degeneration of a 'society of vicious humours which draws to itself a disguised avenger-satirist who hastens its inner tendency to dis-

---

[1] See John Peter, *Complaint and Satire in Early English Literature* (1956), pp. 256–64.

[2] The links with Ben Jonson's plays, especially *Volpone* (1605), in which the characters have type-names like those of *The Revenger's Tragedy*, were emphasized first by Salingar, *loc. cit.*, pp. 415–16. For a treatment of the play in terms of satire, see Alvin Kernan, *The Cankered Muse* (1959).

[3] *Loc. cit.*, p. 417.

solution'.[1] The same problem has been noticed by others in rather different terms. So, for instance, Robert Ornstein found it difficult to reconcile Vindice the moralist with Vindice the satirist treating life as a joke, and thought the play makes life seem futile, since the only three kinds of beings shown in it are 'the completely abandoned, the hypocritical, and the rare, impecunious, malcontented good'; it appeared to him that 'Within his society Vindice represents the only possible moral order, one that is perverse in nature and eminently corruptible because it has no higher purpose than the accomplishment of revenge'.[2] It hardly seems satisfactory to claim after this that an incorruptible moral order finally reveals itself when depravity is punished in Vindice too, but possibly both these critics were too much inclined to identify Vindice with the author, and neither allowed much weight to Castiza and the intrigue, amounting almost to a sub-plot, involving her and Gratiana.

Others have found a greater objectivity in the play, and, stressing its 'moralistic-satiric structure',[3] and the orthodoxy of the views represented in it,[4] have claimed that 'Tourneur is negative in so far as he makes a clean sweep of these vanities, silks, money, camphire and the rest, but his implications are obviously positive, and orthodox'.[5] A Christian audience would recognize these implications, especially as reflected in the scenes involving Castiza and Gratiana, and would find the final reversal from evil to good in Antonio's sentencing of Vindice and Hippolito an event growing 'naturally from the whole ethos of the play'.[6] It has been argued, too, that the manifold ironies of the action and language are used as a means of objectifying its moral attitudes, and, in particular,

---

[1] Salingar, 'Tourneur and the Tragedy of Revenge', in *The Age of Shakespeare*, edited by Boris Ford (1955), pp. 334–54. The quotation is from p. 344.

[2] 'The Ethical Design of *The Revenger's Tragedy*', *E.L.H.*, xxi (1954), 86.

[3] Ewbank, *loc. cit.*, p. 497.

[4] Ornstein thought the play expressed the 'intense, but only temporary, disillusion of a very orthodox and very conservative mind' (*loc. cit.*, p. 82), but others, like John Peter, have agreed with him in finding the orthodoxy, while seeing no reason to talk of disillusion.

[5] Peter, *Complaint and Satire*, p. 264.

[6] *Ibid.*, p. 267; see also Irving Ribner, *Jacobean Tragedy* (1962), who argues that 'Tourneur's answer to social corruption and human debasement is in a return to a primitive Christianity' (p. 72).

keep us aware of the moral basis of Vindice's actions, until the final irony is laid bare, and 'that moral balance on whose behalf he has sinned so earnestly is restored only with his death'.[1]

In a recent attempt to settle the argument about the moral character of the play, T. B. Tomlinson refines on Salingar's point that it fails to establish new positive values (a failure exemplified in the downfall of Vindice) by developing the view that the moral positives of the play are not secure. *The Revenger's Tragedy*, he says, shows too much fascination with evil, and

> must stand as a play that clings to limited moral maxims simply because it is triumphing only precariously over incipient decadence. Its real strength lies in the consistency with which it achieves, not a moral superiority over lust and corruption, but an ability to realise and place its own attraction to them.[2]

On this view a measure of objectivity is obtained only with difficulty, as the author 'sacrifices' a Vindice in whom he is involved, and who, in turn, is 'dangerously involved in what he condemns';[3] and it is further assumed, firstly, that the play is a comment on the 'imminent corruption' of Tourneur's Elizabethan world, which fails to establish new values; and, secondly, that the trite verse and strict metre in which many of the moral statements of the play are expressed show merely 'dullness and dutiful obeisance to morality'.[4] It seems to me that no settlement of the critical argument is reached here, and that perhaps a fuller understanding of the play may be gained by reconciling the strong points of both sides, and rejecting the weak. It is important, when stressing the conventional and orthodox nature of the play's moral attitudes, to note also the frequent triteness of expression, and the degree to which Vindice, so often a moral commentator on the actions of others, is fascinated by and involved in what he condemns. It is equally important,

---

[1] Peter Lisca, '*The Revenger's Tragedy*: A Study in Irony', *P.Q.*, XXXVIII (1959), 242–51; the quotation is from p. 251.

[2] 'The Morality of Revenge: Tourneur's Critics', *Essays in Criticism*, X (1960), 134–47; the quotation is from p. 143. Unfortunately, Tomlinson had evidently not seen the important essays by Robert Ornstein and Peter Lisca cited above.

[3] *Ibid.*, p. 144.

[4] *Ibid.*, pp. 136, 142; see also Salingar, '*The Revenger's Tragedy* and the Morality Tradition', pp. 406, 418.

when stressing the precarious balance of the play, to determine how far it is a comment on Jacobean life, and exactly what function the commonplace moral maxims have in its structure and meaning.

Although some sense of 'disillusionment' inevitable to the 'conscious passing of a long period of high civilization'[1] may, after the death of Queen Elizabeth in 1603, have sharpened the satire of Jacobean writers, it is not necessary to see specific reference to attitudes current at this time, or a close analogy with *Volpone*, in Vindice's images of a corrupt court life. The splendours of court-life had for long provided a ready example of worldly vanity, and Vindice's speeches have much in common with, for example, the Satires of Donne:

> Thou which since yesterday hast been
> Almost about the whole world, hast thou seen,
> O Sun, in all thy journey, Vanity,
> Such as swells the bladder of our court? I
> Think he which made your waxen garden, and
> Transported it from Italy to stand
> With us, at London, flouts our Presence, for
> Just such gay painted things, which no sap, nor
> Taste have in them, ours are; And natural
> Some of the stocks are, their fruits, bastard all.
> 'Tis ten a clock and past; All whom the Mews,
> Balloon, tennis, diet, or the stews,
> Had all the morning held, now the second
> Time made ready, that day, in flocks, are found
> In the Presence, and I, (God pardon me.)
> As fresh, and sweet their apparels be, as be
> The fields they sold to buy them; For a King
> Those hose are, cry the flatterers; And bring
> Them next week to the Theatre to sell.
>
> (*Satire IV*, 165–83)

> Who'd sit at home in a neglected room,
> Dealing her short-liv'd beauty to the pictures,
> That are as useless as old men, when those
> Poorer in face and fortune than herself
> Walk with a hundred acres on their backs,
> Fair meadows cut into green foreparts—O,
> It was the greatest blessing ever happen'd to women,

---

[1] U. M. Ellis-Fermor, *Jacobean Drama* (1936), p. 10.

> When farmers' sons agreed, and met again,
> To wash their hands and come up gentlemen;
> The commonwealth has flourish'd ever since.
> Lands that were mete by the rod, that labour's spar'd,
> Tailors ride down, and measure 'em by the yard;
> Fair trees, those comely foretops of the field,
> Are cut to maintain head-tires—much untold,
> All thrives but chastity, she lies a-cold.
>
> (II. i. 213–227)

The similarity of tone is evident; but Donne was writing in 1594, or perhaps in 1597, directly about the 'high civilization' of the court of Queen Elizabeth as full of vanity and lust, and the practice of selling lands in order to buy bravery for display at court was then commonplace enough. Vindice, on the other hand, speaks of an imaginary Italian court; his attack is general, not specific, and although his utterance is individual, his subject-matter has a long ancestry.

The commonplace moral generalizations which occur throughout the play have, I think, a relevance here. The originality and splendour of its poetry have often been remarked upon, yet the finest flights are liable to end in a thumping *sententia* or a sequence of generalizing couplets. Much of the play is in rhyme: in the first act, for instance, there are 59 couplets or triplets, so that more than 120 of its 500 lines are rhyming, and these, too, give a sense of neat summing-up to much that is said. The effect is further reinforced by the way in which one character often approves the comment of another with phrases like 'y' have truly spoke him' (I. i. 91), or 'I'faith, 'tis true too' (I. ii. 135), or 'In troth it is, too' (I. iii. 71), 'Why, well said' (I. iii. 160), and 'You deal with truth, my lord' (I. iv. 24). All the characters tend in this way to pay a ready, if frequently specious, lip-service to morality. Occasionally one of them does so with a certain self-awareness, as the Duke, startled in bed by Lussurioso, his son, presenting a drawn sword at him, is shaken also, for the moment, into a recognition of the state of his soul; he cries out, 'I have great sins' (II. iii. 11), and a little later pardons his son with the thought,

> It well becomes that judge to nod at crimes,
> That does commit greater himself and lives;

> I may forgive a disobedient error,
> That expect pardon for adultery,
> And in my old days am a youth in lust!
> Many a beauty have I turn'd to poison
> In the denial, covetous of all:
> Age hot is like a monster to be seen;
> My hairs are white, and yet my sins are green.
>
> (II. iii. 124–32)

This reflection has no effect on his actions, of course, and the next we hear of him is that he has hired Vindice 'by price to greet him with a lady' (III. v. 12). Such moments of self-awareness are indeed rare among the characters of the court, and are matched at the opposite pole, as it were, by an occasional burst of honesty about a real desire, as the Duke, expecting a new mistress, cries,

> Give me that sin that's rob'd in holiness.
>
> (III. v. 141)

Only the bastard, Spurio, who openly parades his viciousness, and has the courage and attractiveness of a character with convictions, believes in his own evil. The others screen what they do as a rule behind a façade of commonplaces; and Vindice, who is always self-conscious, and thinks he knows himself, satirically exploits the distances between what the courtiers profess and what they do.[1] In this way he becomes often the agent of our awareness. So in I. iii, when he is taken into the service of Lussurioso, he pretends to have been a bawd, and falls in with his master's thoughts, claiming an intimate acquaintance with all forms of lust; he ends,

> Any kin now, next to the rim o' th' sister,
> Is man's meat in these days; and in the morning,
> When they are up and dress'd, and their mask on,
> Who can perceive this ?—save that eternal eye,
> That sees through flesh and all. Well, if anything
> Be damn'd, it will be twelve o'clock at night,
> That twelve will never 'scape;
> It is the Judas of the hours, wherein
> Honest salvation is betray'd to sin.
>
> (I. iii. 62–70)

[1] Indeed, he frequently sees himself as the director of his own play, the contriver of the action, and his inclusive 'our', 'we', or 'here' embraces us as readers or audience in such passages as those at I. iii. 15, II. ii. 149, and III. v. 80–3.

Lussurioso accepts the moral implications, and caps Vindice's couplet with one of his own,

> It is our blood to err, though hell gap'd loud;
> Ladies know Lucifer fell, yet still are proud;

but salvation and sin, hell and Lucifer, mean nothing to him really, as he goes on at once to hire Vindice to seduce his own sister for him.

At the same time, characters tend to fall into rhyme when summing up their serious desires and attitudes, as later in this scene, upon Vindice's recommending marriage to him, Lussurioso retorts,

> I am one of that number can defend
> Marriage is good; yet rather keep a friend.
> Give me my bed by stealth, there's true delight;
> What breeds a loathing in 't, but night by night?
> (I. iii. 103–6)

Vindice responds in an aside, 'A very fine religion!', and here, indeed, is a belief genuinely held by Lussurioso, as his actions show. The neatness of a couplet, or support of some proverb expanded into a sententious utterance, may lend an appearance of justification to vicious inclinations, and an aura of time-honoured wisdom to the nasty satisfactions of revenge. The Duke, Lussurioso, and all the courtiers are experts in the manipulation of such utterances, which punctuate their speech in lines like these:

> I know this, which I never learn'd in schools:
> The world's divided into knaves and fools.
> (II. ii. 4–5)

> this true reason gathers:
> None can possess that dispossess their fathers.
> (II. iii. 85–6)

> The falling of one head lifts up another.
> (III. i. 28)

> True, such a bitter sweetness fate hath given,
> Best side to us is the worst side to heaven.
> (III. v. 209–10)

> Slaves are but nails, to drive out one another.
> (IV. i. 68)

The test of such saws, which come thick and fast through much of the dialogue, is their relation to what the characters do. They continually expose the half-relevance of their sayings, or an ironical application to themselves, or a contradiction between words and deeds, in their actions; as, for instance, Lussurioso, speaker of the first couplet cited above, shows himself to be both knave and fool. If the application of the remark, its hollowness or irony, are not at once evident, Vindice is often by to comment in an aside, or to moralize, as he does, for instance, on Gratiana's promise to work Castiza to Lussurioso's lust:

> *Grat.* . . . I will sway mine own;
> Women with women can work best alone. *Exit.*
> *Vind.* Indeed, I'll tell him so.
> O, more uncivil, more unnatural
> Than those base-titled creatures that look downward!
> Why does not Heaven turn black, or with a frown
> Undo the world ?—why does not earth start up,
> And strike the sins that tread upon 't ?
>
> (II. i. 249–56)

One character, Castiza, does live by the maxims and sententious couplets she utters:

> If maidens would, men's words could have no power;
> A virgin honour is a crystal tower,
> Which, being weak, is guarded with good spirits;
> Until she basely yields, no ill inherits.
>
> (IV. iv. 151–4)

She has one or two bursts of splendid disdain, and can put on lascivious accents in order to test her mother in IV. iv, but these lines nevertheless demarcate her character. They do not reflect, however, merely a 'dutiful obeisance to morality',[1] but simply indicate the extent to which she, like most of the other characters, is an emblematic figure, a moral example. She is too good to be true to life, as the others are too bad to be true to life. She has vitality because she can act the part of a wanton, and is not a mere innocent. The Duke, the Duchess, and their sons also have vitality in their pursuit of their vicious ends, but they are distanced into comic-grotesque figures through the constant return of the dialogue to proverbs,

[1] Tomlinson, *loc. cit.*, p. 142.

maxims, and couplets. Castiza cannot be a tragic figure because she is incorruptible; the courtiers cannot be tragic because they have no real insight into what they are doing, and are not redeemable. Their moral capacity is limited to sententious phrases that prove to be grossly inadequate, grotesquely misapplied, or relevant with an irony they do not comprehend; and their attitudes shift constantly as they are remade for each situation. The generalizing force of their comments suggests a concern for morality and truth which is quite unrelated to their behaviour, and is never tested against principles. It is a mechanical sententiousness, comically horrible.

Vindice's rôle is a special one, for he is given a degree of self-knowledge, and an insight into the true nature of life at the Duke's court. It seems to me, however, a mistake to think of him as representing moral order,[1] as somehow becoming involved with corruption, and having to be sacrificed by the author in order to 'hold the forces and the sense of corruption back at something like a decently poised, ironic distancing'.[2] It is true that his initial love for the dead Gloriana changes into a cynicism about women in general (see, for example, II. ii. 136 ff.), and his justified anger at her death is transformed gradually into a delight in the skilful plotting of vengeance (see, for example, II. iii. 3 ff.), but this is not a change from good to evil in him.[3] From the opening lines of the play he is shown as contaminated by what he condemns, as able to criticize the faults of others, but unable to detect his own evil. His self-knowledge extends at one point, in his famous speeches in III. v, to a sense of his own foolishness in 'doting' on the beauty of his dead mistress, on

---

[1] Ornstein, *loc. cit.*, p. 86.

[2] Tomlinson, *loc. cit.*, p. 144. Since this introduction was written, Mr Tomlinson has amplified his views on the play in his book, *A Study of Elizabethan and Jacobean Tragedy* (1964); he reprints in this the essay I have quoted from, and adds a further chapter stressing especially the vitality and precision of the poetry in *The Revenger's Tragedy*. He sees the play as a 'very great achievement', as the highpoint of tragic writing between the work of Shakespeare and the tragedies of Middleton.

[3] As it is claimed to be by Peter B. Murray in his dissertation, about to be published as a book, *A Study of Cyril Tourneur*, University of Pennsylvania (1962). He sees Vindice as transformed from a good to an evil figure through Lussurioso's gold; Vindice's origin, he says, is in 'the world of chastity' (pp. 253-4). This may perhaps be granted, but Vindice has left that world a long way behind before the play begins.

what must decay into the unsightliness of the skull he holds in his hands; but much of the power of this scene lies precisely in the poignancy of Vindice's approach in it to what he never attains, a full sense of the moral nature of his own actions. In his opening soliloquy, also spoken over the skull of his mistress, he values her not for her virtue, but for her beauty, and measures this by the degree to which it tempted men to sin:

> 'twas a face
> So far beyond the artificial shine
> Of any woman's bought complexion,
> That the uprightest man (if such there be
> That sin but seven times a day) broke custom,
> And made up eight with looking after her.
> O, she was able to ha' made a usurer's son
> Melt all his patrimony in a kiss,
> And what his father fifty years told,
> To have consum'd, and yet his suit been cold.
>
> (I. i. 20–9)

He can only appreciate her beauty according to the way it provoked lust in men, and clearly his own standards are corrupt, as his one thought is for vengeance, not justice.

It is of a piece with the rest of his behaviour that he should be an ambiguous figure here. On the one hand he is a witty and devastatingly ironic commentator on, and manipulator of, the affairs of the Duke, Lussurioso, and the whole court, seeing himself as Heaven's instrument or representative:

> Why does not Heaven turn black, or with a frown
> Undo the world? (II. i. 254–5)

> Forgive me, Heaven, to call my mother wicked!
> (II. ii. 96)

> Nay, Heaven is just, scorns are the hire of scorns.
> (III. v. 187)

> Is there no thunder left, or is 't kept up
> In stock for heavier vengeance? There it goes!
> (IV. ii. 198–9)

At the same time, Vindice is unconscious of the irony of such remarks as the last two passages cited in relation to himself: Heaven's justice, and Heaven's vengeance, await him as well as the Duke and

Lussurioso. Moreover, this is not a kind of irony that emerges only late in the play; from the first, with his excitement in beauty as the instrument of lust, and his devotion to vengeance, he is marked out as hero-villain. Hippolito comes to him with a message from Lussurioso, who seeks a villain to serve him:

> such a blood,
> A man that were for evil only good—
> To give you the true word, some base-coin'd pander.
>
> (I. i. 79–81)

Vindice takes on the office:

> I'll put on that knave for once,
> And be a right man then, a man o' th' time;
> For to be honest is not to be i' th' world.
>
> (I. i. 93–5)

In taking on the rôle, Vindice finds it fits him only too well, and he becomes a man good for evil, and lays aside honesty indeed, though again he is unconscious of the ironical application of the lines. He at once demonstrates his abilities as a pander, a 'man o' th' time', by seducing his own mother, comforting himself when the task looks to be nearly accomplished, with the thought,

> I fear me she's unmother'd, yet I'll venture.
> *That woman is all male, whom none can enter*;
>
> (II. i. 111–12)

and he encourages Gratiana with another maxim,

> this age fears no man;
> *'Tis no shame to be bad, because 'tis common.*
>
> (II. i. 117–18)

For Vindice, too, is addicted to the couplet and the maxim, and finds them to suit all occasions; the first of these is spoken as an aside to the audience, as if from his heart, and yet it flatly contradicts not only his respect for Castiza's rejection of him earlier in the scene, but also his confident couplet about Gratiana,

> I will lay
> Hard siege unto my mother, though I know
> A siren's tongue could not bewitch her so.
>
> (II. i. 51–3)

In other words, Vindice may be able to recognize and comment on the iniquity of others, but he has no principles himself, only a desire to preserve the honour of his family, and a yearning for vengeance. His superiority over the other characters is a moral one only to a limited extent; it is much more a matter of intelligence, so that it is the play's final and appropriate irony that an excessive pride in his cleverness,

> Strike one strain more, and then we crown our wit,
> (v. i. 170)

brings his downfall. He shares with other characters the habit of confident assertion of, or appeal to, maxims, of which he, too, is often the ironic butt.

The triteness or conventionality of many of these quasi-proverbial or rhymed sayings is, then, an aspect of their dramatic function. They are casual and often specious tags relied upon for the criticism of others or the justification of the self in any course of action. Their operation is for the moment, and their meaning frequently recoils at another time devastatingly on the head of the speaker, as when, for instance, Vindice cannot see the application to himself of his aphorism as he murders the Duke:

> When the bad bleeds, then is the tragedy good.
> (III. v. 205)

Such remarks are gestures towards morality arising out of the occasion, not out of principle, and their triteness, their inadequacy as moral comment, their insufficiency in any perspective outside the immediate one, are what makes them the vehicle of much of the play's deepest irony. This may suggest a way out of the difficulty over the location of the play's positive values. Clearly these do not reside in Vindice, who is the victim as well as the agent of many of the ironies of action and dialogue. He is not 'sacrificed', but belongs from the start to the vicious world of the court he criticizes, and his thoughts hardly escape from it. *The Revenger's Tragedy* is confined in setting to the 'accursed palace' of an anonymous Duke; the names of the characters, and two casual references in the dialogue, indicate that the country is Italy; but this is an Italianate, not an Italian play, offering no sense of locality, but relying rather on a conventional, popular image of Italy as 'the Academy of Man-slaughter, the sporting place of murder, the apothecary shop of poison for all nations'.[1] The confinement is also one of atmosphere, due largely to the narrow range of reference in the language,[2] and a consideration of this may help towards a better understanding of the peculiar nature of the play.

The confinement in range of its poetic imagery is evident if its subjects are compared with those common in Shakespeare's plays.[3] Three of the largest groups in Shakespeare's plays are almost entirely lacking in *The Revenger's Tragedy*. There are few images relating to animals, and only two or three that rise above the commonplace, notably

> Does the silk-worm expend her yellow labours
> For thee ?   (III. v. 72–3)

Classical imagery is limited to two references, one to the phoenix (I. iii. 97), the other to the sirens (II. i. 53); and there is hardly any imagery drawn from the natural world. The greater part of the play's imagery relates to three topics. The first, and most important, is the idea of bodily action, or, by means of personification, the bringing into activity of what is inert. Often the force of these images lies in verbs that give a sense of restless activity, emotional and moral as well as physical, to the unfolding of the drama; the following are some characteristic examples:

> Thrown ink upon the forehead of our state.
> (I. ii. 4)

> impartial doom
> Shall take fast hold of his unclean attempt.
> (I. ii. 41–2)

---

[1] Thomas Nashe, *Piers Peniless* (1592), in *Works*, ed. R. B. McKerrow, I. 186. See also S. Schoenbaum, *Middleton's Tragedies*, pp. 6–9.

[2] This has been noted, as by Schoenbaum, *Middleton's Tragedies*, p. 28; and Inga-Stina Ewbank (Ekeblad) has shown how the poetic imagery, especially the personifications and images of activity, function in the play's structure to make an 'exemplum horrendum', in her 'An Approach to Tourneur's Imagery', *M.L.R.*, LIV (1959), 489–98.

[3] I have used for comparison the tables given in Chart V at the end of Caroline Spurgeon's *Shakespeare's Imagery and what it tells us* (1935).

Death too soon steals out of a lawyer's lip.

(I. ii. 69)

This our age swims within him.   (I. iii. 24)

A sight that strikes man out of me. (I. iv. 5)

We have grief too, that yet walks without tongue.

(I. iv. 22)

The personifications seem almost to swell the cast, for as the characters with morality names, like Lussurioso, are developed from living personifications of Luxury and so forth, so the dialogue brings metaphorically alive other figures, like 'Vengeance' (I. i. 39), 'that bald Madam, Opportunity' (I. i. 55), 'Occasion' (I. i. 99), 'Impudence . . . mistress of mistresses' (I. iii. 5-6), 'fool-bashfulness, That maid in the old time' (I. iii. 12-13), 'Grace the bawd' (I. iii. 16), and many more. The characters are, of course, more than personifications, as having feelings and intelligence, being able to plan and intrigue, so that their behaviour is not fully predictable; but there is a potent relationship between the way they are conceived and the range of personifications in the dialogue. This is realized most fully in that central personification, the skull of Gloriana, Vindice's dead mistress, for this becomes an emblem of the corruption underlying wealth and beauty, of the deaths all the characters are moving towards, as they attempt to destroy one another, of death the leveller of all ambitions, and death the mocker of man's enterprise.

The other main groups of images relate to money and to food, which are the vehicles by means of which the lusts and appetites of the characters are stimulated and valued. Gloriana was able

> to ha' made a usurer's son
> Melt all his patrimony in a kiss;
>
> (I. i. 26-7)

a pander is 'base-coin'd' (I. i. 81), women are changed 'Into white money' (II. ii. 28), and Castiza talks of putting herself 'to common usury' (IV. iv. 103). Vindice is paid to tempt his sister, with the promise that

> thou shouldst swell in money, and be able
> To make lame beggars crouch to thee.
>
> (I. iii. 77-8)

He, in turn, holds out the prospect of wealth to Gratiana:

> I would raise my state upon her breast,
> And call her eyes my tenants; I would count
> My yearly maintenance upon her cheeks,
> Take coach upon her lip, and all her parts
> Should keep men after men, and I would ride
> In pleasure upon pleasure;
>
> (II. i. 95–100)

and Gratiana, in turn, tries to tempt Castiza with the cry, 'Fortunes flow to you' (II. i. 171). The Duchess seduces Spurio after sending him letters 'swell'd up with jewels', and gold is the universal measure of things,

> In this luxurious day wherein we breathe.
>
> (I. iii. 110)

The idea of food and drink assists in suggesting a general atmosphere of luxury, and a concern only with satisfying bodily appetites. It also provides a vivid means of conveying by analogy the sensual excesses of sexual gratification:

> I was begot
> After some gluttonous dinner, some stirring dish
> Was my first father. (I. ii. 180–2)

> Any kin now, next to the rim o' th' sister,
> Is man's meat in these days. (I. iii. 62–3)

> a woman; why, 'tis held now no dainty dish.
>
> (I. iii. 154)

> with long lust to eat
> Into my wearing. (I. iv. 32–3)

> And fed the ravenous vulture of his lust.
>
> (I. iv. 44)

There are images of other kinds than these, among the most striking some drawing on legal terms and concepts,[1] but none that recur so frequently;[2] and the heavy concentration of imagery in this narrow range both intensifies and confines the play's atmosphere. This is

[1] See, for example, I. i. 39–40, IV. ii. 64–5, and notes.

[2] A rough count (figures inevitably vary according to the compiler's idea of an 'image') shows 69 personifications, 108 images of activity, some bordering on personification, 44 related to wealth or money, and 31 related to food and drink.

marked further by the repetitiveness of a certain range of vocabulary. Some of this relates to the imagery, as there are over 250 references to the body and its members, notably to the eye (24), hand (20), lip (12), tongue (31), face (9), forehead (10), and heart (30). Some verbs of action or movement also recur, like fall (19), ride (11), strike (11), cut (9), and enter (8); there are other recurrent words relating to riches and poverty, and to food, drink, and revels. Such iterative words spread the connotations of the imagery and increase its force; image and word interact, and work together in establishing the pace and mood of the play.

More common still, however, are repeated words that do not directly reinforce image patterns, but themselves work to establish certain aspects of the play. For it is true, I think, that

> Recurrent schemes of imagery are not, however, the main device on which Tourneur depends. The principal effect of the sustained assault against the triumphant corruption of the life represented by the Duke's court comes from setting its keenest desires and its most cherished values either explicitly or, for the most part, by inference, against the contrasting measure of temperance and virtue, and its vanities against the oblivion of death.[1]

The 'sustained assault' spoken of here is carried on largely by the repetition of words connected with sex in its vicious aspects, with sin and crime, and, opposing these, words relating to judgment in this world and the next, to virtue, chastity, and punishment. The vocabulary used to describe what goes on at the Duke's court implies a moral condemnation in words like lust or lustful (20 occurrences), adultery (8), rape (6), incest (5), and the sense of immorality is further extended in the repeated use of words like bawd, harlot, cuckold, strumpet, whore, pander, slut, and drab. Countering these are terms like chastity (13) and virgin or virginity (9). The opposition suggested here is registered more strongly in the play's more explicitly moral vocabulary, in the constant reference to vice and virtue, and especially to the idea of sin (30); even the old Duke and Spurio are conscious of it,

> Had not that kiss a taste of sin, 'twere sweet.
> (III. v. 207)

[1] Moody Prior, *The Language of Tragedy* (1947), pp. 140–1.

The sense of deceit and wickedness appears in the words false (16), treason (13), base (14), wrong (11), shame (17), villain and villainous (41), fault (9), knave (15)—a heavy repetitiveness stressing the corruption of the palace. The opposition to this comes less in words like good (26) or virtue (6) than in the many allusions to justice, human and divine, and the suggestions of words like doom (9), curse (12), damn and damnation (17), hell (18), devil (15), and heaven (31). Heaven is spoken of usually as an active agency, able to interfere in human affairs, as equivalent to God, who, indeed, seems to take a part in the action by providing thunder (IV. ii. 199) and a 'blazing star' (V. iii. 15): and Vindice likes to see himself as Heaven's instrument, sent

> To blast this villainous dukedom, vex'd with sin.
> (v. ii. 6)

This vocabulary above all creates the tone of moral urgency in the play, which is marked also in the unusually strong emphasis on death and its associations. The words die, dead, and death occur 86 times; kill, murder, poison, and bleed a further 80 times.[1] The emphasis on death is again gathered into the skull of Gloriana, the central image of the play, suggesting the end to which the corrupted energies of the court characters lead, and standing as a reminder of a judgment to come in the next world:

> sure, 'twould fright the sinner,
> And make him a good coward.
> (III. v. 92–3)

If the play's poetic imagery contributes largely to the predominant atmosphere of the court, with its emphasis on luxury and sensual excitements, and its constant business in intrigue and counter-plot, the stress on groups of repeated words goes a long way to providing an implicit moral framework, an array of positive and negative standards in the light of which all actions are presented. The rôle of Vindice perhaps becomes clearer when con-

[1] Some indication of the weight of these words may be gathered by a comparison with *Hamlet*, the tragedy of Shakespeare's in which words relating to death are most prominent: in this the occurrences of die, death, kill, and murder total 77, in *The Revenger's Tragedy* 129. *Hamlet* is a very much longer play.

sidered in relation to the general nature of the imagery and vocabulary. From the beginning he is bound up in what he condemns, attracted by the luxury and lust he despises, and concerned for vengeance, not justice.[1] From the vantage-point of his position as master-plotter, cleverer than the rest, he can fulminate against the viciousness and folly of the court, and yet he belongs to it, just as Lussurioso and the Duke do. He is not the representative of morality, but rather the one character, apart from his more shadowy brother and assistant Hippolito, who bridges good and evil, combining in himself something of both. The other characters are black or white, wholly evil or good, except for Gratiana, who is converted from her viciousness, and made to repent at the point of a dagger. Vindice is a powerful character partly because he contains the possibility of a sane balance in a world that is grotesque to the point of madness. He says himself, at the end of his most famous speech contemplating the way in which everyone devotes his energies to the pursuit of a 'bewitching minute', the momentary gratification of lust:

> Surely we are all mad people, and they
> Whom we think are, are not; we mistake those:
> 'Tis we are mad in sense, they but in clothes.
> (III. v. 80–2)

Appropriately he includes himself in his appraisal of his society,[2] for he too is caught up in this madness of plotting assignations and revenges; while others lie, cheat, perjure themselves, and spend,

---

[1] This is not to imply that Vindice remains a static figure; he changes during the course of the action, as noted above, p. xxxi. Indeed, while remaining an intelligent and caustic commentator on others, he fails to notice how he becomes progressively more like those he condemns. Peter Murray discusses this in *A Study of Cyril Tourneur*, pp. 212–13, noting particularly how this similarity is enforced in the parallelism between IV. iii, where Supervacuo, rapier in hand, and Ambitioso follow their mother off stage intending to punish her by murder for her adultery, and IV. iv, where Vindice and Hippolito, daggers in hand, bring out their mother, threatening her in the same way. He goes on to point out that at the end of the play, when Vindice and Hippolito take part in the masque, they become 'virtually indistinguishable' from Supervacuo and Ambitioso, all of them dancing in similar costumes in the same masque of murder.

[2] His remark embraces the audience, that is, us too, and for comment on this see p. xxviii and n.

to refine a pleasure which is mere corruption, Vindice becomes absorbed in the pleasure of his own cunning intrigues, meriting the comment of Hippolito,

> Brother, I do applaud thy constant vengeance,
> The quaintness of thy malice, above thought.
>
> (III. v. 108–9)

The concentration of the language upon a few repeated themes, the violent activity suggested by the imagery, the confinement of the imaginative atmosphere within a luxurious and corrupt court, all help to define and control the action within a restricted range of reference that excludes not only politics, in the sense in which Shakespeare's tragic figures are involved in the fate of a nation, but some of the most important attributes of human beings, such as their capacity for love and for compassion. The narrowness of focus is deliberate, as the strength of the play depends upon these features, lying as it does in the intensity, speed, and excitement of poetry that exploits to the full an action consisting, as has often been noted, of a series of ironies and ironic reversals. By these means the world of the play is made to seem grotesque, perverted, even mad, and we do not ask for naturalistic character or behaviour. The characters are emblematic figures with morality names, not rounded personages, and the structure of the play allows not only the use of a dramatic symbol like the skull, but devices that in the context of a different mode of drama might seem absurd, like the thunder that is heard at Vindice's demand in IV. ii, and sounds again in v. iii to greet the death of Lussurioso.

From the opening line, where Vindice, holding the skull of his dead mistress in his hand, sees the Duke passing over the stage as the personification of 'grey-hair'd adultery', the action unfolds lust upon lust, death upon death, in a way that cannot be accepted on any ordinary level of credibility. The.Duke has poisoned Gloriana for refusing to submit to his lust, and his retinue contains his bastard son Spurio, the result of another adulterous affair; the Duke's eldest son, Lussurioso, as lustful as his father, seeks to seduce Castiza; the Duchess, fit mate for the Duke, seduces the Duke's own bastard Spurio; and her own younger son is tried, by a law-court supervised by the Duke, for the rape of Antonio's wife.

The Duke's sons, anxious for their father to die, plot against one another for the succession to the dukedom; his Duchess in her adultery with Spurio plots against the Duke, and all in their private intrigues conflict with one another, as each is concerned for himself alone. The Duke, himself guilty of adultery, murder, and worse,

> Many a beauty have I turn'd to poison
> In the denial,   (II. iii. 129–30)

has to judge and sentence the Duchess's youngest son for rape. Lussurioso hires Vindice to work his own sister and mother to satisfy his lust, yet protests a fine indignation over the adultery of the Duchess with Spurio. Lussurioso's step-brothers try to ensure that he is executed for his apparent attempt on his father's life, but their scheme goes astray, and their own younger brother is executed instead. Plots continually recoil on the inventors' heads, culminating in three especially fine twists in the action: one is the death of the Duke, who, expecting the pleasure of a new mistress, is poisoned by kissing the skull of an old one poisoned by him, and in his death-throes is forced to witness the embraces of his wife with his bastard son; the second is the double masque in Act V, where the dance in which the Duchess's sons plan to kill the new Duke Lussurioso is forestalled by Vindice with his own masque, and the Duchess's sons, finding Lussurioso dead, quarrel over the succession, and strike down one another; the third is the moment when Vindice, carried away by his success, and delighted with his own craft, confesses that he and Hippolito contrived the old Duke's death:

> 'twas somewhat witty carried, though we say it. 'Twas
> we two murdered him.   (V. iii. 97–8)

The first of these marks the climax of the sexual intrigues in the play, the second brings the climax of the plots of ambition and revenge, and the third crowns all with the self-exposure of Vindice, the clever manipulator of others. The little sub-plot concerning Castiza and Gratiana is consistent with the rest in its neatly contrived ironies and reversals: Gratiana succumbs to Vindice's temptations, and tries to seduce her chaste daughter, only to find that

Castiza's stubbornness apparently melts at the moment when she repents. So Gratiana and Castiza temporarily change rôles, and both play the parts of temptress and of virtuous woman scorning temptation before they are reconciled in honour. There is in all this a sense of the grotesque, the dancing of madmen in contrived and macabre gyrations, and Vindice, for much of the play a commentator on the action, points this up, sharpening our awareness of the contrivance of plot and counter-plot, and of the grotesque nature of the action, by his macabre jesting, and his sense of artistry. He adopts two different disguises, and plays in them the parts of bawd and malcontent, besides other rôles adopted for the moment, as at his entry with the skull in III. v:

> Madam, his grace will not be absent long.
> Secret ? Ne'er doubt us, madam; 'twill be worth
> Three velvet gowns to your ladyship. . .
>
> (III. v. 43–5)

From his cry 'be merry' in his opening speech, he clowns, exercises his wit in tricks and quibbles, and guides our appreciation of what happens by his satiric remarks, or mocking comments. Of course, he is involved too in his devices, to the point of rejoicing in his skill and losing sight of their horror and evil, as when he delights in the means he has found of killing the Duke,

> O sweet, delectable, rare, happy, ravishing!
>
> (III. v. 1)

But the fact that he sees the action as macabre, even funny at times, and the characters as mad, helps to control our view of the play's events, and ensure that we do not mistake what we see for an illusion of reality.

An image of reality it is and, within the limitations which are also its strength, the play has great power. Its concentration and intensity never relax, as Marston's does in *Antonio's Revenge* and Chettle's in *Hoffman*, into jesting with the audience and self-parody. Vindice's savage humour, and his passionate devotion to revenge, are kept in balance, so that those comments of his that include the audience in their general embrace suggest for a moment that for some of us life is, and for all could be, no more than such an interlude of lust, treachery, revenge, and murder as this play shows:

> Any kin now, next to the rim o' th' sister,
> Is man's meat in these days.   (I. iii. 62–3)

> If every trick were told that's dealt by night,
> There are few here that would not blush outright.
>   (II. ii. 148–9)

>   see, ladies, with false forms
> You deceive men, but cannot deceive worms.
>   (III. v. 97–8)

As a whole, the play does not touch us so nearly, but demands to be taken emblematically as a type of what a human society might be at its worst, all its bestial passions released, and all its store of proverbial wisdom and moral tags made ineffective because unrelated to deeply felt principles. It is a tragic satire, taking us, as it were, to the edge of a precipice, and showing us, in the gulf beyond, a limiting possibility of society, where social, legal, and moral restraints have crumbled away; and we recoil in horror, perhaps stung into a sharper awareness of our deficiencies.[1] The play provides a fearful lesson or moral image, but its limitations as tragedy are apparent by comparison with, say, *Hamlet*, a play with which it has some analogies; in *The Revenger's Tragedy* there is no sense of tragic waste, of potentialities for good denied fulfilment, and no sense of a restorative or compensating element at work. The characters are mostly types, capable of making moral glosses on their actions, but lacking self-realization; they are aspects of a monstrous fantasy, which powerfully succeeds in making its point, but the price paid for its success is a loss of the common touch, of that representative quality which allows the finest tragedy to speak for every man.

Its lack of the common touch may account for the neglect of the play by professional actors since the seventeenth century. The development of a strong literary interest in it during the present century has probably helped to draw the attention of amateur producers to the theatrical qualities of the action and dialogue, and

---

[1] In this respect it has strong analogies with Ben Jonson's *Volpone*, as L. G. Salingar suggested; see above, p. xxiii.

The Revenger's Tragedy has been staged a number of times, usually by groups associated with colleges or universities. Two of these productions have been noticed in *The Times*: the first, a joint effort by the Marlowe Society and the Cambridge Amateur Dramatic Club in 1937, appeared pallid to the reviewer, and the second, at the Toynbee Hall Theatre in 1954, seemed to him to expose the plot as ludicrous, but on each occasion the reviewer was much impressed by the play's mastery of dramatic language.[1] There is nothing to suggest that either of these productions was very good, and the first provoked the comment, 'Jacobean savagery falls on the ear like an oath from the lips of a mild-mannered curate'. No doubt it is difficult for not very experienced actors to cope with the bitter and savage quality of much of the dialogue, to shed a drawing-room mildness and accept a convention of violence, but at least the attempt to do this, and to bring out the ironic humour of the play, was made in the recent production by Corpus Dramatic Society, Oxford, in May 1964. The director of this, Roger Nicholls, felt afterwards that the play, as 'black comedy', had been theatrically most effective. There have also been college productions of the play in the United States, the most recent which has come to my notice being that at Jonathan Edwards College, Yale University, in March 1964. The play is being staged by a professional company, under the direction of Brian Shelton, at the Pitlochry Festival, Scotland, in the summer of 1965.

2. CYRIL TOURNEUR AND THOMAS MIDDLETON

The Revenger's Tragedy, published anonymously in 1607 or 1608, has usually been assigned to one of two authors, Cyril Tourneur and Thomas Middleton. The careers of these men are described in other volumes in this series,[2] and the brief outline given here of what is known about them is intended to serve as preface to a more detailed consideration of the text of the play and the problem of authorship.

---

[1] *The Times*, 9 March 1937 and 19 February 1954.
[2] In Tourneur's *The Atheist's Tragedy*, edited Irving Ribner (1964), pp. xx–xxiii, and in Middleton's *The Changeling*, edited N. W. Bawcutt (1958), pp. xviii–xxi.

Little is known of Cyril Tourneur's life. He spent some time abroad, saw action as a soldier in the Netherlands, and served, or was patronized by, Sir Francis Vere and the important Cecil family; among his writings are an elegy on the death of Vere (1609), and a character of Robert Cecil, Earl of Salisbury, who died in 1612.[1] Few other works by Tourneur survive in print, and he was perhaps never a fully professional writer. However, he seems for a period of some years to have had a close connection with the stage. His name was first linked with *The Revenger's Tragedy* in the middle of the seventeenth century, but his *The Atheist's Tragedy* was printed in 1611, a lost play of his called *The Nobleman* was acted by the King's Men in 1612, and Robert Daborne gave him an act of another play now lost to write in 1613.[2] In this period, Tourneur also wrote an elegy on the death of Prince Henry (1612), which was published in 1613 together with elegies by two other dramatists, Thomas Heywood and John Webster.

Tourneur's connection with the stage seems, then, to have been a relatively short one, extending perhaps over six or seven years of occasional writing, although it is very possible that more plays by him have not survived. As it is, only one play acknowledged to be by him remains, *The Atheist's Tragedy*. His hand has been detected in *The Honest Man's Fortune*, a play written about 1613 by several authors,[3] and some have argued that he wrote *The Second Maiden's Tragedy* of about 1611, which survives in a manuscript, and is indebted for features of its plot to *The Revenger's Tragedy*;[4] but in neither case is the evidence more than conjectural, and in neither case has it been widely accepted. It is difficult to argue from one play about an author's stylistic habits or other characteristics, which may have changed rapidly; but the conscious literary artist of *The Atheist's Tragedy*, imitating Shakespeare, and remembering George Chapman's plays about Bussy D'Ambois, could be the same

---

[1] The fullest account of the evidence concerning Tourneur's life and career is given by Allardyce Nicoll, in the Introduction to his edition of the *Works* (1930).

[2] See Chambers, *E.S.*, III. 500, and W. W. Greg, *Henslowe Papers* (1907), p. 72.

[3] See the edition by J. Gerritsen (Groningen, 1952), pp. lxxxix–xci.

[4] See Samuel Schoenbaum, *Middleton's Tragedies* (1955), pp. 186–8.

man as the author of *The Revenger's Tragedy*, which also borrows from Shakespeare, and has links with plays by John Marston.

Thomas Middleton was born in 1580, was entered at Oxford University in 1598, and by 1601 was consorting with players in London. He wrote or collaborated in a few plays for the Admiral's Men, as Philip Henslowe's *Diary* testifies,[1] but his main work in the early part of his career as a dramatist was for the companies of boy actors, and he wrote a number of comedies for them between 1602 and 1607 or so. After this period he continued to write comedies and tragi-comedies for various adult companies, including the King's Men. Late in his career he turned to tragedy, and produced his best-known plays, *The Changeling* (1622, written in collaboration with William Rowley) and *Women Beware Women* (?1623). Middleton was also engaged in his later years on writing for masques, and for Lord Mayor's pageants, and in 1620 he became chronologer to the City of London, with the task of recording memorable events. He died in 1627, after a long career as a dramatist, and a large number of plays by him survive.

Thus, after his early work, mainly collaborative, for the Admiral's Men, Middleton turned to the composition of sophisticated city comedies for the children's companies, and his interest in tragicomedy, and then in tragedy, seems to have developed later, when he was writing for adult companies. However, critics have claimed to recognize his hand in a number of anonymous plays, among them those also associated with the hand of Tourneur, and including *The Revenger's Tragedy*. He has one immediate link with this play: it was entered in the Stationers' Register together with one of his comedies, *A Trick to Catch the Old One*, and the plays were printed at about the same time by the same printer. Middleton left a substantial body of writings, affording evidence of his habits of style, and other peculiarities of usage, many of which have been found in the text of *The Revenger's Tragedy*. Either Tourneur or Middleton could have written the play, and the evidence concerning their respective claims to be the author is considered fully below in the section on 'Authorship'.

[1] See *Henslowe's Diary*, edited R. A. Foakes and R. T. Rickert (1961), pp. 201–17; all but one of the entries belong to 1602, the other to 1604.

3. AUTHORSHIP

The Quarto does not name an author, and the play was not assigned to Cyril Tourneur until the middle of the seventeenth century. When two rather obscure Elizabethan plays were reprinted in 1656 and 1661, the publishers included by way of advertisement lists of titles, as one of them, Francis Kirkman, claimed, of 'all the Plays that were ever yet printed'; among them *The Revenger's Tragedy* was named.[1] The attributions in these lists cannot be relied on; for example, in Archer's list of 1656, Middleton's *A Trick to Catch the Old One*, printed by George Eld at roughly the same time as *The Revenger's Tragedy*, was assigned to Shakespeare. Nevertheless, it is odd that this play should be attributed to an author as obscure as Tourneur, unless the similarity between the title and that of *The Atheist's Tragedy* was sufficient to suggest an identity of authorship.[2] The attribution to Tourneur began to be challenged late in the nineteenth century, and after one or two attempts to bring Marston or Webster[3] in as outsiders, a sort of official opposition party representing the claims of Thomas Middleton as the author became established in the present century.

If there is little external evidence for Tourneur's authorship, none at all has been found for Middleton's. Indeed, some evidence which gives no positive information about the author yet goes against Middleton: the title-page of *The Revenger's Tragedy* states that it was acted by the King's Men, a company of adult players, while all eight plays by Middleton printed between 1602 and 1608

[1] The first list was added by Edward Archer to a reprint of *The Old Law*, and the second by Francis Kirkman to a reprint of *Tom Tyler and his Wife*. In Archer's list, *The Revenger's Tragedy* is ascribed to 'Tourneur', and *A Trick to Catch the Old One* to Shakespeare; Kirkman, who claimed to have given great care to preparing his list, assigned the former to 'Cyrill Tourneur', the latter, correctly, to Middleton; see W. W. Greg, *A Bibliography of the English Printed Drama to the Restoration*, III (1957), pp. 1338 ff.

[2] These points were made by S. Schoenbaum, *Middleton's Tragedies*, pp. 157–8, and by Marco Mincoff, *The Authorship of The Revenger's Tragedy* (Sofia, 1939), p. 6.

[3] Possibly the earliest ascription of the play was to Webster, for 'John W' is scrawled on the margin of B2ᵛ in the British Museum copy of the Quarto catalogued as C.34.e.11. The handwriting appears to belong to the early 17th century.

were performed by one or both of the companies of boy actors, for whom Middleton seems to have written as long as they were active.[1] All of the plays from this period known to be by Middleton are comedies. However, he claimed, in defending a law-suit brought against him by Robert Keysar, that he had handed to the plaintiff, in payment of a bond, a tragedy called 'The Viper and her Brood'. It has been asserted that this was another name for *The Revenger's Tragedy*;[2] but Keysar was manager of the Children of the Revels, and what the affair seems to show is that if Middleton wrote a tragedy by 1608, as he says he did, he passed it to a company of boy actors, not to the King's Men.

For many years discussion about the play's authorship was concerned almost exclusively with two topics. One was the relation of *The Revenger's Tragedy* to *The Atheist's Tragedy*. Certain similarities of a general kind between the plays are apparent, in title, in their exploration of the theme of revenge,[3] in their 'moral atmosphere',[4] and it has been strongly argued that a maturing of thought and style can be traced from one play to the other.[5] There are also resemblances in the poetic imagery and the way it is used in both plays.[6] Supporters of the attribution of *The Revenger's Tragedy* to Middleton have stressed rather the differences between this and *The Atheist's Tragedy*, with its slower, more relaxed verse, its less impassioned utterance, its more discursive nature, and, as has sometimes been felt, its general inferiority as poetry. A different and more formal style could have been worked out by an author for the later play to suit its action, and it seems to me that differences of usage, often in quite small details such as colloquial contractions

<hr>

[1] See R. C. Bald, 'The Chronology of Middleton's Plays', *M.L.R.*, XXXII (1937), 33–43.

[2] See H. N. Hillebrand, 'Thomas Middleton's "The Viper's Brood"', *M.L.N.*, XLII (1927), 35–8, and W. D. Dunkel, 'The Authorship of *The Revenger's Tragedy*', *P.M.L.A.*, XLVI (1931), 781–5.

[3] See H. H. Adams, 'Cyril Tourneur on Revenge', *J.E.G.P.*, XLVIII (1949), 72–87.

[4] See M. H. Higgins, 'The Influence of Calvinistic Thought in Tourneur's *The Atheist's Tragedy*', *R.E.S.*, XIX (1943).

[5] In the excellent essay 'Cyril Tourneur' by Harold Jenkins, *R.E.S.*, XVII (1941).

[6] This is well argued by Inga-Stina Ewbank (Ekeblad), 'An Approach to Tourneur's Imagery', *M.L.R.*, LIV (1959), 489–98.

and habitual spellings, are more significant evidence against Tourneur's authorship of both plays.[1] It is true that the plays were
printed in different shops, by compositors with different habits,
and the copy for them supplied to the printer may not have been
in the author's hand; nevertheless, many of Tourneur's peculiarities of spelling can be traced in *The Atheist's Tragedy*, and few in
The Revenger's Tragedy.

All such considerations, however, are at best negative, and the
adherents to the Middleton party have properly paid far more attention to another matter, the links they could discover between
The Revenger's Tragedy and Middleton's known plays. These links
have also been found chiefly in details of usage, some spellings, the
recurrence of certain words, like the exclamation 'Push!', a variant,
or an individual spelling, of 'Pish!', and a number of parallel passages.[2] It has been argued, too, that in certain larger features, such
as the use of disguise in *The Revenger's Tragedy*, or the play's 'ironic
method', it has close similarities with Middleton's city comedies.[3]
It is necessary to be wary in weighing such 'evidence'. For parallel
passages may turn out to be commonplaces, traceable in slightly
varying forms in the works of many authors; words habitually used
by Middleton, and appearing in *The Revenger's Tragedy*, may, like
''Sfoot', be found just as often in the mouths of Marston's characters; and it may prove difficult to show that particular dramatic
techniques are not staple and freely available elements of the good
playwright's stock-in-trade in the period. Altogether, it seems to
me that the arguments for Middleton based on parallels between

---

[1] Several individual disparities have been separately noticed, like the
spellings 'hable' and 'habilitie', which are common in Tourneur's acknowledged works, but do not appear in *The Revenger's Tragedy* (see the letter
by B. Wagner in *T.L.S.*, 23 April 1931); these, and others, among them
some not previously noticed, are tabulated and discussed in Peter B.
Murray's essay 'The Authorship of *The Revenger's Tragedy*', *Papers of the
Bibliographical Society of America*, LVI (1962), 195–218.

[2] The evidence, as identified up to the year 1953, is collected and sifted
in S. Schoenbaum, *Middleton's Tragedies*, pp. 166–82; see also Murray,
loc. cit. It should be noted that there are spellings in *The Revenger's Tragedy*
that seem to be characteristic of Tourneur—a free use of 'y' for 'i', 'weare'
for 'were', 'ould' for 'old' in various words, and some others; see Allardyce
Nicoll, *Works*, pp. 36–7.

[3] See Schoenbaum, *op. cit.*, pp. 169, 171.

his plays and *The Revenger's Tragedy* are unconvincing, especially when it is borne in mind that the latter borrows from *Hamlet* and from plays by Marston, and may well borrow from Middleton too. After reading through the essays, often partisan and impassioned, that have been devoted to presenting arguments of the kind just described, one can only heave a sigh of relief, and agree with Samuel Schoenbaum's sensible comments:

> the external evidence does not sweep all before it, and the situation, as it stands, is that neither Middleton's nor Tourneur's advocates have been able to bring forward the kind of proof to which one party or the other must submit. Hence the seemingly endless exchanges of replies and counter-replies in our journals. Whatever his personal *feeling* about the attribution may be, the task of the historian is, as I see it, to record the fact of uncertainty.[1]

However, the argument does not rest there. For stronger support for the attribution of the play to Middleton has come from the bibliographical analysis of the Quarto recently undertaken by two investigators. One has shown that the punctuation of *The Revenger's Tragedy*, the rather casual stage-directions, and a number of spellings and contractions in the text correspond pretty well with Middleton's habits as revealed in the holograph manuscript of his play *A Game at Chess*, and in the printed text of *A Trick to Catch the Old One*, which was also printed in George Eld's house in 1608.[2] The other has studied 'certain pronouns, verb forms and colloquial contractions', and compiled tables of preferred linguistic forms and spellings in plays printed by Eld in 1607–8, and in *The Atheist's Tragedy*, printed in 1611 by Thomas Snodham. Again he was able

---

[1] 'Internal Evidence and the Attribution of Elizabethan Plays', *Bulletin of the New York Public Library*, LXV (1961), 122. In this essay, Schoenbaum, who had presented the case for Middleton's authorship of *The Revenger's Tragedy* in his book *Middleton's Tragedies* (1955), announced the revision of his views illustrated in the passage cited.

[2] George R. Price, 'The Authorship and the Bibliography of *The Revenger's Tragedy*', *The Library*, 5th series, XV (1960), 262–77. He also draws attention to the appearance of speech-headings consisting merely of numbers (1., 2., 3., and so on) for some minor characters; it certainly seems to have been Middleton's practice to identify unnamed characters in this way, but it is not uncommon in plays by other dramatists, and I have noted a number of examples, for example, in Marston's *The Dutch Courtezan*, signatures G1ᵛ–G2ᵛ, and in *The Two Noble Kinsmen*, E3–E3ᵛ.

to show that many of Middleton's preferred spellings and forms occur in *The Revenger's Tragedy*, whereas those found in *The Atheist's Tragedy* conform with the preferences shown in Tourneur's other acknowledged works.[1] In addition, he demonstrated that Eld's compositors tended to reproduce, though not consistently, spellings and contractions found in their copy; those in *The Revenger's Tragedy* show 'a good relation' with Middleton's 'average practice', and can be differentiated from the habits revealed in plays by Chapman, Marston, Barnabe Barnes, Dekker, and Webster that were also printed by Eld.[2] He believes that the positive correlation between the habits shown in *The Revenger's Tragedy* and those known to be Middleton's point to one of three conclusions, that the latter

> *wrote The Revenger's Tragedy*, that he *revised* it, or that he made a copy of it which was in the line of transmission of the text to the printer, in which he systematically altered the author's forms and imposed his own.[3]

This accumulation of evidence is strong, but not conclusive. There remain some discrepancies between the usages in Middleton's plays and those in *The Revenger's Tragedy*. In this play, for instance, the headings for Acts I, II, and IV vary the formula '*ACT.1.SCAE.1.*', the third act is marked '*ACT.3*', and the heading for Act V is omitted. Middleton, however, liked to write 'Incipit' at the beginning of an act, as in *A Trick to Catch the Old One*, and to close an act with such a formula as 'Finit Actus Secundus', as in *Michaelmas Term* (1607).[4] Some contracted forms, like 'o' th', ''tis', and ''t' (for 'it'), are found in greater abundance than is usual in Middleton's plays.[5] Some features of the printing of *The Revenger's Tragedy*, the long rules used for dashes, commas at the end of sentences where the reader expects a period, speeches continuously printed and not begun with a new line in the text, and a casual regard for the distinction between prose and verse, seem characteristic of the compositor or compositors who set up the text of this

---

[1] Peter B. Murray, 'The Authorship of *The Revenger's Tragedy*', *Papers of the Bibliographical Society of America*, LVI (1962), 195–218.

[2] *Ibid.*, p. 204.   [3] *Ibid.*, p. 207.

[4] This was noted by G. R. Price, *loc. cit.*, p. 264.

[5] See Murray, *loc. cit.*, Table V, p. 217.

play, *A Trick to Catch the Old One*, Webster and Dekker's *North-ward Hoe*, and Marston's *What You Will*, but not of other plays printed by Eld, and perhaps more study of the workings of his printing-house is needed. One thing is certain: the controversy over the authorship will continue as long as no convincing external proof is available. For all arguments based on similarities, parallel usages, or habits of writing necessarily leave a final uncertainty, a further question to be answered.

Two factors must be set in the balance against all the weight of the bibliographical evidence, which is necessarily of a detailed kind, mostly concerned with minutiae of linguistic usages. Firstly, many critics have had the conviction, which is one I share, that in its general temper, its sense of moral urgency, and its character as a revenge play, *The Revenger's Tragedy* has, as a whole, much in com-mon with the plays of Marston to which it is indebted, and with *The Atheist's Tragedy*, and differs from the comedies Middleton wrote in the first decade of the seventeenth century, and from the tragedies he wrote much later. Secondly, *The Revenger's Tragedy* was acted by the King's Men,[1] at a time when Middleton is not known to have had any connection with them, and when he was, indeed, a principal author for their rivals, the Children's companies. Since the evidence is inconclusive, the traditional attribution to Tourneur is retained on the title-page of this edition of the play.

Yet in the end it is necessary simply to 'record the fact of un-certainty, which in this case is the only certainty';[2] and then it is wise to consider, with Allardyce Nicoll, the virtues of anonymity. In his recent reconsideration of the arguments about the play, he wrote:

> *The Revenger's Tragedy* stands as an achievement in its own right, and I would suggest that we may come to understand it best, not by contrasting and comparing it only with *The Atheist's Tragedy* or with Middleton's works, but by focusing attention upon its

[1] Inga-Stina Ewbank (Ekeblad) has drawn attention to the use of a blaz-ing star as a stage effect in v. iii, and points out that the Globe Theatre, at which the King's Men played, was noted for this particular effect; see her 'A Note on "The Revenger's Tragedy"', *Notes and Queries*, cc(1955), 98–9.

[2] Schoenbaum, 'Internal Evidence and the Attribution of Elizabethan Plays', p. 122.

position in the larger contexts of dramatic and theatrical history. We shall be fully justified in pursuing the authorship problem still further, just as we are justified in exploring the lives of all the play-wrights of the time, so long as, in doing so, we keep our minds open to the consideration of other approaches—especially that which would appreciate the plays themselves in their dramatic and thea-trical relationships, without thought of the particular dramatists responsible.[1]

4. THE TEXT

On 7 October 1607, George Eld, the printer, entered as his copy in the Stationers' Register two plays, one *The Revenger's Tragedy*, the other *A Trick to Catch the Old One*. Both were published with-out ascription to an author, and were printed apparently on the same stock of paper and in the same fount of type. Some copies of *The Revenger's Tragedy* are dated 1607 on the title-page, but this was corrected during the printing to 1608; all known copies of *A Trick to Catch the Old One* are dated 1608. A second issue of this play, also dated 1608, has a different title-page, naming the author as 'T.M.', presumably Thomas Middleton, and claiming not mere-ly that it had been acted 'both at Paules and the Blackfryers', but that it had been honoured with a performance at court 'on New yeares night last'. This is generally taken to signify 1 January 1609, when the Children of Blackfriars are known to have played at court; and in the Old Style of dating, still in common use, the year began on 25 March, so that the date 1608 could include the first quarter of 1609. However, the appearance of the quartos suggests that *The Revenger's Tragedy* and Middleton's play were printed in close sequence.[2] The title-page of the former reads:

> THE REVENGERS TRAGÆDIE. *As it hath beene sundry times Acted, by the Kings Maiesties Seruants.* [Pair of ornaments] AT LONDON Printed by G. ELD, and are to be sold at his house in Fleete-lane at the signe of the Printers-Presse. 1607. [Variant date 1608]

[1] 'The Revenger's Tragedy and the Virtue of Anonymity', *Essays on Shakespeare and Elizabethan Drama in Honor of Hardin Craig* (1962), pp. 309–16; the quotation is from pp. 315–16.

[2] This is an inference, and it has not been proved: see George R. Price, 'The Authorship and the Bibliography of *The Revenger's Tragedy*', *The Library*, 5th series, XV (1960), 271 and n.

The variant on the title-page is one of 29 significant variants that have been discovered scattered through six of the nine sheets on which the play was printed. Most of these variants (18) are concentrated in one sheet, H, which alone has corrections in both inner and outer formes.[1] Many of the corrections are of a minor nature, adjustments of spacing, alterations of punctuation, and the like; they seem to represent the casual emendations of a reader, perhaps the compositor, who glanced through the sheets as they came off the press, noticing a few errors, but missing many more, and making no check against the manuscript. However, the corrections in sheet H are of a different kind: many of these are substantive and important corrections of the text, such as could hardly have been made without reference to the manuscript of the play. The outer forme was corrected twice during the printing, so that one line appears in three states:

(1) Wee will make you blush and change to red:

(2) Wet will make you blush and change to red:

(3) Wet will make yron blush and change to red:

(IV. iv. 43)

This, and other variants affecting the text, are recorded in the collation to this edition;[2] there the first state of the Quarto is referred to as Q^a, the second as Q^b, and the third as Q^c.

[1] This information was gathered by George R. Price, *loc. cit.*, pp. 273–6, where the more important of the variants are listed. He has kindly supplied me with a complete list of the others he found. Many are of slight consequence, but some are substantive changes of great importance. I have checked through the copies of the play in the British Museum (C.34.e.11, dated 1607, which has nearly all variants in their second or final stage, and the one at IV. iv. 43 in its third state; C.12.f.8, dated 1608, which has the variants mostly in the first state; and 644.c.80, also dated 1608, which has many in the second state: both the second and third of these show the line at IV. iv. 43 in its first state) and also those in the library of Dulwich College (O.a.2, dated 1607, which is similar in its characteristics to the British Museum copy C.12.f.8, and O.a.5, lacking the title-page, which is similar to the British Museum copy 644.c.80). I have noticed what may be a further variant on signature H1ᵛ, a displacement of letters in the word 'now', corrected in the British Museum copy C.34.e.11, but this is of no significance.

[2] It should be noted that, of earlier editors, only Allardyce Nicoll was aware of the main variants (*Works*, pp. 305–6), and he incorporated the major corrected readings and variants of sheet H into his text or collation.

Me thought by'th Dukes sonne to kill that pandar,
Shall when he is knowne be thought to kill the Duke.

Vind. Neither, O thankes, it is substantiall
For that disguize being on him, which I wore,
It wil be thought I, which he calls the Pandar, did kil the Duke,
& fled away in his apparell, leauing him so disguiz'd, to auoide
swift pursuite·   *Hip.* Firmer, and firmer.

Vind. Nay doubt not tis in graine, I warrant it hold collour.
Hip. Lets about it.

Vind. But by the way too, now I thinke on't, brother,
Let's coniure that base diuill out of our Mother.   *Exeunt.*

Enter the Dutches arme in arme with the Bastard: he seemeth lasci-
uiously to her, after them, Enter Superuacuo, *running with a ra-*
pier, his Brother stops him.

Spuri. Madam, vnlock your selfe, snould it be seene,
Your arme would be suspected.

Duch. Who ist that dares suspect, or this, or these?
May not we deale our fauours where we please?

Spu. I'me confident, you may.   *Exeunt.*

Amb. Sfoot brother hold.

Sup. Woult let the Bastard shame vs?

Amb. Hold, hold, brother? there s fitter time then no w.

Sup. Now when I see it.   *Amb.* Tis too much seene already.

Sup. Scene and knowne,
The Nobler she's, the baser is shee growne.

Amb. If she were bent lasciuiously, the fault
Of mighty women, that sleepe soft,--O death,
Must she needes chuse such an vnequall sinner:
To make all worse.

Sup. A Bastard, the Dukes Bastard, Shame heapt on shame.

Amb. O our disgrace.
Most women haue small waste the world through-out,
But there desires are thousand miles about.   *Exeunt.*

Sup. Come stay not here, lets after, and preuent,
Or els theile sinne faster then weele repent.

Enter Vindice and Hippolito, *bring ing out there Mother*
one by one shoulder, and the other by the other, with
daggers in their hands.

                                Vind.

The play is printed on rough paper, and crammed into nine sheets. The compositor tended to crowd as much as he could on to each forme, and, like *A Trick to Catch the Old One* and some other quartos printed at about this time by Eld, it suggests a printing-house job done with the utmost economy.[1] Something of the appearance of the text can be gathered from the reproduction opposite of a page of the Quarto, H1[v], showing the text from IV. ii. 216[2] to the opening direction of IV. iv. The stage-directions are not spaced out from the text, but are printed almost as if they were part of it; speeches are often printed continuously, sometimes two being cramped into one line, as at IV. iii. 7–8; and the compositor did not pay much attention to the lineation of the verse, which is often printed without regard to the proper division of the lines, as at IV. ii. 222:

    (Quarto)   . . . to auoide
       swift pursuite. *Hip*. Firmer, and firmer.
    Vind. Nay, doubt not tis in graine, I warrant it hold collour.
    Hip. Lets about it.

    (This edition)   . . . to avoid swift pursuit.
    Hipp. Firmer, and firmer.
    Vind.   Nay, doubt not, 'tis in grain;
      I warrant it hold colour.
    Hipp.   Let's about it.

[1] Eld had a large business, and in 1607–8 he printed some fine large folios, like E. Grimestone's *History of the Netherlands* (1608); he also printed some plays on fine paper, with ample spacing and careful setting-out, like Samuel Daniel's *The Queen's Arcadia* (1606) and the anonymous *Caesar's Revenge* (1606–7), plays which are also carefully divided into acts and scenes.

[2] Sheets H and I, which bring the play to an end, are especially crowded with text, and the compositor (as nowhere else in the play) three times increased his usual measure of 38 lines to 39 (on H2[v], H3[v], and I3[r]), and once to 40 (H4[r]). It was necessary to cram up the text in order to squeeze the play into nine sheets, and in these last two sheets the compositor may have been driven to omit directions or even some text. It is significant in this respect that no heading appears in the text for Act V, which is usually thought to begin with the entry of Vindice and Hippolito on H4[v].

Opposite: a page of the Quarto, reproducing the text from IV. ii. 216 to the opening direction of IV. iv. This is signature H1[v] in the British Museum copy C.12.f.8.

This casual treatment of lineation, and continuous printing of speeches, are noticeable in other quartos of plays printed in this period, and may be attributable partly to the habits of the compositor or requirements of the printer, who wished to save paper by crowding as much as he could into a page.[1] However, there are passages where verse shades off into prose, or prose into verse, in a way that may have looked confusing in the manuscript, and perhaps the editor's most difficult task is to decide on lineation.

Most editors of the play have made some attempt to deal with this problem, with widely differing results. It has been a general tendency to put as much as possible of the play into verse, by dividing up passages printed as prose. Although the casual treatment of lines in the Quarto makes it necessary to work out the lineation for much of what evidently is meant to be verse, the borderline between prose and verse is often indistinct; and I suspect that the author, in the heat of composition, fell into blank-verse rhythms when writing prose, as Shakespeare was inclined to do.[2] It happens, then, that some passages of prose contain sections that will go readily enough into rough verse, but do not as a whole seem to flow as verse. A good example is a passage in Act I, which is printed in the Quarto as follows:

> *Spu.* Ifaith 'tis true too; Ime an vncertaine man,
> Of more vncertaine woman; may be his groome 'ath stable be-
> got me, you know I know not, hee could ride a horse well, a
> shrowd suspition marry—hee was wondrous tall, hee had his
> length yfaith, for peeping ouer halfe shut holy-day windowes,
> Men would desire him light, when he was a foote,
> He made a goodly show vnder a Pent-house,
> And when he rid, his Hatt would check the signes, and clatter
> Barbers Basons.[3]

---

[1] See, for example, Middleton's *Your Five Gallants* (1608) and Marston's *What You Will* (1607), both printed by Eld. It may be that texts by authors like Middleton, whose prose is liable to shade off into verse, lent themselves to casual printing and irregular setting-out; see, for example, the quarto of *A Mad World, my Masters* (1608), printed by H. B. for Walter Burre.

[2] See E. K. Chambers, *William Shakespeare. A Study of Facts and Problems*, 2 vols. (1930), I. 181–3.

[3] In the Quarto, this passage appears on signature B2^r; in this edition it is I. ii. 135–43.

Collins put the last two lines into verse, and later editors have divided the whole passage, producing lines like these:

> O' the stable begot me; you know I know not!
> He could ride a horse well, a shrewd suspicion, marry!

A case can perhaps be made for regarding such lines as irregular blank verse, but it seems to me that where the text can only be turned into verse by doing violence to the natural rhythmic flow of a passage like the one cited, it is better to treat it entirely as prose, and it is so printed in this edition.

The proper lineation of some verse passages, especially those containing many short phrases or half-lines printed continuously in the Quarto, is not always easy to decide. The difficulty is the greater because the author was inclined to intersperse extra-metrical asseverations and incomplete lines within the regular sequence of lines. Too often editors have not taken the trouble to think out the right rearrangement, but have been content to chop the text up rather mechanically into lines of five feet. A crude example of this in the 'Mermaid' edition of J. A. Symonds shows a failure to notice a buried couplet:

(Quarto)
> *Hip.* Brother, how happy is our vengeance.
> *Vin.* Why it hits, past the apprehension of indifferent wits.

(Symonds)
> *Hip.* Brother, how happy is our vengeance!
> *Vind.* Why, it hits past the apprehension of
>   Indifferent wits.

(This edition)
> *Hipp.* Brother, how happy is our vengeance!
> *Vind.*   Why, it hits
>   Past the apprehension of indifferent wits.
>   (v. i. 133–4)

In this there is some question whether the word 'Brother' should not be regarded as extra-metrical, as a line on its own, for the author, like Shakespeare, frequently allows phrases of commentary, approval, ejaculation, and the like to stand by themselves as lines interrupting the regular flow of verse; but a slurring of 'happy is' reduces the line as printed to regularity.

The compositor, possibly reproducing his manuscript, was casual in his treatment of such phrases, and, as he tended to fill out the measure of the line when the opportunity offered, odd half-lines are liable to be printed along with a full verse-line, thus:

> I know 'twas but some peevish Moone in him: goe, let him be
> releasd.

> Tis true too; here then, receive this signet, doome shall passe.

Editors have usually rearranged passages of this kind, and most of them correctly alter the first one to:

> *Duke.* I know 'twas but some peevish moon in him;
>   Go, let him be releas'd.
> *Super.*   'Sfoot, how now, brother?

Where something more than cutting off the line after the first ten syllables is involved, editors have not always bothered to work out the necessary alteration; so Collins and Harrison leave the second passage as they found it in the Quarto, while Symonds and Oliphant print it thus:

> 'Tis true too; here, then, receive this signet,
> Doom shall pass;
> Direct it to the judges, he shall die.

It seems merely insensitive to create such a clumsy line as the first of these, when there are plenty of parallels for treating the Duke's phrase of assent as extra-metrical; so elsewhere in the play we find:

> But to the purpose:
> Last evening, predecessor unto this,
> (I. i. 65–6)

and here the arrangement clearly should be:

> 'Tis true too.
> Here then, receive this signet, doom shall pass;
> Direct it to the judges, he shall die. . .
> (II. iii. 98–100)

These examples may serve to show that the matter of lineation has not received adequate attention from editors of the play,[1] and I

---

[1] I have treated this question more fully in an essay 'On the Authorship of *The Revenger's Tragedy*', *M.L.R.*, XLVIII (1953), 130–4.

have attempted in the present edition to arrange the text in the way that seems best to fulfil the rhythmic patterns and expectations established in the dialogue.

One unusual feature of the treatment of lineation perhaps deserves further comment. On several occasions the author makes a character speak by way of cry or interjection, interrupting with an extra-metrical phrase a blank-verse line spoken by another character. The Quarto treats these in its usual casual way, and editors have generally been content to chop such passages into rough verse. So at II. iii. 9–11, the Quarto prints:

> *Duk* You vpper Guard defend vs. *Duch*. Treason, treason.
> *Duk*. Oh take mee not in sleepe I haue great sins I must
>   haue daies,
> Nay months deere sonne, with penitential heaues,

All editors have interpreted the Quarto's arrangement of the first two speeches as indicating two parts of a blank-verse line, and they have either kept the next line as an unusually long one, a heptameter, or chopped it up into two lines, thus:

> O take me not in sleep!
> I have great sins, I must have days ...
>   (Thorndike)
>
> O take me not in sleep, I have great sins,
> I must have days,   (Oliphant)

They seem not to have noticed that the Duchess's cry interrupts the flow and is not part of it; so in the present edition the passage is printed thus:

> *Duke*. You upper guard defend us—
> *Duchess*. Treason, treason!
> *Duke*.   —O take me not
> In sleep; I have great sins, I must have days,
> Nay, months, dear son, with penitential heaves, ...

This treatment preserves the regular pattern and urgent flow of the Duke's speech, and accounts simply and economically for what appears in the Quarto to be a heptameter. Such passages[1] are numbered as two lines, the phrase interjected being taken as one line, and the split blank-verse line as the other.

[1] For other examples, see II. i. 73–4 and II. iii. 112–13.

The problems of division into prose and verse, and of lineation, are the most difficult of those posed by the Quarto, and they are of importance because they affect our estimate of the poetry of the play: properly set out it begins to look much less irregular than some critics have supposed it to be. For the rest, the text is a good one, showing many minor errors, but no major cruces. Some muddles there are: for instance, the allocation of speeches associated with the deaths in the masque of murderers at v. iii. 49–55 does not make sense, and must be incorrect. It is possible, too, that at a number of places the compositor misrepresented the original as clumsily as he certainly did at IV. iv. 43, which happens to have been press-corrected. The stage-directions are inadequate for a performance in the theatre, since many entrances and exits are not given in the Quarto.[1] The play is partly divided into acts, but the heading for Act V is omitted. Some of the stage-directions in the Quarto appear to be of a literary kind, like that marking the entry of Antonio (I. iv) as 'the discontented Lord Antonio, whose wife the Duchess's youngest son ravished', or 'Enter Castiza the sister' (II. i); in both the descriptive phrases are of help to a reader, but not to a producer or actor. Nothing about the text requires us to think that it was printed from a manuscript that had been used in the theatre; and the haphazard presence of necessary directions, the casual omission of the heading to Act V, and the suggestions of a literary descriptiveness in directions giving information unnecessary for staging the play all seem to indicate that the copy for this text stemmed from a manuscript of the author's, which was not carefully prepared, or transcribed, for the printer.[2]

In this edition the text is based on that of the Quarto. Many additions to stage-directions, or new directions, have been included, perhaps rather more than in previous editions, for the action often needs to be clarified, and, in particular, it is important to indi-

---

[1] Price, *loc. cit.*, p. 263, says that 18 entrances are lacking, together with numerous exits, and at least 18 other directions necessary to the action. Lack of space in pages crowded with text may have driven the compositor to make some omissions; see above, p. lvii and n.

[2] Price, *loc. cit.*, p. 263, thinks it 'reasonable to describe the manuscript as a fair copy in the author's hand'; this goes with an argument that the author was Middleton. See above, p. li.

cate the numerous asides, which provide one of the main means of unfolding the play's multiple ironies. All material added is placed in square brackets, and a note is made in the collation. The collation also records alterations of lineation from the Quarto, lists some of the odder spellings found in it, which occasionally involve matters of interpretation, as at II. i. 232, where 'loue' (Quarto) has been read as 'low' and as 'love', and notes corrections made in the Quarto as it was being printed.

5. SOURCES AND DATE

No source has as yet been found for *The Revenger's Tragedy*, if by a source is meant a work that provided an outline of and detailed suggestions for plot, action, and dialogue. Nevertheless, the play is not, as was for long supposed, an original invention. Its sensational image of an Italian court devoted to treachery, lust, and revenge fits in well enough with a common Elizabethan popular image of life there, and the play distils the essence of that conception of Italy where flourish

> the art of atheism, the art of epicurising, the art of whoring, the art of poisoning, the art of Sodomitry. The only probable good thing they have to keep us from utterly condemning it is that it maketh a man an excellent Courtier, a curious carpet knight: which is, by interpretation, a fine close lecher, a glorious hypocrite.[1]

The particular circumstances of the plot of *The Revenger's Tragedy* have some connection with the story of Duke Alessandro de' Medici, who was assassinated in 1537.[2] The tale of his death was narrated as the twelfth novel of the second day in the *Heptameron* of Marguerite of Navarre, a collection of seventy-two stories con-

---

[1] Thomas Nashe, *The Unfortunate Traveller* (1594), in *Works*, edited R. B. McKerrow, II. 301; I have modernized the text.

[2] This seems to have been noticed first by J. A. Symonds, in *The Renaissance in Italy* (7 vols., 1881 edn), v. 118, where he remarks that 'Varchi's account of Lorenzino de' Medici affecting profligacy and effeminacy in order to deceive Duke Alessandro, and forming to his purpose the ruffian Scoronconcolo from the dregs of the prisons, furnishes a complete justification for even Tourneur's plots. The snare this traitor laid for Alessandro, when he offered to bring his own aunt to the Duke's lust, bears a close resemblance to Vendice's scheme in *The Revenger's Tragedy*.'

ceived, on the analogy of Boccaccio's *Decameron*, as told in turn by a group of courtiers at the rate of ten a day. Marguerite died in 1549, without completing her work, and since the events described in this particular 'nouvelle' were, so to speak, completed only in 1548 with the assassination of Lorenzino de' Medici, it was very much contemporary history; the author herself makes this clear by beginning with the phrase, 'About ten years ago . . .'. In the English translation included in William Painter's *The Palace of Pleasure* (1567), a collection of tales drawn from a variety of authors, this opening phrase is omitted, but otherwise the translation sticks pretty closely to the original. Alexander and Lorenzino are not named in either account, but are referred to simply as a Duke of Florence and a Gentleman, his servant. The Duke, it is said, fell in love with the sister of a gentleman, whose help he begged in order to seduce her. The gentleman promised aid, and shortly reported to the Duke that he had persuaded his sister to receive him in her bed at night. When the night arrived, the Duke was taken to a bed and laid in it, whereupon the gentleman and one of his servants murdered the Duke in the bed by stabbing him, and fled the house and city. The story corresponds pretty well in the circumstances of his death with the murder of Alexander, Duke of Florence, by his nephew Lorenzino, aided by an accomplice Scoronconcolo. It has analogies in the play with Vindice's promise to procure his sister Castiza for Lussurioso, and his later revenge on the Duke.[1]

Another story that has links with part of the play's action appears in Giraldi Cinthio's *Hecatommithi* (1565), a collection of tales in which one concerns a plan by Don Ercolo d'Este, later Duke Ercole II of Ferrara, to seduce the beautiful but poor Lucilla, with the aid

[1] For the French text, which begins, 'Depuis dix ans en ça, en la ville de Florence, y avoit un duc de la maison de Medicis', see Marguerite de Navarre, *L'Heptameron*, edited Michel François (Paris, 1950), p. 90. There it is the 12th story of the second day. The translation in William Painter's *The Palace of Pleasure* is reprinted in the Appendix to this edition. Its connections with *The Revenger's Tragedy* were pointed out independently by N. W. Bawcutt, '*The Revenger's Tragedy* and the Medici Family', *Notes and Queries*, CXCVII (1957), 192–3, and by Pierre Legouis, 'Réflexions sur la Recherche des Sources à propos de la "Tragédie du Vengeur"', *Etudes Anglaises*, XII (1959), 47–55.

of her widowed mother. Although in the story as told here, and as freely translated by Barnabe Rich in his *Farewell to Military Profession* (1581), the emphasis is placed on the virtue of Lucilla when startled naked in her bed by the prince, and on the magnanimity of the prince, who persuades his father to provide Lucilla with a dowry so that she may marry Nicander, whom she loves, it may nevertheless have helped to suggest the behaviour of Gratiana to Castiza, in acting as bawd to her own daughter, and the virtue of Lucilla is matched by that of Castiza.[1]

The names of the characters in *The Revenger's Tragedy* are, in the main, Italian words,[2] and it is possible that the author read Italian. If so, he may, as L. G. Salingar suggests, not only have browsed through the other tales of the Este family, coloured by intrigues among brothers legitimate and illegitimate, in Decade VI of the *Hecatommithi*, but he may also have read a story of the same family in Matteo Bandello's *Novelle* (1554), I. 37. This concerns Duke Niccolò III, who took a young second wife, Parisina, when already father of a number of children, one of whom, Ugo, was as old as the bride. When Niccolò neglected Parisina for various mistresses, she fell in love with Ugo, now her stepson, and seduced him; but their affair became known to Niccolò, who, in revenge, had them beheaded. Although Niccolò is not shown in this story as old and vicious, he is like the Duke in *The Revenger's Tragedy* in being notorious for his adulteries. Although the ages and moral nature of the figures are different, the Duchess in the play seduces the Duke's bastard son Spurio, just as Parisina seduced Ugo. In Bandello, Ugo is the legitimate son, who has cause to fear his father's bastard children, so that if the dramatist borrowed from the tale, he altered what he found there to suit his plot, and did not follow it in detail, or use it as a source-book. Nevertheless, apart from the general similarity of the Niccolò–Parisina–Ugo tale

---

[1] The analogy was pointed out by Louis Berthé in his book on Giraldo Cinthio (1920), p. 208 n. It is discussed in detail by L. G. Salingar in his essay '*The Revenger's Tragedy*: Some Possible Sources', *M.L.R.*, LX (1965), 3–12; and I am greatly indebted to him for providing me with a typescript of this in advance of publication. In Cinthio the story appears as Decade VI, Novel 3; in Barnes, as 'Of Nicander and Lucilla'.

[2] See below, p. 2.

and the Duke–Duchess–Spurio intrigue, the dramatist might have found hints for the general atmosphere of his play in the sexual licence and vengefulness of the Este family, and for the Duchess's wooing of Spurio in Parisina's speeches of pleading to Ugo.

One episode in *The Revenger's Tragedy* has been traced to another source. In II. iii Lussurioso rushes into the ducal bedchamber, expecting to find the Duchess in bed with her stepson, the bastard Spurio; instead, he finds himself standing with a drawn sword in front of his father, the Duke. 'Amaz'd to death', he does not resist as the Duke calls a guard, and has him taken off to prison. There is a similar episode in the story of Cnemon in Book I of the *Æthiopica* by Heliodorus, which was translated into English by Thomas Underdowne, and published in 1587 as *An Æthiopian History*. Here Cnemon, expecting to find his stepmother in bed with an adulterer, surprises instead his own father, who, like the Duke in the play, at first cries for mercy, and then, as Cnemon stands 'amazed', has him arrested and bound.[1]

If no other 'sources' have been found, it is important to note that the play is derivative in other ways, for the author was clearly familiar with, and borrowed ideas, names, and vocabulary from, the work of other dramatists of the time. Some of these debts are noted in section I of this Introduction,[2] and further examples are set out here with the aim not only of illustrating an important aspect of the play's background, but as determining its date of composition. To start with, verbal echoes of a number of plays by Middleton have been observed, collected, and tabulated by the advocates of Middleton's authorship of *The Revenger's Tragedy*.[3] Some of these appear to be pretty commonplace, like ''tis in grain; I warrant it hold colour' (IV. ii. 223–4), which occurs also in *A Mad World, my Masters* (printed 1608), III. iii. 81; others suggest a more individual turn of phrase, like 'cut off a great deal of dirty way' (II. i. 17–18), which appears in the same play by Middleton (I. i. 75). This

---

[1] See G. K. Hunter, 'A Source for *The Revenger's Tragedy*', *R.E.S.*, new series, x (1959), 181–2. The relevant passage is reprinted in the Appendix to this volume.

[2] See above, p. xxi; see also the section on Authorship, pp. xlviii ff.

[3] A useful list is given in S. Schoenbaum's *Middleton's Tragedies* (1955), pp. 177–81.

play was written probably between 1604 and 1606, but not published until the end of 1608. Most of the phrases that are at all closely paralleled in plays by Middleton could be echoes, since their counterparts are found mainly in this writer's early city comedies, like *The Phoenix* (written about 1602). However, apart from *Blurt, Master Constable* (printed 1602), all were published in 1607 or 1608, so close in time to the printing of *The Revenger's Tragedy* that echoes in this play would presumably have been picked up by ear, not from the written page.[1] There are echoes of *The Revenger's Tragedy* in later plays by Middleton, though fewer of any consequence, and it is conceivable that Middleton remembered this play, or read it, when it was published in 1607–8, or transcribed it for the press, or that he wrote it, though this is not a view I share.[2] In any case, these parallels are of little or no use in dating *The Revenger's Tragedy*.

What may encourage the thought that the author of this play caught up and used some of Middleton's tricks of phrase is his evident familiarity with, and echoing of, other plays of the period. In one or two episodes Vindice suggests an analogy with the Prince in *The Phoenix*;[3] in both plays a noticeable feature is the approval given by one character to what another says:

> Brother, y' have spoke that right.
> > (*The Revenger's Tragedy*, III. v. 66)
>
> Your grace hath spoke it right;
> > (*The Phoenix*, I. i)

and the character names Lussurioso and Castiza appear in both plays. There are similar resemblances to John Marston's *Antonio's Revenge* (1602): Antonio (like Malevole in *The Malcontent* of 1604) is a forerunner of Vindice as revenger, tool-villain, hero, and malcontent all combined; some characteristic words and phrases of Marston's are recalled, like 'juiceless', 'upon the stroke', ''Sfoot!', all apparently first used by him; and the character-names Piero and Antonio appear in both plays. The name Dondolo seems to have

---

[1] R. C. Bald, 'The Chronology of Middleton's Plays', *M.L.R.*, XXXII (1937), 33–43, provides a guide which is still pretty reliable for the dating of Middleton's work.

[2] See above, p. liii.   [3] See Schoenbaum, *op. cit.*, pp. 71–2.

been borrowed from Marston's *The Fawn* (written 1604–5; printed 1606), where he is listed as a 'bald fool'. There seem too to be some links between Henry Chettle's *Hoffman* and *The Revenger's Tragedy*, though these are less important.[1]

Perhaps the most pervasive reminiscences are of plays by Shakespeare, especially *Hamlet*. A number of features of this play are recalled. Hamlet's meditations over a skull may have suggested the use of one by Vindice, and influenced his thoughts too:

> Does every proud and self-affecting dame
> Camphor her face for this ?   (III. v. 84–5)

> . . . get you to my lady's chamber, and tell her, let her
> paint an inch thick, to this favour she must come.
>   (*Hamlet*, v. i. 187–9)

The device of swearing over a drawn sword in Act I of *Hamlet* may have seemed effective to the author of *The Revenger's Tragedy*, where it is repeated twice: in I. iii, when Lussurioso makes Vindice swear to be true to him, and in the following scene, where a concerted oath to revenge the rape of Antonio's wife is taken over Hippolito's sword. There is a further parallel between the 'closet' scene in *Hamlet* and the scene in which Vindice and Hippolito arraign their mother:

> *Grat.* What means my sons ? What, will you murder me ?
>   (IV. iv. 2)

> *Queen.* What wilt thou do ? Thou wilt not murder me ?
>   (*Hamlet*, III. iv. 21)

Gratiana pretends ignorance, then eventually admits her guilt and repents; the image she uses is similar to Gertrude's:

> *Grat.* O you heavens,
>   Take this infectious spot out of my soul.
>   (IV. iv. 50–1)

> *Queen* . . . Thou turn'st my eyes into my very soul;
>   And there I see such black and grained spots
>   As will not leave their tinct.
>   (*Hamlet*, III. iv. 89–91)

Vindice's feigned madness, his railing against corruption, and his

[1] These are noted above, p. xxi.

speaking in prose when playing the part of a melancholic possibly also owe something to Hamlet.[1] The play may also echo *King Lear*, as perhaps in Vindice's tirade beginning,

> Here's a cheek keeps her colour, let the wind
> Go whistle;
> Spout rain, we fear thee not; be hot or cold,
> All's one with us. . .   (III. v. 60-3)

This speech recalls Lear's outbursts in the storm, 'Blow, winds, and crack your cheeks', and 'Spit, fire; spout, rain' (III. ii).

If a connection with this group of plays be granted, then we have confirmation of a probable date for *The Revenger's Tragedy*. For all the plays mentioned as relating to it were probably written and acted between 1600 and 1605. *Antonio's Revenge* was available in print in 1602, *Hamlet* in its full text in 1604, *The Malcontent* in 1604, and *The Fawn* in 1606. *King Lear* is usually dated in 1605, although it was not printed until 1608. It seems very likely that *The Revenger's Tragedy* was written in 1605-6, since it may owe something not only to *King Lear*, but to *Volpone* (written 1605, published 1607) in its satirical tone and its characters with type-names.[2] Even if these debts be discounted, it can hardly have been written much earlier because of its connections with *Hamlet* and with plays by Marston; it is without doubt a play conceived and staged in the early years of the reign of James I.

---

[1] Various links with Shakespeare have been pointed out by critics since E. E. Stoll first drew attention to some of them in his *John Webster* (1905); see especially Allardyce Nicoll, *Works*, pp. 6-7; a study of the influence of *Hamlet* and *King Lear* on Tourneur by L. L. Schücking in *Englische Studien*, L (1916-17), 80-105; and D. J. McGinn, *Shakespeare's Influence on the Drama of his Age Studied in Hamlet* (1938).

[2] See above, p. xxiii.

THE REVENGER'S TRAGEDY

[DRAMATIS PERSONAE

The DUKE.

LUSSURIOSO, *the Duke's son, by a previous marriage, and his heir.*

SPURIO, *the Duke's bastard son.*

AMBITIOSO, *the Duchess's eldest son.*

SUPERVACUO, *the Duchess's second son.*

JUNIOR BROTHER, *the Duchess's youngest son.*

ANTONIO, \
PIERO, *noblemen attending at the Duke's court.*

VINDICE, *in one of his disguises known as* PIATO, *brother of Castiza.*

HIPPOLITO, *also once called* CARLO, *another brother of Castiza.*

DONDOLO, *servant to Gratiana.*

NENCIO, \
SORDIDO, *followers of Lussurioso.*

The DUCHESS.

GRATIANA, *mother of Castiza.*

CASTIZA.

Nobles, Judges, Gentlemen, a Guard, a Prison-Keeper, Officers, and Servants.

SCENE: *An unnamed court and its environs, somewhere in Italy.*]

Dramatis Personae] first listed, incompletely, by Collins.

Lussurioso . . . Castiza] The names of many of these characters are Italian words, or derive from Italian words, and though the meanings of some of them may be clear enough, the definitions provided by John Florio in his dictionary, *A World of Words* (1598), illustrate what the dramatist had in mind: *Lussurioso*, lecherous, riotous; *Spurio*, a bastard; *Ambitioso*, ambitious, very desirous of honour; *Supervacuo*, superfluous, vain; *Vindice*, a revenger of wrongs, a redresser of things and abuses; *Dondolo*, a gull, a fool, a thing to make sport; *Nencio*, a fool, an idiot; *Sordido*, a niggard, a dodger, a covetous wretch; *Gratiana*, from *gratia*, grace; *Castiza*, from *casta*, chaste; *Piato*, flat, squat, cowered down, hidden.

Carlo] See I. i. 108 and n.

The Revenger's Tragedy

Act I

ACT I, SCENE i

Enter VINDICE [*holding a skull; he watches as*] *the* Duke, Duchess, LUSSURIOSO *his son,* SPURIO *the bastard, with a train, pass over the stage with torch-light.*

Vind. Duke; royal lecher; go, grey-hair'd adultery;
    And thou his son, as impious steep'd as he;
    And thou his bastard, true-begot in evil;
    And thou his duchess, that will do with devil.
    Four excellent characters—O, that marrowless age   5
    Would stuff the hollow bones with damn'd desires,
    And 'stead of heat, kindle infernal fires
    Within the spendthrift veins of a dry duke,
    A parch'd and juiceless luxur. O God!—one
    That has scarce blood enough to live upon,   10
    And he to riot it like a son and heir?
    O, the thought of that
    Turns my abused heart-strings into fret.

ACT I, SCENE i] Q (*ACT*. I. *SCÆ*. I.).   0.1. *Vindice*] Vendici Q.   0.2. his] Dodsley 2; her Q.   6. Would] Q; Should Dodsley I.

---

   1. i. 4. *do*] copulate.
   5. *excellent characters*] ironically commenting on their moral qualities as shown in their appearance (the common meaning of 'character': cf. *Cor.*, v. iv. 26); the word was not used until the 18th century to signify 'dramatic personage'.
   9. *luxur*] lecher.
   13. *fret*] passionate anger (as in the phrase 'fever and fret'); playing also on *fret* = a ring of gut placed on the fingerboard of a stringed musical instrument to regulate the fingering: cf. *H8*, III. ii. 105.

Thou sallow picture of my poison'd love,
My study's ornament, thou shell of death,   15
Once the bright face of my betrothed lady,
When life and beauty naturally fill'd out
These ragged imperfections,
When two heaven-pointed diamonds were set
In those unsightly rings—then 'twas a face   20
So far beyond the artificial shine
Of any woman's bought complexion,
That the uprightest man (if such there be
That sin but seven times a day) broke custom,
And made up eight with looking after her.   25
O, she was able to ha' made a usurer's son
Melt all his patrimony in a kiss,
And what his father fifty years told,
To have consum'd, and yet his suit been cold.
But O, accursed palace!   30
Thee when thou wert apparel'd in thy flesh
The old duke poison'd,
Because thy purer part would not consent
Unto his palsy-lust; for old men lustful
Do show like young men, angry, eager, violent,   35
Outbid like their limited performances.
O 'ware an old man hot and vicious:
Age, as in gold, in lust is covetous.

---

14. *picture*] He addresses the skull he is holding.
28. *years*] a disyllable: cf. *Tp.*, I. ii. 53, and Abbott, 480.
   told] counted, i.e., saved up.
36. *Outbid*] i.e., outbidden; the general sense here is: lustful old men
behave like young men who are violent because they have been outbidden,
have failed in a love suit; and outbid themselves because their performance
in love is limited. Cf. I. ii, 149.
38.] Commas mark off this line in Q as a 'sentence' (Latin *sententia*), a
pithy saying worthy to be noted down by the reader in his 'commonplace'
book. Commas, or a hand in the margin, were used to draw attention to
lines in a number of plays of this period; see G. K. Hunter, 'The Marking
of *Sententiae* in Elizabethan Printed Plays, Poems, and Romances', *The
Library*, 5th series, VI (1951), 171–88. This line recalls the proverb, 'Like
a leek he has a white head and a green tail' (Tilley, L177, and cf. L589).

Vengeance, thou murder's quit-rent, and whereby
Thou show'st thyself tenant to Tragedy,   40
O, keep thy day, hour, minute, I beseech,
For those thou hast determin'd!—hum, who e'er knew
Murder unpaid? Faith, give Revenge her due,
Sh' has kept touch hitherto—be merry, merry,
Advance thee, O thou terror to fat folks,   45
To have their costly three-pil'd flesh worn off
As bare as this—for banquets, ease and laughter,
Can make great men, as greatness goes by clay;
But wise men little are more great than they.

Enter his brother HIPPOLITO.

Hipp. Still sighing o'er death's vizard?
Vind.   Brother, welcome;   50
    What comfort bring'st thou? how go things at court?
Hipp. In silk and silver, brother; never braver.
Vind. Puh,
    Thou play'st upon my meaning. Prithee say,
    Has that bald Madam, Opportunity,   55
    Yet thought upon 's? Speak, are we happy yet?
    Thy wrongs and mine are for one scabbard fit.
Hipp. It may prove happiness.
Vind.   What is 't may prove?

47. laughter,] *Q*^b^; laughter *Q*^a^.   49.1. *his*] *Dodsley 1; her Q.*   50.
death's] *Q*^b^; death *Q*^a^.   vizard?] *Dodsley 1;* vizard. *Q.*

39. *quit-rent*] properly, rent paid by a freeholder of land in lieu of services required of him; vengeance, so to speak, is the due of murder.
40. *tenant to Tragedy*] continuing the metaphor from 'quit-rent'. With this reference to tragedy, cf. III. v. 99, 205.
42. *determin'd*] settled on, judged.
45. *thee*] i.e., the skull.
46. *three-pil'd*] alluding to three-piled velvet, in which the loops are formed by three threads, producing a very thick pile.
49. *wise . . . they*] Cf. Tilley, W526, 'Wisdom is better than riches'; 'little' means 'of low rank'.
55. *bald Madam*] alluding to the common personification and emblem figure; cf. Tilley, T311, 'Take Occasion by the forelock, for she is bald behind', and ll. 99–100 below.

Give me to taste.

Hipp.   Give me your hearing then.
You know my place at court.

Vind.   Ay, the duke's chamber;   60
But 'tis a marvel thou'rt not turn'd out yet!

Hipp. Faith, I have been shov'd at, but 'twas still my hap
To hold by th' duchess' skirt—you guess at that;
Whom such a coat keeps up can ne'er fall flat.
But to the purpose: 65
Last evening, predecessor unto this,
The duke's son warily inquir'd for me,
Whose pleasure I attended. He began
By policy to open and unhusk me
About the time and common rumour;   70
But I had so much wit to keep my thoughts
Up in their built houses, yet afforded him
An idle satisfaction without danger.
But the whole aim and scope of his intent
Ended in this, conjuring me in private   75
To seek some strange-digested fellow forth,
Of ill-contented nature, either disgrac'd
In former times, or by new grooms displac'd
Since his stepmother's nuptials; such a blood,
A man that were for evil only good—   80
To give you the true word, some base-coin'd pander.

Vind. I reach you, for I know his heat is such,
Were there as many concubines as ladies,
He would not be contain'd, he must fly out.
I wonder how ill-featur'd, vile-proportion'd   85

---

62. I have] *Q;* I've *Symonds.*

---

76. *strange-digested*] oddly constituted, or perhaps at odds with the prevailing order: cf. 'strange-composed', l. 96.

78. *grooms*] servants.

79. *blood*] man of hot spirit, a roisterer.

81. *base-coin'd*] perhaps debased (base coin), and suggesting mean or illegitimate birth.

82. *reach*] understand.

That one should be, if she were made for woman,
Whom at the insurrection of his lust
He would refuse for once; heart, I think none;
Next to a skull, though more unsound than one,
Each face he meets he strongly doats upon.   90

Hipp. Brother, y' have truly spoke him.
He knows not you, but I'll swear you know him.

Vind. And therefore I'll put on that knave for once,
And be a right man then, a man o' th' time;
For to be honest is not to be i' th' world.   95
Brother, I'll be that strange-composed fellow.

Hipp. And I'll prefer you, brother.

Vind.   Go to, then;
The small'st advantage fattens wronged men.
It may point out Occasion; if I meet her,
I'll hold her by the foretop fast enough,   100
Or, like the French mole, heave up hair and all.
I have a habit that will fit it quaintly.
Here comes our mother.

Hipp.   And sister.

Vind.   We must coin.
Women are apt, you know, to take false money;

88. none;] *Dodsley 1;* none, *Q.*   97. to] *Q* (too).   103. coin] *Q*
(quoyne).

88–9. *none . . . skull*] i.e., his lust would stop short only at necrophily;
cf. I. iii. 62–3.
89. *skull*] again drawing attention to the object he holds.
91. *spoke*] described.
94. *right*] orthodox, fitting the accepted standards.
95. *For . . . i' th' world*] i.e., one cannot live in society and remain honourable.
96. *strange-composed*] Cf. l. 76 above.
99–100. *Occasion . . . enough*] See l. 55 above and n.; 'foretop' means
forelock.
101. *French . . . all*] alluding to one of the effects of syphilis, known as
'the French disease'; cf. *MND.*, I. ii. 86–7.
102. *habit*] costume.
quaintly] finely, cleverly.
103. *coin*] make pretence, counterfeit.

But I dare stake my soul for these two creatures,   105
Only excuse excepted—that they'll swallow
Because their sex is easy in belief.

[*Enter* GRATIANA *and* CASTIZA.]

Grat. What news from court, son Carlo?
Hipp.   Faith, mother,
   'Tis whisper'd there, the duchess' youngest son
   Has play'd a rape on lord Antonio's wife.   110
Grat. On that religious lady!
Cast. Royal blood! Monster, he deserves to die,
   If Italy had no more hopes but he.
Vind. Sister, y' have sentenc'd most direct and true;
   The law's a woman, and would she were you.   115
   Mother, I must take leave of you.
Grat.   Leave? for what?
Vind. I intend speedy travel.
Hipp. That he does, madam.
Grat.   Speedy indeed!
Vind. For since my worthy father's funeral,
   My life's unnatural to me, e'en compell'd   120
   As if I liv'd now when I should be dead.
Grat. Indeed, he was a worthy gentleman,
   Had his estate been fellow to his mind.

---

106. excepted—that] *Nicoll;* excepted that *Q;* excepted, that *Dodsley 1.*
107.1. *Enter . . . Castiza.*] *Dodsley 1; not in Q.*   108. *Grat.*] *Moth. Q*
(*Moth., Mot., or Mo. to end of scene*).   112. Royal blood! Monster] *Q*
(Royall bloud: monster)*;* Royal-blood monster! *Collins.*   116. Leave?
for] *This ed., after Dodsley 1;* Leaue for *Q.*   120. unnatural] *Dodsley 1;*
vnnaturally *Q.*

105–7.] i.e., Vindice is sure Gratiana and Castiza will see through and
reject hypocrisy or deceit, with one exception—they will believe a good
excuse, for women are credulous that way.

108. *Carlo*] the only occurrence of this name in the play, perhaps a relic
of the author's first idea for naming the character Hippolito.

115. *law's a woman*] probably alluding to the familiar image of Justice as
a goddess holding scales or a sword; cf. *Oth.,* v. ii. 17.

120. *compell'd*] forced on me; an extension of the normal senses.

Vind. The duke did much deject him.
Grat.   Much!
Vind.   Too much.
    And through disgrace, oft smother'd in his spirit   125
    When it would mount, surely I think he died
    Of discontent, the nobleman's consumption.
Grat. Most sure he did!
Vind.   Did he? 'lack, you know all,
    You were his midnight secretary.
Grat.   No.
    He was too wise to trust me with his thoughts.   130
Vind. I'faith, then, father, thou wast wise indeed;
    Wives are but made to go to bed and feed.

    Come, mother, sister; you'll bring me onward, brother?
Hipp. I will.
Vind.   I'll quickly turn into another.   *Exeunt.*

[I. ii]

Enter the old Duke, LUSSURIOSO *his son, the* Duchess, [SPURIO] *the
bastard, the Duchess's two sons* AMBITIOSO *and* SUPERVACUO, *the
third, her youngest* [Junior Brother] *brought out with* Officers *for the
rape; two* Judges.

Duke. Duchess, it is your youngest son. We're sorry
    His violent act has e'en drawn blood of honour,
    And stain'd our honours;
    Thrown ink upon the forehead of our state,
    Which envious spirits will dip their pens into   5

125. through] *Q;* though *Dodsley 1.*

___

124. *deject*] humble, deprive of high estate.
125-7. *through . . . discontent*] The sense seems to be 'he died of discontent, fostered by disgrace which was often choked down in his temper of mind, instead of being allowed to mount (and vent itself in words or actions)'.
129. *secretary*] confidant; cf. *Spanish Tragedy,* III. ii. 12.
130-2.] alluding to the proverbial inability of women to keep secrets; cf. Tilley, S196; W347a, 677-8. For the italicizing of l. 132, cf. l. 38 above and n.

After our death, and blot us in our tombs.
For that which would seem treason in our lives
Is laughter when we're dead; who dares now whisper
That dares not then speak out, and e'en proclaim
With loud words and broad pens our closest shame?   10
1.Judge. Your grace hath spoke like to your silver years,
Full of confirmed gravity; for what is it to have
A flattering false insculption on a tomb,
And in men's hearts reproach? The bowell'd corpse
May be cer'd in, but—with free tongue I speak—   15
The faults of great men through their cerecloths break.
Duke. They do. We're sorry for 't, it is our fate
To live in fear, and die to live in hate.
I leave him to your sentence—doom him, lords,
The fact is great—whilst I sit by and sigh.   20
Duchess. My gracious lord, I pray be merciful.
Although his trespass far exceed his years,
Think him to be your own, as I am yours;
Call him not son-in-law. The law, I fear,
Will fall too soon upon his name and him.   25
Temper his fault with pity!   [*She kneels.*]
Luss.   Good my lord,

11. *1.Judge.*] Symonds (subs.); *Iud.* Q.   15. cer'd] *Q* (seard).   16. *cere-*
cloths] *Q* (searce clothes).   19. sentence—doom] *This ed.;* sentance
dome *Q;* sentence, doom *Dodsley 1.*   20. great—] *This ed.;* great; *Q.*
26. *She kneels.*] *Oliphant; not in Q.*

7–10.] Cf. Tilley, M591, 'Dead men have no friends'.
10. *closest*] most secret.
13. *insculption*] carved inscription.
14. *bowell'd*] disembowelled.
15. *cer'd in*] sealed up by being embalmed and wrapped in a cerecloth or
a winding-sheet; *seard* (Q) was a common spelling, as 'seare' at *Cym.*, I. i.
116.
16.] varying the proverb 'Murder (truth) will out'; cf. IV. ii. 207 below,
and Tilley, M1315; T591. For the italics, marking a 'sentence', cf. I. i. 38
and n.
19. *doom him*] sentence him.
20. *fact*] crime.
24. *son-in-law*] step-son; a proper, but now obsolete, use of the word.

    Then 'twill not taste so bitter and unpleasant
    Upon the judges' palate, for offences
    Gilt o'er with mercy show like fairest women,
    Good only for their beauties, which wash'd off,   30
    No sin is uglier.

Ambit.   I beseech your grace,
    Be soft and mild; let not relentless Law
    Look with an iron forehead on our brother.

Spurio. [*Aside*] He yields small comfort yet; hope he shall die,—
    And if a bastard's wish might stand in force,   35
    Would all the court were turn'd into a corse.

Duchess. No pity yet? must I rise fruitless then,
    A wonder in a woman? are my knees
    Of such low metal that without respect—

1. Judge. Let the offender stand forth.   40
    'Tis the duke's pleasure that impartial doom
    Shall take fast hold of his unclean attempt.
    A rape! why 'tis the very core of lust,
    Double adultery!

Junior Bro.   So, sir.

2. Judge.   And which was worse,
    Committed on the Lord Antonio's wife,   45
    That general-honest lady. Confess, my lord,
    What mov'd you to 't?

Junior Bro.   Why, flesh and blood, my lord;
    What should move men unto a woman else?

30–1. Good . . . uglier] *so Thorndike; one line in Q.*   34. Aside] *Symonds; not in Q.*   38. woman? are] *This ed.;* woman are *Qᵃ;* woman; are *Qᵇ;* woman! are *Dodsley 1.*   39. low metal that] *Q* (lowe—mettall—that).   42. fast] *Dodsley 1; first Q.*   46. general-honest] *This ed.;* Generall honest *Q.*

---

35. *And if*] = if; see *O.E.D.*, 'and', C.1b, and Abbott, 103–5.
36. *corse*] This early Middle English form of the word corpse was still common in the 17th century, and is required here by the rhyme.
39. *low metal*] i.e., base metal, poor worth.
41. *doom*] judgment.
42. *attempt*] assault.
46. *general-honest*] invariably chaste and upright.

Luss. O, do not jest thy doom; trust not an axe
  Or sword too far. The law is a wise serpent,   50
  And quickly can beguile thee of thy life.
  Though marriage only has made thee my brother,
  I love thee so far, play not with thy death.
Junior Bro. I thank you, troth; good admonitions, faith,
  If I'd the grace now to make use of them.   55
1.Judge. That lady's name has spread such a fair wing
  Over all Italy, that if our tongues
  Were sparing toward the fact, judgement itself
  Would be condemn'd, and suffer in men's thoughts.
Junior Bro. Well then, 'tis done, and it would please me well   60
  Were it to do again. Sure, she's a goddess,
  For I'd no power to see her and to live;
  It falls out true in this, for I must die.
  Her beauty was ordain'd to be my scaffold,
  And yet methinks I might be easier 'sess'd;   65
  My fault being sport, let me but die in jest.
1.Judge. This be the sentence—
Duchess. O keep 't upon your tongue, let it not slip;
  Death too soon steals out of a lawyer's lip.
  Be not so cruel-wise!
1.Judge.   Your grace must pardon us,   70
  'Tis but the justice of the law.
Duchess.   The law
  Is grown more subtle than a woman should be.

60. well] Q^b; well. Q^a.   65. 'sess'd] *Dodsley 1;* ceast *Q.*

---

 49. *jest*] i.e., jest about.
 58. *fact*] crime; cf. l. 20.
 62. *live*] go on living, implying that he had to 'die' in the consumma-
tion of sexual intercourse with her, a common idea in the poetry of the
time; cf. Shakespeare, *Sonn.* xcii. 12, 'Happy to have thy love, happy to
die'.
 65. *'sess'd*] assessed, judged; *cess* was a common aphetic form of the verb
until the 19th century; but the spelling *ceast* in Q suggested to Nicoll
'ceased', and perhaps a quibble on the meaning 'brought to rest' (*O.E.D.* 7)
is intended.
 71–2. *law . . . woman*] Cf. I. i. 115 and n.

Spurio. [*Aside*] Now, now he dies; rid 'em away!
Duchess. O what it is to have an old-cool duke
    To be as slack in tongue as in performance.   75
1. Judge. Confirm'd, this be the doom irrevocable—
Duchess. O!
1. Judge. To-morrow early—
Duchess.   Pray be abed, my lord.
1. Judge. Your grace much wrongs yourself.
Ambit.   No, 'tis that tongue,
    Your too much right, does do us too much wrong.   80
1. Judge. Let that offender—
Duchess.   Live, and be in health.
1. Judge. Be on a scaffold—
Duke.   Hold, hold, my lord.
Spurio. [*Aside*]   Pox on 't,
    What makes my dad speak now?
Duke. We will defer the judgment till next sitting.
    In the meantime let him be kept close prisoner;   85
    Guard, bear him hence.
Ambit. [*Aside*]   Brother, this makes for thee;
    Fear not, we'll have a trick to set thee free.
Junior Bro. [*Aside*] Brother, I will expect it from you both,
    And in that hope I rest.
Super.   Farewell; be merry.
                      Exit [Junior Brother] *with a guard.*
Spurio. [*Aside*] Delay'd, deferr'd—nay then, if judgment have 90
    Cold blood, flattery and bribes will kill it.
Duke. About it then, my lords, with your best powers;

73, 82, 86, 88. *Aside*] Symonds; *not in* Q.   82. Pox] *Dodsley 1;* Pax *Q.*
88–9. both, / And . . . hope I] *Dodsley 2;* both; and . . . hope / I *Q.*   90.
Aside] Oliphant; *not in* Q.   90–1. have /Cold blood, flattery] *so Harrier;*
haue cold bloud, / Flattery *Q.*

---

  75. *performance*] i.e., in bed; cf. I. i. 36.
  79. *wrongs*] dishonours.
  80. *Your . . . right*] i.e., the excessive privilege you have, as a judge, to
speak.
  82. *Pox*] Pax (Q) is a common corruption of the expletive.
  86. *makes for*] favours, helps.

More serious business calls upon our hours.

Exeunt [all but the] Duchess.

Duchess. Was 't ever known step-duchess was so mild
    And calm as I ? some now would plot his death   95
    With easy doctors, those loose-living men,
    And make his wither'd grace fall to his grave,
    And keep church better.
    Some second wife would do this, and dispatch
    Her double-loathed lord at meat or sleep.   100
    Indeed, 'tis true, an old man's twice a child.
    Mine cannot speak; one of his single words
    Would quite have freed my youngest, dearest son
    From death or durance, and have made him walk
    With a bold foot upon the thorny law,   105
    Whose prickles should bow under him; but 'tis not,
    And therefore wedlock faith shall be forgot.
    I'll kill him in his forehead, hate there feed;
    That wound is deepest, though it never bleed.

[*Enter* SPURIO *at a distance.*]

    And here comes he whom my heart points unto;   110
    His bastard son, but my love's true-begot.
    Many a wealthy letter have I sent him,
    Swell'd up with jewels, and the timorous man
    Is yet but coldly kind.

93.1. *Exeunt . . . Duchess.*] *so Symonds; Exe. manet Du. Q.*   100. double-
loathed] *Thorndike;* double loathd *Q.*   or] *Dodsley 1;* and *Q.*   109.1.
Enter . . . distance.] *This ed.; not in Q.*

---

    98. *keep church better*] attend church more regularly and devoutly, being
buried there, than he does while alive.

    99. *Some*] some one or other: cf. II. iii. 76.

    100. *or sleep*] Nicoll keeps 'and sleep' (Q), interpreting the lines, 'might
kill her lord as he is eating, and sleep quietly after'; but I suspect the word
'and' was caught in error by the compositor from the line above.

    101. *old . . . child*] a common proverb; Tilley, M570, and cf. *Ham.*,
II. ii. 380.

    108. *kill . . . forehead*] i.e., by cuckolding him. The cuckold's horns pro-
verbially sprouted from the forehead (cf. Tilley, H624–5), and the husband's suffering was naturally located there: see *Oth.*, III. iii. 288.

That jewel's mine that quivers in his ear,   115
Mocking his master's chillness and vain fear.
'Has spy'd me now.
Spurio.   Madam, your grace so private?
My duty on your hand.
Duchess. Upon my hand, sir! troth, I think you'd fear
To kiss my hand too, if my lip stood there.   120
Spurio. Witness I would not, madam.   [*Kisses her.*]
Duchess.   'Tis a wonder,
For ceremony has made many fools;
It is as easy way unto a duchess
As to a hatted dame (if her love answer),
But that by timorous honours, pale respects,   125
Idle degrees of fear, men make their ways
Hard of themselves—what, have you thought of me?
Spurio. Madam, I ever think of you in duty,
Regard, and—
Duchess. Puh, upon my love, I mean.
Spurio.   I would   130
'Twere love, but 'tis a fouler name than lust.
You are my father's wife; your grace may guess now
What I could call it.
Duchess.   Why, th' art his son but falsely;
'Tis a hard question whether he begot thee.
Spurio. I'faith, 'tis true too; I'm an uncertain man, of more 135

117. now.] *Q; now. Enter Spurio. Dodsley 1.*   121. *Kisses her.*] *Symonds;
not in Q.*   127. what, have] *Symonds;* what haue *Q.*   130–1. would /
'Twere . . . name than] *This ed.;* would 'twere . . . name / Then *Q.*   135.]
This ed.; as verse in Q, line ending man (*so Symonds, omitting* too). 135–
40. of . . . windows] *so Q; as verse Symonds, lines ending* groom / . . . not! /
. . . marry!— / . . . i'faith / . . . windows.

124. *hatted dame*] unexplained. *O.E.D.* seems wide of the mark in guess-
ing 'peasant-woman'; the phrase is more likely to refer generally to women
of a lower class. So in Middleton, *Your Five Gallants,* V. I. 7 (*Works,* III.
230), a courtesan says to a merchant's wife, 'You have a privilege from
your hat, forsooth, / To walk without a man and no suspicion, / But we
poor gentlewomen that go in tires / Have no such liberty'. The duchess,
as a gentlewoman, no doubt wore 'tires', or a head-dress: see II. i. 226
below.

uncertain woman. Maybe his groom o' th' stable begot
me, you know I know not; he could ride a horse well, a
shrewd suspicion, marry; he was wondrous tall, he had
his length, i'faith, for peeping over half-shut holiday
windows; men would desire him 'light. When he was   140
afoot, he made a goodly show under a penthouse, and
when he rid, his hat would check the signs, and clatter
barbers' basins.

Duchess. Nay, set you a-horseback once, you'll ne'er 'light off.

Spurio. Indeed, I am a beggar.   145

Duchess. That's more the sign th' art great—but to our love.
      Let it stand firm both in thy thought and mind
      That the duke was thy father, as no doubt then
      He bid fair for 't: thy injury is the more,
      For had he cut thee a right diamond,   150
      Thou hadst been next set in the dukedom's ring,
      When his worn self, like age's easy slave,
      Had dropp'd out of the collet into th' grave.
      What wrong can equal this? canst thou be tame
      And think upon 't?

Spurio.   No, mad and think upon 't.   155

Duchess. Who would not be reveng'd of such a father,

140–6. men . . . love] *This ed.; as irregular verse in Q, lines ending* a foote, /
. . . Pent-house, / . . . Basons. / . . . once, / . . . beggar. / . . . loue; *so Thorndike, lines ending* afoot / . . . pent-house; / . . . signs, / . . . once, / . . . beggar. /
. . . great.— / . . . love.   147. thy] *Dodsley 1; not in Q.*

138–40. *he . . . windows*] i.e., he was so tall that when he sat on horseback
he could peep over half-shut windows, and so intrude into the privacy of
people relaxing on holidays.

140. *'light*] alight.

141. *penthouse*] the awning over a shop or stall.

142. *signs*] shop-signs, hung out over the street.

143. *basins*] shaving-dishes, broad-edged, and with a semi-circular opening for the neck, allowing the chin to reach into the bowl. They were commonly used for barbers' shop-signs.

144–5.] alluding to the common proverb (Tilley, B238–9).

149. *bid fair for*] made a good attempt at: cf. I. i. 36.

153. *collet*] socket; the setting of a jewel in a ring.

156. *of*] i.e., on; see Abbott, 175.

E'en in the worst way ? I would thank that sin
That could most injury him, and be in league with it.
O what a grief 'tis, that a man should live
But once i' th' world, and then to live a bastard,   160
The curse o' the womb, the thief of nature,
Begot against the seventh commandment,
Half-damn'd in the conception, by the justice
Of that unbribed everlasting law.

Spurio. O, I'd a hot-back'd devil to my father.   165

Duchess. Would not this mad e'en patience, make blood rough ?
Who but an eunuch would not sin, his bed
By one false minute disinherited ?

Spurio. [*Aside*] Aye, there's the vengeance that my birth was
    wrapp'd in.
I'll be reveng'd for all; now hate begin,   170
I'll call foul incest but a venial sin.

Duchess. Cold still ? in vain then must a duchess woo ?

Spurio. Madam, I blush to say what I will do.

Duchess. Thence flew sweet comfort. [*She kisses him.*] Earnest,
    and farewell.

Spurio. O, one incestuous kiss picks open hell.   175

Duchess. Faith now, old duke, my vengeance shall reach high;
I'll arm thy brow with woman's heraldry.   *Exit.*

Spurio. Duke, thou didst do me wrong, and by thy act
Adultery is my nature.
Faith, if the truth were known, I was begot   180

---

158. injury] *Q; injure Dodsley 1.*   162. commandment] *Q* (commande-
ment).   167–8. sin, . . . disinherited ?] *This ed.;* sinne ? . . . disinherited. *Q.*
169. Aside] *This ed.; not in Q.*   174. She . . . him.] *Symonds; not in Q.*

---

158. *injury*] a common form of the verb in the 17th century; cf. Heywood, *Woman Killed with Kindness*, edited R. W. Van Fossen (Revels Plays,
1961), xi. 99.
162. *commandment*] *Exodus*, **xx.** 14, forbidding adultery. The spelling in
Q, and the demands of the metre, indicate that the word was here pronounced as four syllables.
166. *make . . . rough*] stir the blood (i.e., temper) to anger.
174. *Earnest*] Her kiss is a foretaste of more to come.
177. *heraldry*] i.e., cuckold's horns: cf. l. 108 above.

After some gluttonous dinner, some stirring dish
Was my first father, when deep healths went round,
And ladies' cheeks were painted red with wine,
Their tongues as short and nimble as their heels,
Uttering words sweet and thick; and when they rose,   185
Were merrily dispos'd to fall again,—
In such a whisp'ring and withdrawing hour,
When base male-bawds kept sentinel at stair-head,
Was I stol'n softly; O, damnation met
The sin of feasts, drunken adultery.   190
I feel it swell me; my revenge is just;
I was begot in impudent wine and lust.
Step-mother, I consent to thy desires,
I love thy mischief well, but I hate thee,
And those three cubs thy sons, wishing confusion,   195
Death and disgrace may be their epitaphs.
As for my brother, the duke's only son,
Whose birth is more beholding to report
Than mine, and yet perhaps as falsely sown
(Women must not be trusted with their own),   200
I'll loose my days upon him, hate all I;
Duke, on thy brow I'll draw my bastardy.
For indeed a bastard by nature should make cuckolds,
because he is the son of a cuckold-maker.   *Exit.*

185. rose] *Dodsley 1;* rise *Q.*   189. met] *Q;* meet *Dodsley 1.*   203–4.]
so this ed.; verse in Q, divided at Cuckolds, / Because.

181. *stirring*] stimulating, stirring to action: cf. II. i. 200–2.
184. *short*] lisping, inarticulate; but also alluding to a common phrase
descriptive of a wanton woman. Tilley, S397, cites Chester, *Love's Martyr*
(1601), p. 91, 'Be not short-heel'd with every wind to fall'.
185–6. *rose . . . fall again*] suggesting not only that they were drunk, but
that they were ready to lie with any man.
197. *only son*] Lussurioso, the duke's only legitimate son.
201. *loose . . . him*] i.e., devote my time to persecuting him.
202.] Cf. l. 177 and n.
203–4.] See collation. After the couplets expressing his venom, Spurio
drops at the end into sardonic humour, and his last two lines seem to me
to be best regarded as prose.

[I. iii]

Enter VINDICE *and* HIPPOLITO, *Vindice in disguise to attend Lord*
Lussurioso, the Duke's son.

Vind. What, brother? am I far enough from myself?
Hipp. As if another man had been sent whole
    Into the world, and none wist how he came.
Vind. It will confirm me bold, the child o' th' court.
    Let blushes dwell i' th' country. Impudence,   5
    Thou goddess of the palace, mistress of mistresses,
    To whom the costly-perfum'd people pray,
    Strike thou my forehead into dauntless marble,
    Mine eyes to steady sapphires; turn my visage,
    And if I must needs glow, let me blush inward,   10
    That this immodest season may not spy
    That scholar in my cheeks, fool-bashfulness,
    That maid in the old time, whose flush of grace
    Would never suffer her to get good clothes.
    Our maids are wiser, and are less asham'd;   15
    Save Grace the bawd, I seldom hear grace nam'd!
Hipp. Nay, brother,
    You reach out o' th' verge now—'sfoot, the duke's son;
    Settle your looks.
Vind.   Pray let me not be doubted.

                [*Enter* LUSSURIOSO.]

Hipp. My Lord—
Luss.   Hippolito? [*To Vindice*] Be absent; leave us.
                [*Vindice withdraws to one side.*]

I. iii. 5. country. Impudence] *Dodsley 1;* Country impudence *Q.*   17–19.
Nay . . . looks] *so this ed.; prose in Q; verse in Dodsley 1, divided at* now— |
'Sfoot; *in Collins, divided at* 'Sfoote, | The.   19.1. *Enter Lussurioso.*]
Dodsley 1; not in Q.   20. *To Vindice*] *This ed.; not in Q.*   20.1. *Vindice*
. . . *side.*] *This ed. (after Oliphant); not in Q.*

    I. iii. 1. *far . . . myself*] i.e., well enough disguised.
    6. *mistresses*] quibbling on the sense 'paramour'.
    18. *You . . . verge*] i.e., you go beyond the limit (the modern phrase); you
are being fanciful.

Hipp. My lord, after long search, wary inquiries,   21
          And politic siftings, I made choice of yon fellow,
          Whom I guess rare for many deep employments;
          This our age swims within him, and if time
          Had so much hair, I should take him for time,   25
          He is so near kin to this present minute.

Luss. 'Tis enough.
          We thank thee; yet words are but great men's blanks.
          Gold, though it be dumb, does utter the best thanks.

                              [*Gives Hippolito money.*]

Hipp. Your plenteous honour!—an excellent fellow, my lord.   30

Luss. So, give us leave. [*Exit* HIPPOLITO.] Welcome, be not
          far off, we must be better acquainted. Push, be bold with
          us; thy hand.

Vind. With all my heart, i'faith; how dost, sweet musk-cat?
          When shall we lie together?

Luss. [*Aside*]   Wondrous knave!   35
          Gather him into boldness?—'sfoot, the slave's
          Already as familiar as an ague,
          And shakes me at his pleasure. [*To Vindice*] Friend, I can

29.1. *Gives . . . money.*] so Symonds; not in Q.   31. *Exit Hippolito.*] Dodsley
2; not in Q.   35. *Aside*] Thorndike; not in Q.   38. *To Vindice*] This ed.;
not in Q.

---

22. *siftings*] close questionings.

23. *rare*] excellent.

24. *our . . . him*] i.e., he is in touch with all that goes on; cf. ll. 75, 109–10.

24–5. *time . . . hair*] Time was commonly personified as bald; cf. Tilley,
T311.

28. *words . . . blanks*] i.e., expressions of gratitude have no current value.
'Blanks' may refer to documents left with a space for signature or instruc-
tions; or the word may allude to metal cut and shaped for coins, but not
yet stamped with a value.

31. *give us leave*] leave us.

32. *Push*] the same as 'Pish!'; it occurs in several plays by Middleton,
in *Timon of Athens*, and in other plays of the period.

34. *musk-cat*] commonly applied to a fop or a courtesan, as these were
likely to use perfume: cf. Ben Jonson, *Every Man out of his Humour*, II. i.
97, 'he sleeps with a musk-cat every night'.

36. *Gather . . . boldness*] Lussurioso means that there was no need to
'gather' Vindice by taking his hand (l. 33). Presumably Vindice embraces
him here.

Forget myself in private, but elsewhere
I pray do you remember me.   40

Vind. O, very well, sir—I conster myself saucy.

Luss. What hast been, of what profession?

Vind. A bone-setter.

Luss. A bone-setter?

Vind. A bawd, my lord; one that sets bones together.   45

Luss. Notable bluntness!
Fit, fit for me, e'en train'd up to my hand.
Thou hast been scrivener to much knavery then?

Vind. Fool to abundance, sir; I have been witness to the sur-
renders of a thousand virgins, and not so little. I have seen   50
patrimonies washed a-pieces, fruit-fields turned into bastards, and, in a world of acres, not so much dust due to the
heir 'twas left to, as would well gravel a petition.

Luss. [*Aside*] Fine villain! Troth, I like him wondrously;
He's e'en shap'd for my purpose. [*To Vindice.*] Then thou
know'st   55
I' th' world strange lust?

Vind.   O, Dutch lust, fulsome lust!

40–6.] *so Q; as verse Thorndike, lines ending* sir— / . . . been? / . . . bone-
setter. / . . . lord— / . . . bluntness!   42.] *so this ed.; two lines in Q, divided
at* beene, / Of.   45.] *so this ed.; two lines in Q, divided at* Lord, / One.
49–53.] *so this ed.; irregular verse in Q, lines ending* witnesse / . . . virgins, /
. . . little, / . . . peices / . . . bastards, / . . . Acres, / . . . too / . . . petition!
49. Fool] *Q;* S'foote *Collins.*   54. *Aside*] *Symons; not in Q.*   55. *To
Vindice*] *This ed.; not in Q.*

---

40. *remember me*] i.e., pay the respect due to one of my rank.

41. *conster*] a common form of 'construe' until the 19th century, reflecting a pronunciation which (as this line demands) stressed the first syllable.

48. *scrivener to*] i.e., secretary to, agent for.

49. *Fool*] accessory, or 'voluntary dupe' (Nicoll). The word was perhaps
suggested by the proverbial linkage between knaves and fools: see Tilley,
F446, K129, 144, and II. ii. 5 below. 'Fool to abundance' may mean 'I have
been the necessary complement to abundance of knavery'. Collins emends
to 'Sfoot', which might just possibly have been misread by a compositor
as 'Fool'.

51. *washed a-pieces*] wrecked, as by a rough sea.

53. *gravel a petition*] sand, in order to dry the ink of, a petition or suit
in law for the recovery of lost property.

56. *Dutch lust*] The Dutch, or Germans, were proverbially regarded as

Drunken procreation, which begets so many drunkards.
Some father dreads not (gone to bed in wine)
To slide from the mother, and cling the daughter-in-law;
Some uncles are adulterous with their nieces,   60
Brothers with brothers' wives. O, hour of incest!
Any kin now, next to the rim o' th' sister,
Is man's meat in these days; and in the morning,
When they are up and dress'd, and their mask on,
Who can perceive this ?—save that eternal eye,   65
That sees through flesh and all. Well, if anything
Be damn'd, it will be twelve o'clock at night,
That twelve will never 'scape;
It is the Judas of the hours, wherein
Honest salvation is betray'd to sin.   70

Luss. In troth it is, too; but let this talk glide.
It is our blood to err, though hell gap'd loud;
Ladies know Lucifer fell, yet still are proud.
Now, sir; wert thou as secret as thou'rt subtle,
And deeply fathom'd into all estates,   75
I would embrace thee for a near employment,
And thou shouldst swell in money, and be able
To make lame beggars crouch to thee.

Vind.   My lord,
Secret ? I ne'er had that disease o' th' mother,
I praise my father. Why are men made close,   80

58–9.] *so Oliphant; divided in Q at* mother, / And.   66–8.] *so this ed.; divided in Q at* dambd ? / It . . . twelue / Will.   72. loud] *Q;* wide *Dodsley 1.*

---

heavy drinkers, and 'drunken procreation' may be regarded as equivalent
to this phrase.

62–3. *Any . . . days*] Cf. I. i. 88–9 and n.

62. *rim*] womb (properly the peritoneum, or membrane lining the belly),
and limit (from the 'rim' or edge, as of a wheel).

72. *gap'd*] yawned, alluding perhaps to *Isaiah*, v. 14, and shouted or
bawled.

75. *all estates*] all sorts of people; cf. *R3*, III. vii. 213.

76. *near*] i.e., intimately concerning me.

79. *disease o' th' mother*] i.e., of talking too much; see I. i. 130–2 and n.
There is a quibble also on the disease called 'the mother', a form of hysteria;
see II. i. 126 and n.

But to keep thoughts in best ? I grant you this,
Tell but some woman a secret overnight,
Your doctor may find it in the urinal i' th' morning.
But my lord—

Luss.   So; thou'rt confirm'd in me,
And thus I enter thee.   [*Gives him money.*]

Vind.   This Indian devil   85
Will quickly enter any man—but a usurer;
He prevents that, by ent'ring the devil first.

Luss. Attend me: I am past my depth in lust,
And I must swim or drown. All my desires
Are levell'd at a virgin not far from court,   90
To whom I have convey'd by messenger
Many wax'd lines, full of my neatest spirit,
And jewels that were able to ravish her
Without the help of man; all which, and more,
She, foolish-chaste, sent back, the messengers   95
Receiving frowns for answers.

Vind.   Possible ?
'Tis a rare phoenix, whoe'er she be.
If your desires be such, she so repugnant,
In troth, my lord, I'd be reveng'd and marry her.

Luss. Push!   100
The dowry of her blood, and of her fortunes,
Are both too mean,—good enough to be bad withal.
I am one of that number can defend

---

82. woman] *Q;* women *Symonds.*   85. *Gives . . . money.*] *Dodsley 3; not
in Q.*   95. foolish-chaste] *This ed.;* foolish chast *Q.*   100–1.] *so this ed.;
one line in Q.*   103. I am] *This ed.;* Ime *Q.*

---

84. *confirm'd in me*] established in my trust.
85. *enter*] initiate, admit; in the next line Vindice picks up the play on
the usual sense of the word.
Indian] referring to the Indies (East or West) as sources of gold and
silver.
92. *wax'd lines*] sealed letters (Nicoll).
neatest spirit] purest ardour.
98. *repugnant*] resisting.
101. *blood*] family.

Marriage is good; yet rather keep a friend.
Give me my bed by stealth, there's true delight;   105
What breeds a loathing in 't, but night by night?

Vind. A very fine religion!

Luss.   Therefore thus:
I'll trust thee in the business of my heart,
Because I see thee well experienc'd
In this luxurious day wherein we breathe.   110
Go thou, and with a smooth enchanting tongue,
Bewitch her ears, and cozen her of all grace;
Enter upon the portion of her soul,
Her honour, which she calls her chastity,
And bring it into expense; for honesty   115
Is like a stock of money laid to sleep,
Which, ne'er so little broke, does never keep.

Vind. You have gi'en it the tang, i'faith, my lord.
Make known the lady to me, and my brain
Shall swell with strange invention; I will move it   120
Till I expire with speaking, and drop down
Without a word to save me; but I'll work—

Luss. We thank thee, and will raise thee. Receive her name,
it is the only daughter to Madam Gratiana, the late
widow.   125

Vind. [*Aside*] O, my sister, my sister!

Luss. Why dost walk aside?

Vind. My lord, I was thinking how I might begin, as thus:

---

118. gi'en it] *so Symonds;* gint *Q.*   123–5.] *so Q; as verse Symonds, lines
ending* thee.— / . . . Madam / . . . widow.   126. *Aside*] *Dodsley 3; not in
Q.*   128–30.] *so this ed.; verse in Q, lines ending* begin / . . . deuices, /
. . . in.

---

104. *friend*] lover; cf. *LLL.*, v. ii. 404.

110. *luxurious*] lecherous.

113. *portion*] marriage-portion or dowry, linking with 'expense', l. 115,
meaning spending, as of money.

118. *gi'en . . . tang*] caught its very flavour, described it accurately.

120. *move*] urge.

123. *raise*] advance; but with amusingly literal suggestions following on
'drop down', l. 121.

'O lady—', or twenty hundred devices; her very bodkin
  will put a man in.   130

Luss. Ay, or the wagging of her hair.

Vind. No, that shall put you in, my lord.

Luss. Shall 't? why, content. Dost know the daughter then?

Vind. O, excellent well by sight.

Luss. That was her brother that did prefer thee to us.   135

Vind. My lord, I think so; I knew I had seen him somewhere—

Luss. And therefore prithee let thy heart to him
  Be as a virgin, close.

Vind.   O, my good lord.

Luss. We may laugh at that simple age within him.

Vind. Ha, ha, ha.   140

Luss. Himself being made the subtle instrument
  To wind up a good fellow—

Vind.   That's I, my lord.

Luss. That's thou.
  To entice and work his sister.

Vind.   A pure novice!

Luss. 'Twas finely manag'd.

Vind.   Gallantly carried;   145
  [*Aside*] A pretty perfum'd villain.

Luss.   I've bethought me
  If she prove chaste still and immovable,
  Venture upon the mother, and with gifts,
  As I will furnish thee, begin with her.

135.] *so this ed.; two lines in Q, divided at* brother / That.   136.] *so this
ed.; two lines in Q, divided at* so, / I.   138. my] *Dodsley 1;* me *Q.*   146.
Aside] *This ed.; not in Q.*

---

  130. *put a man in*] serve as a topic for him to begin his address to her.

  139. *simple age*] innocent (and foolish) stage of life.

  142. *wind up*] incite; an expression borrowed probably from Marston,
Antonio's Revenge; see v. ii. 7 below and n.

  144. *work*] prevail upon.

  146. *perfum'd*] Cf. l. 34 above; it was the mark of a courtier to use perfume; cf. *AYL.*, III. ii. 56–7.

  148. *Venture upon*] make trial of.

  149–50. *begin . . . end*] implying the proverbial 'to begin at the wrong
end'; see Tilley, E132.

Vind. O fie, fie, that's the wrong end, my lord. 'Tis mere   150
   impossible that a mother by any gifts should become a
   bawd to her own daughter.

Luss. Nay then, I see thou'rt but a puny in the subtle mys-
   tery of a woman; why, 'tis held now no dainty dish. The
   name   155
   Is so in league with age that nowadays
   It does eclipse three quarters of a mother.

Vind. Does 't so, my lord?
   Let me alone then to eclipse the fourth.

Luss. Why, well said; come, I'll furnish thee, but first   160
   Swear to be true in all.

Vind.   True?

Luss.   Nay, but swear!

Vind. Swear?
   I hope your honour little doubts my faith.

Luss. Yet for my humour's sake, 'cause I love swearing.

Vind. 'Cause you love swearing, 'slud, I will.

Luss.   Why, enough.   165
   Ere long look to be made of better stuff.

Vind. That will do well indeed, my lord.

Luss.   Attend me.   [*Exit.*]

Vind. O!
   Now let me burst; I've eaten noble poison.
   We are made strange fellows, brother, innocent villains;   170
   Wilt not be angry when thou hear'st on 't, think'st thou?
   I'faith, thou shalt. Swear me to foul my sister!
   Sword, I durst make a promise of him to thee;

153–5.] *so Q; verse in Symonds, lines ending* puisne / . . . woman. / . . . name.
158. Does 't] *Q* (Dost).   160–1.] *so Symonds; as prose Q.*   162–3.] *so
Thorndike; one line in Q.*   167. Exit.] *Dodsley 2; not in Q.*

---

153. *puny*] novice; cf. *1H6*, IV. vii. 36.
155. *name*] i.e., of bawd.
156. *age*] i.e., middle or old age.
165. *'slud*] a form of *'sblood* (God's blood), a common oath.
167. *Attend me*] i.e., wait on me as a regular attendant.
170. *fellows*] partners, accomplices.
172. *foul*] debauch; an extension of the normal senses.

Thou shalt dis-heir him, it shall be thine honour.
And yet, now angry froth is down in me,   175
It would not prove the meanest policy
In this disguise to try the faith of both;
Another might have had the self same office,
Some slave, that would have wrought effectually,
Ay, and perhaps o'erwrought 'em. Therefore I,   180
Being thought travell'd, will apply myself
Unto the self same form, forget my nature,
As if no part about me were kin to 'em,
So touch 'em—though I durst almost for good
Venture my lands in heaven upon their blood.   *Exit.* 185

[I. iv]

Enter the discontented Lord ANTONIO, *whose wife the Duchess's
youngest son ravished; he discovering the body of her dead to* [PIERO,]
certain Lords, *and* HIPPOLITO.

Ant. Draw nearer, lords, and be sad witnesses
Of a fair, comely building newly fall'n,
Being falsely undermined. Violent rape
Has play'd a glorious act; behold, my lords,
A sight that strikes man out of me.   5
Piero. That virtuous lady!
Ant.   Precedent for wives!

185. blood] *Dodsley 1; good Q.*

I. iv. 0.2. Piero] *Symonds; not in Q.*

___

174. *dis-heir*] i.e., make him cease to be the duke's heir, by killing him.
180. *o'erwrought*] won over.
181–2. *apply . . . form*] adapt myself to appear like that (i.e., like the 'slave'
of l. 179).
184. *touch*] test; cf. *Tim.*, III. iii. 6; so the fineness of gold was tested by
rubbing it on a touchstone.
184–5. *I . . . blood*] The meaning seems to be, 'I dare almost for good
and all stake my hopes of salvation on their disposition (or strength of
character)'.

I. iv. 4. *play'd . . . act*] suggesting a stage action, and sharpening our
awareness of the play as play; cf. I. i. 40.

Hipp. The blush of many women, whose chaste presence
    Would e'en call shame up to their cheeks, and make
    Pale wanton sinners have good colours.
Ant.   Dead!
    Her honour first drunk poison, and her life,   10
    Being fellows in one house, did pledge her honour.
Piero. O grief of many!
Ant.   I mark'd not this before—
    A prayer-book the pillow to her cheek;
    This was her rich confection, and another
    Plac'd in her right hand, with a leaf tuck'd up,   15
    Pointing to these words:
    Melius virtute mori, quam per dedecus vivere.
    True and effectual it is indeed.
Hipp. My lord, since you invite us to your sorrows,
    Let's truly taste 'em, that with equal comfort,   20
    As to ourselves, we may relieve your wrongs;
    We have grief too, that yet walks without tongue:
    Curae leves loquuntur, maiores stupent.
Ant. You deal with truth, my lord.
    Lend me but your attentions, and I'll cut   25
    Long grief into short words. Last revelling night,
    When torchlight made an artificial noon
    About the court, some courtiers in the masque,
    Putting on better faces than their own,

8–9.] *so Dodsley 3; divided in Q at* cheekes, / And.   15. Plac'd] *Q* (Plastc'd).

---

14. *confection*] preservative; from the medicinal sense of the word, as a compound of drugs.

17. Melius . . . vivere] 'Better to die in virtue than to live in dishonour'; a commonplace tag of the period, the source of which is not known.

18. *effectual*] to the point; cf. *2H6*, III. i. 41.

23. Curae . . . stupent] 'Small cares speak out, greater ones are struck dumb'; a tag misquoted from Seneca, *Hippolytus*, l. 607, where the correct reading is 'ingentes' (huge) for 'maiores'. This was a favourite tag of Jacobean dramatists, referred to at *Mac.*, IV. iii. 209–10; and in Webster's *White Devil*, II. i. 278; it was cited by Florio in his translation of Montaigne's *Essays*, I. 2, and passed into proverb lore (Tilley, G449).

28–9. *masque . . . own*] alluding to the masks worn by the performers in court entertainments.

Being full of fraud and flattery—amongst whom,   30
The duchess' youngest son (that moth to honour)
Fill'd up a room; and with long lust to eat
Into my wearing, amongst all the ladies,
Singled out that dear form, who ever liv'd
As cold in lust as she is now in death   35
(Which that step-duchess' monster knew too well);
And therefore, in the height of all the revels,
When music was heard loudest, courtiers busiest,
And ladies great with laughter—O, vicious minute,
Unfit but for relation to be spoke of!—   40
Then, with a face more impudent than his vizard,
He harried her amidst a throng of panders
That live upon damnation of both kinds,
And fed the ravenous vulture of his lust
(O death to think on 't!). She, her honour forc'd,   45
Deem'd it a nobler dowry for her name
To die with poison than to live with shame.

Hipp. A wondrous lady, of rare fire compact;
    Sh' has made her name an empress by that act.
Piero. My lord, what judgment follows the offender?   50
Ant. Faith, none, my lord; it cools and is deferr'd.
Piero. Delay the doom for rape?
Ant.   O, you must note
    Who 'tis should die:

---

36. step-duchess' monster] *Q* (step Duches-Monster).   52–3. O . . . die]
so Oliphant; one line in Q.

30.] The broken syntax suggests the speaker's passion.
31. *moth*] as the moth destroys by eating away.
32. *room*] place.
40. *but for relation*] if it were not for its essential place in my narrative.
42. *harried*] violated.
43. *damnation . . . kinds*] presumably by sinning themselves, and by cor-
rupting others.
46. *dowry*] endowment.
47.] This is virtually a translation of the tag at l. 17.
49. *empress*] or perhaps 'impress', emblem.
52. *doom*] Cf. I. ii. 41.

The duchess' son; she'll look to be a saver;
Judgement in this age is near kin to favour.   55
Hipp. Nay then, step forth thou bribeless officer.

                                        [*Draws his sword.*]

I bind you all in steel to bind you surely;
Here let your oaths meet, to be kept and paid,
Which else will stick like rust, and shame the blade.
Strengthen my vow, that if, at the next sitting,   60
Judgment speak all in gold, and spare the blood
Of such a serpent, e'en before their seats
To let his soul out, which long since was found
Guilty in heaven.
All.   We swear it, and will act it.
Ant. Kind gentlemen, I thank you in mine ire.   65
Hipp. 'Twere pity
The ruins of so fair a monument
Should not be dipp'd in the defacer's blood.
Piero. Her funeral shall be wealthy, for her name
Merits a tomb of pearl. My lord Antonio,   70
For this time wipe your lady from your eyes;
No doubt our grief and yours may one day court it,
When we are more familiar with revenge.
Ant. That is my comfort, gentlemen, and I joy
In this one happiness above the rest,   75
Which will be call'd a miracle at last;
That, being an old man, I'd a wife so chaste.   *Exeunt.*

56.1. *Draws . . . sword.*] *Symonds; not in Q.*

---

54. *she'll . . . saver*] i.e., the Duchess will expect to save him.
56–64.] This ceremonious swearing of an oath over drawn swords was
perhaps suggested by *Ham.*, I. v. 145 ff., where Hamlet makes his com-
panions swear on his sword to keep an oath of silence.
72. *court it*] be shown at court.

Act II

Enter CASTIZA, *the sister.*

Cast. How hardly shall that maiden be beset,
    Whose only fortunes are her constant thoughts;
    That has no other child's-part but her honour,
    That keeps her low and empty in estate.
    Maids and their honours are like poor beginners;   5
    Were not sin rich, there would be fewer sinners.
    Why had not virtue a revenue ? well,
    I know the cause, 'twould have impoverish'd hell.

[Enter DONDOLO.]

    How now, Dondolo ?
Don. Madonna, there is one, as they say, a thing of flesh and   10
    blood, a man I take him by his beard, that would very
    desirously mouth to mouth with you.
Cast. What's that ?
Don. Show his teeth in your company.
Cast. I understand thee not.   15
Don. Why, speak with you, Madonna.
Cast. Why, say so, madman, and cut off a great deal of dirty

ACT II, SCENE i] *Q* (*ACTVS.* 2. *SCAE.* 1.).   8.1. *Enter Dondolo.*] Dodsley
1; not in Q.

   II. i. 1. *beset*] besieged by temptations; cf. l. 52.
   3. *child's-part*] share in an inheritance.
   9. *Dondolo*] a type name for a foolish character; see notes to the list of
characters, p. 2. The play is indebted to *Hamlet* (see Intro., p. lxviii), and
Osric may lie behind this affected courtier, but the immediate suggestion
for him probably came from John Marston's *The Fawn* (printed 1606),
which has 'Dondolo, a bald fool' among its characters.
   17-18. *cut . . . way*] a fanciful way of saying 'avoid tediousness'; cf.

way; had it not been better spoke in ordinary words, that
one would speak with me?

Don. Ha, ha; that's as ordinary as two shillings. I would   20
strive a little to show myself in my place; a gentleman-
usher scorns to use the phrase and fancy of a serving-
man.

Cast. Yours be your own, sir. Go, direct him hither;

                                        [*Exit* DONDOLO.]

I hope some happy tidings from my brother   25
That lately travell'd, whom my soul affects.
Here he comes.

Enter VINDICE *her brother, disguised.*

Vind. Lady, the best of wishes to your sex,
     Fair skins and new gowns.   [*Presents her with a letter.*]
Cast.   O, they shall thank you, sir.
     Whence this?
Vind.   O, from a dear and worthy friend,   30
     Mighty!
Cast.   From whom?
Vind.   The duke's son.
Cast.   Receive that!
                         A box o' th' ear to her brother.

I swore I'd put anger in my hand,
And pass the virgin limits of myself,
To him that next appear'd in that base office,

24. own] *Dodsley 1;* one *Q.*   24.1. *Exit Dondolo.*] *Symonds; not in Q.*
29. *Presents . . . letter.*] *This ed., after Oliphant; not in Q.*   33. myself]
Q; my sex *Symonds.*

Middleton, *A Mad World my Masters* (1608), I. i. 75, 'to be short, and cut
off a great deal of dirty way'.
     21. *place*] office.
     25–6.] A nice touch, for her brother comes, disguised, with bad news,
and to meet hate (l. 36), not love.
     26. *affects*] loves, is drawn to.
     30. *this*] Vindice clearly gives her something, presumably a letter.
     32.] The line is a syllable short, the irregularity reflecting the passion and
abruptness of the speaker.

To be his sin's attorney. Bear to him   35
That figure of my hate upon thy cheek
Whilst 'tis yet hot, and I'll reward thee for 't;
Tell him my honour shall have a rich name
When several harlots shall share his with shame.
Farewell; commend me to him in my hate!   *Exit.*   40

Vind. It is the sweetest box that e'er my nose came nigh,
The finest drawn-work cuff that e'er was worn!
I'll love this blow for ever, and this cheek
Shall still henceforward take the wall of this.
O, I'm above my tongue! most constant sister,   45
In this thou hast right honourable shown;
Many are call'd by their honour that have none.
Thou art approv'd for ever in my thoughts.
It is not in the power of words to taint thee;
And yet for the salvation of my oath,   50
As my resolve in that point, I will lay
Hard siege unto my mother, though I know
A siren's tongue could not bewitch her so.
Mass, fitly here she comes; thanks, my disguise.
Madam, good afternoon.

[*Enter* GRATIANA.]

41.] *so Collins; two lines in* Q, *divided at* Boxe, / That.   55.1. *Enter*
Gratiana.] *Dodsley 2; not in* Q.

41–6.] Cf. I. iii. 84–7, where Vindice had accepted Lussurioso's money;
his strong approval of his sister's rejection of Lussurioso's suit sorts oddly
with his own acceptance of service under the duke's son.

41. *box*] a quibble, alluding to the common meaning, a box of sweet-
smelling ointment.

42. *drawn-work cuff*] a cuff decorated in patterned threads, but alluding
also to the blow (cuff) that has decorated his cheek.

44. *take the wall of*] be privileged over; the phrase properly referred to
a person's insisting on walking on the inside, the wall side, hence the cleaner
and safer side, of a roadway or sidewalk.

46. *right honourable*] a quibble on the form of address proper to peers, or
daughters of peers, below the rank of marquess, to Privy Councillors, and
certain other dignitaries.

50. *oath*] See I. iii. 164–5.

51. *As . . . point*] i.e., as it was his plan to 'try the faith of both' daughter
and mother; see I. iii. 176–7.

Grat.   Y' are welcome, sir.   55
Vind. The next of Italy commends him to you,
    Our mighty expectation, the duke's son.
                       [Presents her with a letter.]
Grat. I think myself much honour'd that he pleases
    To rank me in his thoughts.
Vind.   So may you, lady.
    One that is like to be our sudden duke—   60
    The crown gapes for him every tide—and then
    Commander o'er us all. Do but think on him;
    How blest were they now that could pleasure him
    E'en with anything almost.
Grat.   Ay, save their honour!
Vind. Tut, one would let a little of that go too,   65
    And ne'er be seen in 't—ne'er be seen in 't, mark you;
    I'd wink, and let it go—
Grat.   Marry, but I would not.
Vind. Marry, but I would, I hope; I know you would too,
    If you'd that blood now which you gave your daughter.
    To her indeed 'tis, this wheel comes about;   70
    That man that must be all this, perhaps e'er morning
    (For his white father does but mould away),
    Has long desir'd your daughter—
Grat. Desir'd?
Vind.   —Nay, but hear me:

56–7.] Vindice here greets Gratiana much as he did Castiza, and probably hands her too a letter, rather than beginning with gifts, as Lussurioso suggested at I. iii. 148. Vindice gives her money later, at ll. 120 ff.

60. *to . . . duke*] suddenly to become duke.

61. *tide*] hour or season (as in 'eventide', etc.).

66. *ne'er . . . 't*] never be observed in doing it (in other words, keep it secret).

70. *wheel*] suggesting the wheel of Fortune, now turning to bring her prosperity.

72. *white*] white-haired.

He desires now that will command hereafter;   75
Therefore be wise, I speak as more a friend
To you than him. Madam, I know y' are poor,
And 'lack the day,
There are too many poor ladies already;
Why should you vex the number? 'tis despis'd;   80
Live wealthy, rightly understand the world,
And chide away that foolish country-girl
Keeps company with your daughter, chastity.
Grat. O fie, fie; the riches of the world cannot hire a mother
    to such a most unnatural task!   85
Vind. No, but a thousand angels can;
Men have no power, angels must work you to 't.
The world descends into such base-born evils
That forty angels can make fourscore devils.
There will be fools still I perceive, still fools;   90
Would I be poor, dejected, scorn'd of greatness,
Swept from the palace, and see other daughters
Spring with the dew o' th' court, having mine own
So much desir'd and lov'd—by the duke's son?
No, I would raise my state upon her breast,   95
And call her eyes my tenants; I would count
My yearly maintenance upon her cheeks,
Take coach upon her lip, and all her parts
Should keep men after men, and I would ride
In pleasure upon pleasure.   100
You took great pains for her, once when it was,
Let her requite it now, though it be but some:

78–9.] *so Symonds; one line in* Q.   84–5.] *so* Q; *as verse Symonds, divided
at* hire / A.   90. still fools] *Collins;* still foole Q.

---

80. *vex*] afflict, by adding to it.
86. *angels*] gold coins, bearing the figure of St Michael; a common
quibble: see *Sh. England*, I. 342.
91. *dejected*] lowly, abased; cf. *Lr.*, IV. i. 3.
95. *state*] social status, suggesting a splendid manner of living.
102. *though . . . some*] though only partially.

You brought her forth, she well may bring you home.
Grat. O heavens!
    This overcomes me.
Vind. [*Aside*]   Not, I hope, already!   105
Grat. [*Aside*] It is too strong for me, men know that know us:
    We are so weak, their words can overthrow us.
    He touch'd me nearly, made my virtues bate,
    When his tongue struck upon my poor estate.
Vind. [*Aside*] I e'en quake to proceed, my spirit turns edge;   110
    I fear me she's unmother'd, yet I'll venture.
    That woman is all male, whom none can enter.
    [*To her*] What think you now, lady ? speak, are you wiser ?
    What said advancement to you ? Thus it said:
    The daughter's fall lifts up the mother's head.   115
    Did it not, madam ? But I'll swear it does:
    In many places, tut, this age fears no man;
    'Tis no shame to be bad, because 'tis common.
Grat. Ay, that's the comfort on 't.
Vind.   The comfort on 't ?
    I keep the best for last; can these persuade you   120
    To forget heaven—and—   [*Gives her money.*]

104–5. O . . . me] *This ed.; one line in* Q.   105, 106, 110. *Aside*] *Dodsley;
not in* Q.   113. *To her*] *This ed.; not in* Q.   116–17. does: / . . . places,]
This ed.; does / . . . places, Q; does / . . . places; *Dodsley.*   121. *Gives . . .
money.*] *Symonds; not in* Q.

---

103. *bring you home*] i.e., make you rich (*O.E.D.*, *home* sb. 7, first citation
1760).

108. *nearly*] closely.

   bate] abate, weaken.

110. *turns edge*] becomes blunt. He is loth to press the attack for fear she
will surrender.

111. *she's unmother'd*] She has lost the natural feelings of a mother for
her child.

   venture] pronounced 'venter', a true rhyme with 'enter'; see Kökeritz,
p. 271.

112.] a line marked as a 'sentence' or epigram to be noticed; it varies the
familiar proverb 'All women may be won', Tilley, W681.

118.] like l. 112, marked as a 'sentence'; the idea may be developed from
the commonplace, 'Flesh is frail' (Tilley, F363; *Matthew*, xxvi. 41).

Grat. Ay, these are they—

Vind. O!

Grat.   —that enchant our sex, these are
  The means that govern our affections.
  That woman   125
  Will not be troubled with the mother long,
  That sees the comfortable shine of you;
  I blush to think what for your sakes I'll do.

Vind. [*Aside*] O suff'ring heaven, with thy invisible finger,
  E'en at this instant turn the precious side   130
  Of both mine eyeballs inward, not to see myself!

Grat. Look you, sir.

Vind.   Holla!

Grat.   Let this thank your pains.

Vind. O, you're a kind madam.

Grat. I'll see how I can move.

Vind.   Your words will sting.

Grat. If she be still chaste, I'll ne'er call her mine.   135

Vind. Spoke truer than you meant it.

Grat. Daughter Castiza.

[*Enter* CASTIZA.]

Cast. Madam.

Vind. O, she's yonder; meet her.
  [*Aside*] Troops of celestial soldiers guard her heart.   140
  Yon dam has devils enough to take her part.

Cast. Madam, what makes yon evil-offic'd man

123–5. that . . . woman] *Symonds; two lines in Q, divided at* sexe, / These.
129. *Aside*] *Dodsley 1; not in Q.*   133. madam] *Dodsley 1;* Mad-man *Q.*
137.1. *Enter Castiza.*] *Dodsley 2; not in Q.*   139–40. yonder; meet her. /
Troops] *Collins;* yonder. / Meete her: troupes. *Q.*   140. *Aside*] *Harrison;
not in Q.*

---

126. *mother*] maternal affection and responsibility; quibbling on the
commoner meaning of 'hysteria', thought of as a disease rising from the
womb.

129. *finger*] Cf. *Exodus*, viii. 19 and *Luke*, xii. 20, for the phrase 'the finger
of God'.

In presence of you?
Grat.   Why?
Cast.   He lately brought
    Immodest writing sent from the duke's son
    To tempt me to dishonourable act.   145
Grat. Dishonourable act?—good honourable fool,
    That wouldst be honest 'cause thou wouldst be so,
    Producing no one reason but thy will.
    And 't has a good report, prettily commended,
    But pray, by whom?—mean people, ignorant people;   150
    The better sort I'm sure cannot abide it.
    And by what rule should we square out our lives,
    But by our betters' actions? O if thou knew'st
    What 'twere to lose it, thou would never keep it;
    But there's a cold curse laid upon all maids;   155
    Whilst others clip the sun, they clasp the shades.
    Virginity is paradise, lock'd up.
    You cannot come by your selves without fee,
    And 'twas decreed that man should keep the key.
    Deny advancement? treasure? the duke's son?   160
Cast. I cry you mercy, lady, I mistook you;
    Pray, did you see my mother? Which way went she?
    Pray God I have not lost her.
Vind. [*Aside*]   Prettily put by.

---

152. should] *Dodsley 1;* shouldst *Q.*   156. others] *Dodsley 1;* other *Q.*
162. she] *This ed.;* you *Q.*   163. *Aside*] *Dodsley 3; not in Q.*

---

147. *honest*] virtuous.

152. *square out*] frame, or mark out as in a plan.

156. *Whilst . . . shades*] i.e., while others embrace life (in this context, the Prince also, as the sun is a common figure for the ruler; cf. *1H4*, I. ii. 190), they embrace unreal appearances (in this context, death, as uncooperative maids, like Vindice's betrothed, are killed, and as 'shades' refers to the darkness of the dwelling of the dead, Hades).

158. *come by your selves*] become possessed of yourselves (i.e., of 'paradise').

fee] reward (as 'treasure', l. 160, will be given to her).

158–9.] varying the proverb 'Women receive perfection by men'; see Tilley, W718. This proverb is cited in Marston, *Ant. Rev.*, III. iv (M.S.R., l. 1224).

Grat. Are you as proud to me as coy to him ?
  Do you not know me now ?
Cast.   Why, are you she ?   165
  The world's so chang'd, one shape into another,
  It is a wise child now that knows her mother!
Vind. [*Aside*] Most right, i'faith.
Grat.   I owe your cheek my hand
  For that presumption now, but I'll forget it;
  Come, you shall leave those childish haviours,   170
  And understand your time. Fortunes flow to you;
  What, will you be a girl ?
  If all fear'd drowning that spy waves ashore,
  Gold would grow rich, and all the merchants poor.
Cast. It is a pretty saying of a wicked one,   175
  But methinks now
  It does not show so well out of your mouth,
  Better in his.
Vind. [*Aside*] Faith, bad enough in both,
  Were I in earnest, as I'll seem no less—
  [*To her*] I wonder, lady, your own mother's words 180
  Cannot be taken, nor stand in full force.
  'Tis honesty you urge; what's honesty ?
  'Tis but heaven's beggar, and what woman is
  So foolish to keep honesty,
  And be not able to keep herself ? No,   185

---

168. *Aside*] *Dodsley 3; not in Q.* 175-6.] *so this ed.; one line in Q.* 178.
Aside] *Dodsley 1; not in Q.* 180. *To her*] *This ed.; not in Q.* 183-4.]
so Dodsley 2; one line in Q.

---

164. *coy*] disdainful.
167.] varying the common proverb 'It is a wise child that knows his own father' (Tilley, C309).
170. *haviours*] ways of behaving.
173-4. *If . . . poor*] i.e., if all those on shore feared drowning when they saw waves (at sea), money (gold) would become plentiful (rich), because no one would venture his money in trade, and so merchants would grow poor.
183-5. *'Tis . . . herself*] inverting the proverbial advice that a woman who loses her honesty has nothing else worth losing; see Tilley, S271, W662, M1033.

Times are grown wiser, and will keep less charge;
A maid that has small portion now intends
To break up house, and live upon her friends.
How blest are you, you have happiness alone;
Others must fall to thousands, you to one,   190
Sufficient in himself to make your forehead
Dazzle the world with jewels, and petitionary people
Start at your presence.
Grat.   O, if I were young,
I should be ravish'd.
Cast.   Ay, to lose your honour.
Vind. 'Slid, how can you lose your honour to deal with my   195
    lord's grace?
He'll add more honour to it by his title,
Your mother will tell you how.
Grat.   That I will.
Vind. O, think upon the pleasure of the palace;
Secured ease and state; the stirring meats,   200
Ready to move out of the dishes, that
E'en now quicken when they're eaten;
Banquets abroad by torch-light, music, sports,
Bare-headed vassals, that had ne'er the fortune
To keep on their own hats, but let horns wear 'em;   205

193–4. O . . . ravish'd] *so this ed.; one line in Q.*   195–6.] *so this ed.; as
verse in Q, divided at* honor? / To.   201–2.] *so Symonds; one line in Q.*
203. music] *Dodsley 1;* Musicks *Q.*   205. wear] *Q* (were).

---

186. *keep . . . charge*] take less care (about honesty or virtue), quibbling,
too, on the sense 'maintain less expense'.

187. *intends*] resolves.

192. *petitionary people*] i.e., people who come to court to beg for favours
or benefits.

194. *ravish'd*] Gratiana means 'filled with delight at such a prospect',
but Castiza takes the word in its more violent sense.

200. *stirring*] physically stimulating; cf. Dekker, *Gull's Hornbook* (Grosart, VIII. 34), 'Capon is a stirring meat sometime' (cited *O.E.D.*), and I. ii.
181 above.

202. *quicken*] excite people; but also suggesting the idea of becoming
pregnant.

203. *abroad*] out of doors.

205.] It was the custom for men to remove their hats at court, though

Nine coaches waiting,—hurry, hurry, hurry.

Cast. Ay, to the devil.

Vind. [*Aside*] Ay, to the devil— [*To her*] To th' duke, by my faith.

Grat. Ay, to the duke. Daughter, you'd scorn to think o' th'
    devil and you were there once.   210

Vind. [*Aside*] True, for most there are as proud as he for his
    heart, i'faith.—

    [*To Castiza*] Who'd sit at home in a neglected room,
    Dealing her short-liv'd beauty to the pictures,
    That are as useless as old men, when those   215
    Poorer in face and fortune than herself
    Walk with a hundred acres on their backs,
    Fair meadows cut into green foreparts—O,
    It was the greatest blessing ever happen'd to women,
    When farmers' sons agreed, and met again,   220
    To wash their hands and come up gentlemen;
    The commonwealth has flourish'd ever since.
    Lands that were mete by the rod, that labour's spar'd,

208. *Aside*] Symonds; *not in* Q.   *To her*] *This ed.; not in* Q.   211. *Aside*]
Dodsley *1; not in* Q.   213. *To Castiza*] *This ed.; not in* Q.   223. mete]
Q (meat).

---

these were commonly worn elsewhere, as in the home, or at church. There
is an undertone of bawdy in the line, a suggestion of cuckoldry, as if 'hats'
might suggest 'wives'.

   210. *and*] if.

   211–12. *proud . . . heart*] i.e., proud in the extreme; 'for his heart' is equivalent to 'for (at the expense of) his life'; cf. *Shr.,* I. ii. 37, 'And could not
get him for my heart to do it'. So I take the phrase here to mean, 'proud
enough to risk his life for the sake of his pride'. 'As proud as Lucifer' (or
as the devil) was a common proverbial saying (Tilley, L572).

   217–18. *Walk . . . foreparts*] The idea is common; cf. *John,* II. i. 70, *H8,*
I. i. 84, and Camden, *Remains* (1605), p. 221, 'A Nobleman . . . having
lately sold a Manor . . . came ruffling into the Court in a new suit saying:
Am not I a mightie man, that bear an hundred houses on my back?' 'Foreparts' were stomachers, ornamental coverings for the breast.

   220. *met again*] presumably a rough equivalent for 'agreed again'; perhaps the author was hard driven for a rhyme here.

   221. *come up gentlemen*] i.e., rise in rank, and come to court.

   223. *mete*] measured.

   rod] a measure of length (5½ yards), and of area (160 rods to the
acre).

    Tailors ride down, and measure 'em by the yard;
    Fair trees, those comely foretops of the field,   225
    Are cut to maintain head-tires—much untold,
    All thrives but chastity, she lies a-cold.
    Nay, shall I come nearer to you? mark but this:
    why are there so few honest women, but because 'tis the
    poorer profession? That's accounted best that's best 230
    followed; least in trade, least in fashion; and that's not
    honesty, believe it; and do but note the low and dejected
    price of it:
    Lose but a pearl, we search and cannot brook it.
    But that once gone, who is so mad to look it?   235
Grat. Troth, he says true.
Cast.   False, I defy you both.
    I have endur'd you with an ear of fire;
    Your tongues have struck hot irons on my face.
    Mother, come from that poisonous woman there!
Grat. Where?   240
Cast. Do you not see her? she's too inward, then.
    [*To Vindice*] Slave, perish in thy office. You heavens, please
    Henceforth to make the mother a disease,
    Which first begins with me; yet I've outgone you.   *Exit.*
Vind. [*Aside*] O angels, clap your wings upon the skies,   245

232. low] *Q* (loue); love *Dodsley 1.*   242. *To Vindice*] *This ed.; not in Q.*
245. *Aside*] *Symonds; not in Q.*

---

    224. *yard*] tailor's or cloth-yard.
    225. *foretops*] The image is of the lock of hair that grows at the front of the head, and was sometimes arranged to adorn the forehead; cf. *Sh. England*, II. 168.
    226. *head-tires*] head-dresses.
    untold] not reckoned; i.e., much more might be said.
    227. *chastity . . . a-cold*] Cf. the proverb 'As chaste as ice' (Tilley, I1); here the implication is that to be chaste is to be poor.
    234. brook it] put up with its loss.
    235. look] look into, take trouble about.
    243. *make . . . disease*] a quibbling allusion to 'mother' as a term for hysteria; cf. l. 126 above, and note.
    244. *outgone*] perhaps = circumvented, if 'you' refers to Gratiana and Vindice; but the exact sense is not clear.

And give this virgin crystal plaudities!

Grat. Peevish, coy, foolish!—but return this answer:
My lord shall be most welcome, when his pleasure
Conducts him this way. I will sway mine own;
Women with women can work best alone.   *Exit.*   250

Vind. Indeed, I'll tell him so.
O, more uncivil, more unnatural
Than those base-titled creatures that look downward!
Why does not Heaven turn black, or with a frown
Undo the world?—why does not earth start up,   255
And strike the sins that tread upon 't? O,
Were 't not for gold and women, there would be no
damnation; Hell would look like a lord's great kitchen
without fire in 't:
But 'twas decreed before the world began,   260
That they should be the hooks to catch at man.   *Exit.*

[II. ii]

    Enter LUSSURIOSO, *with* HIPPOLITO, *Vindice's brother.*

Luss. I much applaud
Thy judgment; thou art well-read in a fellow,
And 'tis the deepest art to study man.
I know this, which I never learn'd in schools:
The world's divided into knaves and fools.   5

257–9.] *so this ed.; as verse in Q, divided at* damnation, / Hell.

II. ii. 1–2.] *so Symonds; one line in Q.*

---

246. *crystal plaudities*] clear-ringing applause. The word 'crystal' alludes also to the crystalline sphere supposed, in Ptolemaic astronomy, to be one of the heavenly spheres revolving between God's throne and earth, and so is an appropriate location for angels. There is a reference to it in Milton's *Paradise Lost*, III. 482.

247. *Peevish*] headstrong, perverse.

250.] This looks proverbial, but is not recorded by Tilley.

252. *uncivil*] barbarous.

258–9. *Hell . . . in 't*] i.e., without gold and women, there would be no fuel for the fires of hell, which would then resemble the kitchen of a great house without its huge open fires, steam, and smoke.

II. ii. 5.] proverbial; see Tilley, K144 (first citation 1659).

Hipp. [*Aside*] Knave in your face, my lord—behind your back.

Luss. And I much thank thee, that thou hast preferr'd
      A fellow of discourse, well-mingled,
      And whose brain time hath season'd.

Hipp.   True, my lord;
      [*Aside*] We shall find season once, I hope. O villain,   10
      To make such an unnatural slave of me—but—

Luss. Mass, here he comes.

[*Enter* VINDICE *disguised.*]

Hipp. [*Aside*] And now shall I have free leave to depart.

Luss. Your absence; leave us.

Hipp. [*Aside*]   Are not my thoughts true?
      I must remove, but brother, you may stay;   15
      Heart, we are both made bawds a new-found way!   *Exit.*

Luss. Now,
      We're an even number; a third man's dangerous,
      Especially her brother. Say, be free,
      Have I a pleasure toward?

Vind.   O, my lord.   20

Luss. Ravish me in thine answer; art thou rare?
      Hast thou beguil'd her of salvation,
      And rubb'd hell o'er with honey? Is she a woman?

Vind. In all but in desire.

Luss.   Then she's in nothing—
      I bate in courage now.

6. *Aside*] *Dodsley 1; not in Q.*   10. *Aside*] *This ed.; not in Q.*   12.1.
Enter . . . disguised.] *Symonds; not in Q.*   13. *Aside*] *Dodsley 2; not in Q.*
14. *Aside*] *Dodsley 1; not in Q.*   17–18.] *so this ed.; one line in Q.*   24–5.
Then . . . now] *so Thorndike; one line in Q.*

8. *discourse*] good conversation.

well-mingled] 'mingled' was perhaps pronounced as three syllables, so
making the line regular: 'mingell' was a common spelling of the verb.

10. *find . . . once*] find an opportunity one day (i.e., to deal with Lussurioso).

21. *rare*] full of merit, as having succeeded.

25. *bate in courage*] lose something of my desire for her. For 'courage' in
this sense, *O.E.D.* cites Barnabe Barnes, *Works* (1573), p. 329, 'priests are
so hot of courage, and can not keep their chastity'.

Vind.   The words I brought   25
　　Might well have made indifferent-honest naught;
　　A right good woman in these days is chang'd
　　Into white money with less labour far.
　　Many a maid has turn'd to Mahomet
　　With easier working; I durst undertake,   30
　　Upon the pawn and forfeit of my life,
　　With half those words to flat a puritan's wife.
　　But she is close and good—yet 'tis a doubt
　　By this time. O, the mother, the mother!

Luss. I never thought their sex had been a wonder   35
　　Until this minute. What fruit from the mother?

Vind. [*Aside*] Now must I blister my soul, be forsworn,
　　Or shame the woman that receiv'd me first;
　　I will be true, thou liv'st not to proclaim;
　　Spoke to a dying man, shame has no shame.—   40
　　[*To him*] My lord!

Luss.   Who's that?

Vind.   Here's none but I, my lord.

Luss. What would thy haste utter?

Vind.   Comfort.

Luss.   Welcome.

Vind. The maid being dull, having no mind to travel
　　Into unknown lands, what did me I straight,

26. indifferent-honest] *This ed.;* indifferent honest, *Q.*　33-4.] *so Symonds;*
prose in Q.　37. *Aside*] *Dodsley 1; not in Q.*　Now] *Q;* How *Collins.*
41. *To him*] *This ed.; not in Q.*　44. me] *Q;* omitted *Collins.*

26. *made . . . naught*] made reasonably virtuous women wicked (or
'naughty').
　28. *white money*] silver coin; i.e., the woman is sold into prostitution.
　29-30. *Many . . . working*] i.e., many a maid has turned pagan and abandoned her religion (not merely her morality) under less pressure.
　32. *flat*] overthrow, with the sense of making her lie down.
　33. *close*] not open to persuasion.
　38. *receiv'd*] greeted me on arrival, i.e., at my birth.
　39. *thou*] Lussurioso.
　proclaim] i.e., publish my mother's shame.
　44. *did me I*] See Abbott, 220; 'me' here seems merely emphatic, as in

But set spurs to the mother; golden spurs   45
Will put her to a false gallop in a trice.

Luss.   Is 't possible that in this
The mother should be damn'd before the daughter?

Vind. O, that's good manners, my lord; the mother for her
age must go foremost, you know.   50

Luss. Thou 'st spoke that true; but where comes in this comfort?

Vind. In a fine place, my lord—the unnatural mother
Did with her tongue so hard beset her honour,
That the poor fool was struck to silent wonder;
Yet still the maid, like an unlighted taper,   55
Was cold and chaste, save that her mother's breath
Did blow fire on her cheeks. The girl departed,
But the good ancient madam, half mad, threw me
These promising words, which I took deeply note of:
'My lord shall be most welcome—'

Luss.   Faith, I thank her.   60

Vind. 'When his pleasure conducts him this way—'

Luss. That shall be soon, i'faith.

Vind.   'I will sway mine own—'

Luss. She does the wiser; I commend her for 't.

Vind. 'Women with women can work best alone.'

Luss. By this light, and so they can; give 'em their due, men 65
are not comparable to 'em.

Vind. No, that's true, for you shall have one woman knit more
in an hour than any man can ravel again in seven and
twenty year.

Luss. Now my desires are happy; I'll make 'em freemen now; 70
Thou art a precious fellow; faith, I love thee.

69. year] *Q* (yeare); years *Dodsley 3*.

'made me no more ado', *1H4*, II. iv. 193–4, and Vindice is calling attention
to his cleverness.

65. *By this light*] a common asseveration; by daylight, or God's good
light.

68. *ravel*] unravel.

70. *make . . . freemen*] as if they had been slaves, kept down by sheer force.

71. *precious fellow*] man of great worth; quibbling on the sense 'fine (i.e.,
as arrant, or wicked) accomplice': cf. l. 127.

> Be wise, and make it thy revenue: beg, leg;
> What office couldst thou be ambitious for?

Vind. Office, my lord? Marry, if I might have my wish, I
   would have one that was never begged yet. 75

Luss. Nay, then, thou canst have none.

Vind. Yes, my lord, I could pick out another office yet, nay,
   and keep a horse and drab upon 't.

Luss. Prithee, good bluntness, tell me.

Vind. Why, I would desire but this, my lord: to have all the 80
   fees behind the arras, and all the farthingales that fall
   plump about twelve o'clock at night upon the rushes.

Luss. Thou 'rt a mad apprehensive knave; dost think to make
   any great purchase of that?

Vind. O, 'tis an unknown thing, my lord; I wonder 't has 85
   been missed so long!

Luss. Well, this night I'll visit her, and 'tis till then
   A year in my desires; farewell—attend:
   Trust me with thy preferment.   *Exit.*

Vind.   My lov'd lord.
   [*Drawing his sword*] O, shall I kill him o' th' wrong side
     now? No; 90
   Sword, thou wast never a back-biter yet.
   I'll pierce him to his face;

---

89. *Exit.*] *Q; after* lord. *Thorndike.*   90. *Drawing . . . sword*] *This ed.; not
in Q.*   92–3.] *so this ed.; one line in Q.*

---

72. *revenue*] accented, as was normal in the 17th century, on the second
syllable.
   beg, leg] beg by bowing, or making a leg.
   81. *fees . . . arras*] i.e., fees for making assignations behind tapestries such
as were commonly hung on the walls of rooms, and stood far enough away
from the walls to allow people to stand in the space between.
   farthingales] hooped petticoats. Clothes were valuable, and could easily
be sold or pawned.
   82. *plump*] roundly, or, in current idiom, smack.
   rushes] commonly used for strewing on the floors of rooms.
   83. *apprehensive*] sharp-witted, perceptive.
   84. *purchase*] profit.
   91. *back-biter*] The personification, and the play on this word, are characteristic of the play's language.

He shall die looking upon me:
Thy veins are swell'd with lust, this shall unfill 'em;
Great men were gods, if beggars could not kill 'em.   95
Forgive me, Heaven, to call my mother wicked!
O, lessen not my days upon the earth.
I cannot honour her; by this I fear me
Her tongue has turn'd my sister into use.
I was a villain not to be forsworn   100
To this our lecherous hope, the duke's son;
For lawyers, merchants, some divines, and all
Count beneficial perjury a sin small.
It shall go hard yet, but I'll guard her honour,
And keep the ports sure.   105

Enter HIPPOLITO.

Hipp. Brother, how goes the world? I would know news
Of you, but I have news to tell you.
Vind.   What,
In the name of knavery?
Hipp.   Knavery faith;
This vicious old duke's worthily abus'd
The pen of his bastard writes him cuckold.   110
Vind. His bastard?
Hipp.   Pray believe it; he and the duchess
By night meet in their linen. They have been seen
By stair-foot panders.
Vind.   O, sin foul and deep!
Great faults are wink'd at when the duke's asleep.

106–8. Brother . . . knavery?] *so this ed.; divided in Q at* you / But . . . you. /
What.

97–8. *lessen . . . her*] an allusion to *Exodus*, xx. 12, 'Honour thy father and
thy mother: that thy days may be long upon the land which the Lord thy
God giveth thee!'
    99. *use*] employment for sexual purposes (*O.E.D.*, sb. 3b), and also profit
(usury): see IV. iv. 103 and n.
    105. *ports*] gates.
    110.] Cf. Middleton, *Phoenix* (printed 1607), I. ii. 100, 'he'll one day
write me cuckold'.

    See, see, here comes the Spurio.

Hipp.   Monstrous luxur!   115

            [*Enter* SPURIO *with two* Servants.]

Vind. Unbrac'd; two of his valiant bawds with him.
    O, there's a wicked whisper; hell is in his ear.
    Stay, let's observe his passage—

Spurio.   O, but are you sure on 't?

1. Serv. My lord, most sure on 't, for 'twas spoke by one
    That is most inward with the duke's son's lust: 120
    That he intends within this hour to steal
    Unto Hippolito's sister, whose chaste life
    The mother has corrupted for his use.

Spurio. Sweet word, sweet occasion! Faith, then, brother,
    I'll disinherit you in as short time   125
    As I was when I was begot in haste;
    I'll damn you at your pleasure—precious deed!
    After your lust, O, 'twill be fine to bleed.
    Come, let our passing out be soft and wary.

                        Exeunt [SPURIO *and* Servants].

Vind. Mark, there, there, that step; now to the duchess.   130
    This, their second meeting, writes the duke cuckold
    With new additions, his horns newly reviv'd.
    Night, thou that look'st like funeral heralds' fees,
    Torn down betimes i' th' morning, thou hang'st fitly

115.1. *Enter . . . Servants.*] *Dodsley 2 (after l. 118); not in Q.*   119.
1. Serv.] *Symonds; Ser. Q.*

---

    115. *luxur*] lecher; cf. I. i. 9.
    116. *Unbrac'd*] with clothes unfastened.
    123. *use*] Cf. l. 99 and n.
    131. *writes . . . cuckold*] continuing the image of l. 110.
    133. *funeral . . . fees*] In Elizabethan London the heralds made a lot of money by the high fees they charged for attending funerals and supervising a display of escutcheons, pennons, and other trappings, in order to advertise the much-prized gentility of a dead man and his family. Here, by a characteristic telescoping of sense, the 'fees' are equated with the canvas escutcheons and other displays, torn down after the funeral. See *Sh. England*, II. 74–5.

To grace those sins that have no grace at all.   135
Now 'tis full sea abed over the world;
There's juggling of all sides. Some that were maids
E'en at sunset are now perhaps i' th' toll-book.
This woman in immodest thin apparel
Lets in her friend by water; here a dame,   140
Cunning, nails leather hinges to a door,
To avoid proclamation; now cuckolds are
A-coining, apace, apace, apace, apace;
And careful sisters spin that thread i' th' night
That does maintain them and their bawds i' th' day.   145

Hipp. You flow well, brother.

Vind.   Puh, I'm shallow yet,
Too sparing and too modest—shall I tell thee?
If every trick were told that's dealt by night,
There are few here that would not blush outright.

Hipp. I am of that belief too.

Vind.   Who's this comes?   150

[*Enter* LUSSURIOSO.]

The duke's son up so late?—brother, fall back,
And you shall learn some mischief.—My good lord.

142–3.] *so this ed.; divided in Q at* proclamation, / Now.   150. *Vind.*] *Q;
omitted Dodsley 3.*   150.1. *Enter Lussurioso.*] *Dodsley 1 (after l. 152); not
in Q.*   151. The] *Nicoll (and catchword in Q on D4ʳ); Vind. The Q.*

---

136. *full sea*] high tide (i.e., in sexual activity).
137. *juggling*] deception.
138. *i' th' toll-book*] i.e., for sale as prostitutes; literally, the toll-book
was the register of animals for sale at a market, with the tolls payable on
them.
140. *by water*] hinting at the River Thames? or Venetian canals?
144. *sisters*] probably = prostitutes (*O.E.D.* cites 'sisters of the Bank',
i.e., Bankside, famous for its brothels, as a phrase meaning this).
147. *modest*] moderate.
150–1. Vind. *Who's . . . The duke's*] In Q, '*Vind.* Whose this comes,' is
the bottom line on page D4ʳ, and the catchword is 'The'; however, the top
line of D4ᵛ begins '*Vind.* The Dukes. . .' I think the catchword is correct,
the second speech-heading an error, and I have given both lines to Vindice.
Many editors regard the first speech-heading as a mistake, and assign
'Who's this comes?' to Hippolito.

Luss. Piato! Why, the man I wish'd for; come,
  I do embrace this season for the fittest
  To taste of that young lady.
Vind. [*Aside*]   Heart, and hell!   155
Hipp. [*Aside*] Damned villain!
Vind. [*Aside*] I ha' no way now to cross it, but to kill him.
Luss. Come; only thou and I.
Vind.   My lord, my lord!
Luss. Why dost thou start us?
Vind.   I'd almost forgot—
  The bastard!
Luss.   What of him?
Vind.   This night, this hour— 160
  This minute, now—
Luss.   What, what?
Vind.   Shadows the duchess—
Luss. Horrible word!
Vind.   And, like strong poison, eats
  Into the duke your father's forehead.
Luss.   O!
Vind. He makes horn-royal.
Luss.   Most ignoble slave!
Vind. This is the fruit of two beds.
Luss.   I am mad.   165
Vind. That passage he trod warily.
Luss.   He did!

155, 156, 157. *Aside*] Symonds; *not in* Q. 159–60. I'd ... bastard] *so this ed.; one line in* Q. 160–1. This ... now] *so this ed.; one line in* Q.

---

153. *Piato*] the first mention of Vindice's assumed name, which means 'hidden'; see above, p. 2.
 159. *start us*] startle me.
 161. *Shadows*] covers.
 163. *forehead*] as expressing shame (*O.E.D.*, 2, cites J. Burges, *Answer Rejoined*, 1631, 'No man can deny it, who hath any forehead left', and cf. *Rom.*, III. ii. 92), but also suggesting the cuckold's horns of the next line.
 164. *horn-royal*] i.e., a royal cuckold.
 165. *fruit ... beds*] the result of the Duke's lechery—lying in another bed besides his own, and so begetting the bastard, Spurio.

Vind. And hush'd his villains every step he took.

Luss. His villains ? I'll confound them.

Vind. Take 'em finely, finely now.

Luss. The duchess' chamber-door shall not control me.   170

Exeunt [LUSSURIOSO *and* VINDICE].

Hipp. Good, happy, swift; there's gunpowder i' th' court,
  Wild-fire at midnight. In this heedless fury
  He may show violence to cross himself;
  I'll follow the event.   *Exit.*

[II. iii]

Enter again [LUSSURIOSO, *with drawn sword, and* VINDICE;
  the Duke *and* Duchess *screened within a bed*].

Luss.   Where is that villain ?

Vind. Softly, my lord, and you may take 'em twisted.

Luss. I care not how.

Vind.   O, 'twill be glorious
  To kill 'em doubled, when they're heap'd. Be soft,
  My lord.

Luss.   Away, my spleen is not so lazy;   5
  Thus, and thus, I'll shake their eyelids ope,
  And with my sword shut 'em again for ever.

172. midnight. In . . . fury] *Dodsley 1;* mid-night, in . . . fury *Q;* mid-night,
in . . . fury. *Nicoll.*

II. iii. 0.1. *Lussurioso . . . Vindice*] *Dodsley 1;* not in *Q.*   *with drawn
sword*] *This ed.;* not in *Q.*   0.2. *the . . . bed.*] *This ed.;* not in *Q.*   4–8.]
so this ed.; four lines in Q, *divided at* Lord. / Away . . . thus, / Ile . . . sword /
Shut.   4. they're] *Q (their).*

172. *Wild-fire*] in war, inflammable material used to start fires; so here
suggesting swift-spreading violence.

173. *He . . . himself*] He may show so much violence as to thwart his own
hopes.

174. *follow the event*] go to see what the outcome is.

II. iii.] Although Hippolito's half-line as he goes off is completed by
Lussurioso as he enters, the stage is cleared here, and a bed must be put
in view, so that it seems proper to begin a new scene. Beds were commonly
provided with curtains, which may have been used here to conceal the duke
and duchess.

Villain! Strumpet!

[*He reveals the Duke and Duchess in bed.*]

Duke. You upper guard defend us—

Duchess. Treason, treason!   10

Duke.   —O, take me not
    In sleep; I have great sins, I must have days,
    Nay, months, dear son, with penitential heaves,
    To lift 'em out, and not to die unclear.
    O, thou wilt kill me both in heaven and here.

Luss. I am amaz'd to death.

Duke.   Nay, villain, traitor,   15
    Worse than the foulest epithet, now I'll gripe thee
    E'en with the nerves of wrath, and throw thy head
    Amongst the lawyers. Guard!

[*The* Guard *enters and seizes Lussurioso.*]

Enter [HIPPOLITO,] *Nobles, and* [AMBITIOSO *and* SUPERVACUO,
            the Duke's] *sons.*

1. Noble. How comes the quiet of your grace disturb'd?

Duke. This boy, that should be myself after me,   20
    Would be myself before me; and in heat
    Of that ambition, bloodily rush'd in,
    Intending to depose me in my bed.

2. Noble. Duty and natural loyalty forfend!

Duchess. He call'd his father villain, and me strumpet,   25
    A word that I abhor to file my lips with.

8.1.] *This ed., after Harrison; not in Q.*   9–11. O . . . days] *so this ed.;
one line in Q.*   18. lawyers. Guard!] *Collins;* Lawyers gard *Q.*   18.1.
The . . . Lussurioso.] This ed.; not in Q.   18.2. Hippolito] *Thorndike; not
in Q.*   18.2–3. Ambitioso . . . Duke's] *Symonds; not in Q.*

---

9. *upper*] innermost, or nearest to the bedchamber, as furthest from the
entrance: cf. *Cor.,* IV. v. 193, 'set at upper end o' th' table', i.e., the end
furthest from the door.

12. *heaves*] groans or sighs; Nicoll compares *Ham.,* IV. i. 1.

13. *unclear*] not free from sins.

17. *nerves*] sinews.

20. *myself*] i.e., duke.

26. *file*] defile.

Ambit. That was not so well done, brother.
Luss.   I am abus'd—
    I know there's no excuse can do me good.
Vind. [*Aside*] 'Tis now good policy to be from sight;
    His vicious purpose to our sister's honour   30
    Is cross'd beyond our thought.
Hipp. [*Aside*]   You little dreamt
    His father slept here.
Vind. [*Aside*]   O, 'twas far beyond me—
    But since it fell so, without frightful words,
    Would he had kill'd him; 'twould have eas'd our swords!
                    [VINDICE *and* HIPPOLITO] *dissemble a flight*
                                        [*and steal away*].
Duke. Be comforted, our duchess, he shall die.   35
                                        [*Exit* Duchess.]
Luss. Where's this slave-pander now ? Out of mine eye,
    Guilty of this abuse.

            Enter SPURIO *with* [*two* Servants,] *his villains.*

Spurio.   You're villains, fablers,

27–8. I am . . . good] *so Oliphant; one line in Q.*   29. *Aside*] *Symonds;
not in Q.*   31, 32. *Aside*] *Oliphant; not in Q.*   31–2. You . . . here] *so
Oliphant; one line in Q.*   33. words] *Dodsley 1;* word *Q.*   34.1–2.
Vindice . . . away.] *so this ed.;* dissemble a flight. (*against ll. 35–6*) *Q;* Exeunt
Vindice and Hippolito. *Symonds.*   35.1. *Exit* Duchess.] *This ed.; not in
Q.*

33. *frightful*] causing fright; the murder of the duke by his own son
should be a frightful thing to wish.
34.1.] The phrase '*dissemble a flight*' is printed against ll. 35 and 36 in Q,
but I think it refers to the way in which Vindice and his brother slink off
here, and not to the duchess; l. 34 is of more than average length, and there
was no space to print '*dissemble*' against it, though it is true too that the
S.D. has no bracket before it to mark it as belonging to the line above, like
'*Exeunt*' at II. ii. 170.
35.1. Exit *Duchess*] No exit is marked for her in Q, and there is no reason
to leave her on stage for the general 'Exeunt' at l. 123.1. It seems appropriate that she should go off with the duke's words of comfort in her ears,
the last words spoken to her in the scene.
36. *Out . . . eye*] i.e., out of sight.

　　You have knaves' chins and harlots' tongues; you lie,
　　And I will damn you with one meal a day!

1. Serv. O good my lord!

Spurio.　　　　　　　'Sblood, you shall never sup!　　40

2. Serv. O, I beseech you, sir!

Spurio.　　　　　　　　To let my sword
　　Catch cold so long and miss him.

1. Serv.　　　　　　　　Troth, my lord,
　　'Twas his intent to meet there.

Spurio.　　　　　　Heart, he's yonder.
　　Ha? what news here? is the day out o' th' socket
　　That it is noon at midnight? the court up?　　45
　　How comes the guard so saucy with his elbows?

Luss. [*Aside*] The bastard here?
　　Nay, then, the truth of my intent shall out.
　　[*To the Duke*] My lord and father, hear me.

Duke.　　　　　　　　　　　　Bear him hence.

Luss. I can with loyalty excuse—

Duke.　　　　　　　Excuse?　　50
　　To prison with the villain!
　　Death shall not long lag after him.

Spurio. [*Aside*] Good i'faith; then 'tis not much amiss.

Luss. Brothers, my best release lies on your tongues;
　　I pray persuade for me.

Ambit.　　　　　　It is our duties;　　55
　　Make yourself sure of us.

Super.　　　　　We'll sweat in pleading.

Luss. And I may live to thank you.　　　　*Exit* [*guarded*].

41–3.] *so Oliphant; divided in* Q *at* sir. / To . . . him. / Troth . . . there /
Heart.　47. *Aside*] *Oliphant; not in* Q　49. *To the Duke*] *This ed.; not
in* Q.　50–1. Excuse? / . . . villain] *so Oliphant; one line in* Q.　53.
Aside] *Harrier; not in* Q.　55–6. It . . . us] *so Oliphant; one line in* Q.
57. *Exit guarded.*] *This ed.; Exeunt.* Q; *Exit with Lords. Symonds.*

　　38. *harlots'*] another term of abuse, equivalent to 'villains' and 'knaves',
and originally applied to men.
　　44. *out o' th' socket*] i.e., out of gear, as might now be said; not fitting into
its proper place in the scheme of things.
　　46. *his elbows*] the elbows of Lussurioso, who is under arrest.

Ambit.   No, thy death
   Shall thank me better.
Spurio. [*Aside*]   He's gone; I'll after him,
   And know his trespass; seem to bear a part
   In all his ills, but with a puritan heart.   *Exit.* 60
Ambit. Now, brother, let our hate and love be woven
   So subtilly together, that in speaking
   One word for his life, we may make three for his death:
   The craftiest pleader gets most gold for breath.
Super. Set on; I'll not be far behind you, brother.   65
Duke. Is 't possible a son should be disobedient as far as the
   sword? It is the highest; he can go no farther.
Ambit. My gracious lord, take pity—
Duke.   Pity, boys?
Ambit. Nay, we'd be loth to move your grace too much;
   We know the trespass is unpardonable,   70
   Black, wicked, and unnatural—
Super. In a son, O, monstrous!
Ambit.   —yet, my lord,
   A duke's soft hand strokes the rough head of law,
   And makes it lie smooth.
Duke.   But my hand shall ne'er do 't.
Ambit. That as you please, my lord.
Super.   We must needs confess   75
   Some father would have enter'd into hate
   So deadly-pointed that before his eyes
   He would ha' seen the execution sound,
   Without corrupted favour.
Ambit.   But my lord,
   Your grace may live the wonder of all times,   80

57–8. No . . . better] *so this ed.; one line in Q.*   58. *Aside*] *Oliphant; not
in Q.*   62–3.] *so Oliphant; divided in Q at* life, / We.   76. father] *Q;*
fathers *Dodsley 1.*

60. *puritan*] hypocritical.
76. *Some*] one or another; cf. I. ii. 99.
78. *sound*] properly (soundly) carried out. Nicoll compares III. iv. 27.
79. *corrupted favour*] implying that any mercy would be corrupt.

    In pard'ning that offence which never yet
    Had face to beg a pardon.
Duke. [*Aside*]   Honey? How's this?
Ambit. Forgive him, good my lord, he's your own son,—
    And I must needs say, 'twas the vilelier done!
Super. He's the next heir—yet this true reason gathers: 85
    None can possess that dispossess their fathers.
    Be merciful—
Duke. [*Aside*]   Here's no stepmother's wit;
    I'll try them both upon their love and hate.
Ambit. Be merciful—although—
Duke.   You have prevail'd;
    My wrath, like flaming wax, hath spent itself.   90
    I know 'twas but some peevish moon in him;
    Go, let him be releas'd.
Super. [*Aside*]   'Sfoot, how now, brother?
Ambit. Your grace doth please to speak beside your spleen;
    I would it were so happy.
Duke.   Why, go, release him.
Super. O my good lord, I know the fault's too weighty,   95
    And full of general loathing; too inhuman,
    Rather by all men's voices worthy death.
Duke. 'Tis true too.
    Here then, receive this signet, doom shall pass;
    Direct it to the judges, he shall die   100
    E'er many days. Make haste.

---

82. *Aside*] Oliphant; *not in* Q.   84. vilelier] Q (vildlier); viler *Dodsley 1.*
87, 92. *Aside*] Symonds; *not in* Q.   91–2. I . . . releas'd] *so Dodsley 2; one
line in* Q.   98–9.] *so this ed.; one line in* Q.

---

82. *Honey?*] i.e., sweet words, instead of the 'envy', l. 104, the duke
expects: cf. 'honey words', *R3*, IV. i. 80.
87. *no stepmother's wit*] The duke sees through their feigned plea for
mercy, as they lack their stepmother's intelligence. He expects them, as
sons of the duchess, to be hostile to Lussurioso, his son by a former
marriage.
91. *peevish moon*] senseless fit of frenzy. Here 'moon' refers to its supposed influence, and the more common word was 'lune', as at *Wint.*, II. ii.
30, giving rise to the modern 'lunacy'.
93. *beside . . . spleen*] leaving your anger aside.

Ambit.   All speed that may be.
    We could have wish'd his burden not so sore;
    We knew your grace did but delay before.
                          Exeunt [AMBITIOSO *and* SUPERVACUO].
Duke. Here's envy with a poor thin cover o'er 't,
    Like scarlet hid in lawn, easily spied through.   105
    This their ambition by the mother's side
    Is dangerous, and for safety must be purg'd.
    I will prevent their envies; sure it was
    But some mistaken fury in our son,
    Which these aspiring boys would climb upon: 110
    He shall be releas'd suddenly.

                    Enter [*two*] *Nobles.*

1. Noble. Good morning to your grace—
Duke. Welcome, my lords.
2. Noble.   —Our knees shall take
    Away the office of our feet for ever,
    Unless your grace bestow a father's eye   115
    Upon the clouded fortunes of your son,
    And in compassionate virtue grant him that
    Which makes e'en mean men happy,—liberty.
Duke. [*Aside*] How seriously their loves and honours woo
    For that which I am about to pray them do,   120
    Which— [*To them*] rise, my lords; your knees sign his release.
    We freely pardon him.
1. Noble. We owe your grace much thanks, and he much duty.
                                  Exeunt [Nobles].

112–14. Our . . . ever] *so Dodsley 2; one line in Q.*   119. Aside] *Oliphant;
not in Q.*   121. Which— [*To them*] rise] *This ed.;* Which—rise *Q;* Arise
Dodsley 1.

_____

    104. *envy*] malicious hatred; the word had a much stronger meaning
than it does now; cf. *Mer. V.,* IV. i. 10.
    105. *scarlet*] a rich red cloth.
    lawn] fine, and so partially transparent, linen.
    108. *prevent*] forestall.
    111. *suddenly*] at once.
    117. *virtue*] power, as of a divine being; cf. *Cor.,* v. ii. 12.

Duke. It well becomes that judge to nod at crimes,
    That does commit greater himself and lives;   125
    I may forgive a disobedient error,
    That expect pardon for adultery,
    And in my old days am a youth in lust!
    Many a beauty have I turn'd to poison
    In the denial, covetous of all: 130
    Age hot is like a monster to be seen;
    My hairs are white, and yet my sins are green.   [*Exit.*]

132. *Exit.*] *Thorndike; not in Q.*

129–30. *turn'd . . . denial*] i.e., I have brought about the poisoning of
many a beautiful woman who denied me. For 'turn to' in this sense, cf.
Cor., III. i. 284, 'turn you to no further harm'.

132.] a line echoed in Middleton, *Roaring Girl*, v. ii. 124, 'Their sins are
green even when their heads are grey'.

Act III

Enter AMBITIOSO *and* SUPERVACUO.

Super. Brother, let my opinion sway you once;
    I speak it for the best, to have him die,
    Surest and soonest. If the signet come
    Unto the judges' hands, why then his doom
    Will be deferr'd till sittings and court-days,   5
    Juries, and further. Faiths are bought and sold;
    Oaths in these days are but the skin of gold.
Ambit. In troth, 'tis true too.
Super.   Then let's set by the judges,
    And fall to the officers; 'tis but mistaking
    The duke our father's meaning, and where he nam'd   10
    'E'er many days', 'tis but forgetting that,
    And have him die i' th' morning.
Ambit.   Excellent!
    Then am I heir—duke in a minute!
Super. [*Aside*]   Nay,
    And he were once puff'd out, here is a pin
    Should quickly prick your bladder!
Ambit.   Blest occasion!   15

ACT III, SCENE i] *Q* (*ACT. 3.*).   13. *Aside*] *Scott; not in Q.*   15. Blest]
Dodsley 1; Blast *Q.*

III. i. 6. *bought and sold*] betrayed for money.

7. *Oaths . . . gold*] i.e., oaths nowadays carry no validity, and serve merely
as a cover for transactions in cash, which alone have weight.

8. *set by*] disregard.

9. *fall to*] apply to.

14. *he*] i.e., Lussurioso.

puff'd out] extinguished (like a flame); but the alternative sense, 'blown
up', no doubt suggested 'bladder' in the next line.

He being pack'd, we'll have some trick and wile
To wind our younger brother out of prison,
That lies in for the rape; the lady's dead,
And people's thoughts will soon be buried.

Super. We may with safety do 't, and live and feed;   20
The duchess' sons are too proud to bleed.

Ambit. We are, i'faith, to say true. Come, let's not linger;
I'll to the officers; go you before,
And set an edge upon the executioner.

Super. Let me alone to grind him.   *Exit.*

Ambit.   Meet! Farewell.   25
I am next now; I rise just in that place,
Where thou 'rt cut off,—upon thy neck, kind brother.
The falling of one head lifts up another.   *Exit.*

[III. ii]

       Enter with the Nobles, LUSSURIOSO, *from prison.*

Luss. My lords,
I am so much indebted to your loves
For this, O, this delivery.

1. Noble.   But our duties,
My lord, unto the hopes that grow in you.

Luss. If e'er I live to be myself, I'll thank you.   5

---

18. lady's] *Q* (Ladies).   21. duchess' sons] *Q* (Duchesse-sonnes).   25.
Meet! Farewell.] *so Nicoll;* Meete farewell, *Q.*

III. ii. 1–2. My . . . loves] *so this ed.; one line in Q.*   3. But] *Q;* Put *Collins.*
3–4. But . . . you] *so Oliphant; one line in Q.*

---

16. *pack'd*] packed off, got rid of.

24. *executioner*] quibbling on the word's original meaning, one who
carries out a deed, especially an evil deed (so Nicoll); in this sense, Supervacuo is himself an 'executioner'. The words 'edge' and 'grind' apply properly to the executioner's axe, but are here transferred to the executioner
himself.

25. *Meet*] fitting. Ambitioso applauds his own idéa.

III. ii. 3. *But*] merely.
5. *myself*] i.e., duke; cf. II. iii. 20–1.

O Liberty, thou sweet and heavenly dame!—
But hell for prison is too mild a name.   *Exeunt.*

[III. iii]

Enter AMBITIOSO *and* SUPERVACUO, *with* Officers.

Ambit. Officers,
    Here's the duke's signet, your firm warrant, brings
    The command of present death along with it
    Unto our brother, the duke's son. We are sorry
    That we are so unnaturally employ'd,   5
    In such an unkind office, fitter far
    For enemies than brothers.
Super.   But you know
    The duke's command must be obey'd.
1. Offic. It must, and shall, my lord—this morning, then,
    So suddenly?
Ambit.   Ay, alas; poor, good soul,   10
    He must break fast betimes; the executioner
    Stands ready to put forth his cowardly valour.
2. Offic. Already?
Super. Already, i'faith. O sir, destruction hies,
    And that is least impudent, soonest dies.   15
1. Offic. Troth, you say true. My lord, we take our leaves;
    Our office shall be sound, we'll not delay .

III. iii. 1–3.] *so this ed.; two lines in Q, divided at* warrant, / Brings.   10.
Ay . . . soul] *Q* (I alasse poore-good-soule,).   15. impudent] *Q;* impru-
dent *Dodsley 4.*   16. true. My lord,] *Dodsley 1;* true my Lord *Q.*

6. *O . . . dame !*] The personification was common.
7. *hell*] a common image for prison: cf. *Err.*, IV. ii. 40, where a sergeant-
at-law describes his office as 'carrying poor souls to hell'.

III. iii. 15. *impudent*] wanting in shame or decency. This word was generally accented on the first syllable, and Dodsley's emendation to 'im-
prudent' has been widely adopted; but the emphasis in the play on impudence (see especially I. iii. 5 ff.) supports the reading of Q as an ironic
comment on Junior Brother. A better emendation would be 'he that' for
'that'.
17. *sound*] properly performed; cf. II. iii. 78.

The third part of a minute.
Ambit.   Therein you show
    Yourselves good men, and upright officers.
    Pray let him die as private as he may;   20
    Do him that favour, for the gaping people
    Will but trouble him at his prayers, and make
    Him curse, and swear, and so die black. Will you
    Be so far kind?
1. Offic.   It shall be done, my lord.
Ambit. Why, we do thank you; if we live to be,   25
    You shall have a better office.
2. Offic.   Your good lordship.
Super. Commend us to the scaffold in our tears.
1. Offic. We'll weep, and do your commendations.
                                        Exeunt [Officers].

Ambit. Fine fools in office!
Super.   Things fall out so fit.
Ambit. So happily; come, brother; ere next clock,   30
    His head will be made serve a bigger block.   *Exeunt.*

[III. iv]

Enter in prison JUNIOR BROTHER.

Junior Bro. Keeper!

[*Enter* Keeper.]

Keeper. My lord.

19. upright officers] *Q*; upright. Officers *Collins.*   22–4.] *so this ed.;
divided in Q at* prayers. / And . . . black. / Will.

III. iv. 0.1. *Enter . . . Brother.*] *Q; Enter . . . Youngest Son and Keeper.
Symonds, after Dodsley 2.*   1.1. *Enter* Keeper.] *This ed.; not in Q.*

21. *gaping*] staring.
23. *black*] wicked, in sin.
25. *live to be*] i.e., duke, as he thinks; cf. III. ii. 5.
28. *commendations*] pronounced as five syllables.
31. *block*] the executioner's block; quibbling on the idea of a 'smaller'
block, a mould for a hat.

Junior Bro. No news lately from our brothers ? Are they un-
 mindful of us ?

Keeper. My lord, a messenger came newly in,   5
 And brought this from 'em.   [*Gives him a letter.*]

Junior Bro.   Nothing but paper comforts ?
 I look'd for my delivery before this,
 Had they been worth their oaths—prithee, be from us.

                    [*Exit* Keeper.]

 Now, what say you, forsooth; speak out, I pray.

                    [*He begins to read the letter.*]

 'Brother, be of good cheer'—'slud, it begins like a whore,   10
 with good cheer; 'thou shalt not be long a prisoner'—not
 five and thirty year, like a bankrupt; I think so! 'We have
 thought upon a device to get thee out by a trick'—by a
 trick ? Pox o' your trick, and it be so long a-playing! 'And
 so rest comforted; be merry, and expect it suddenly.' Be   15
 merry! Hang merry, draw and quarter merry; I'll be
 mad! Is 't not strange that a man should lie in a whole
 month for a woman ? Well, we shall see how sudden our
 brothers will be in their promise. I must expect still a
 trick; I shall not be long a prisoner.   20

[*Enter* Keeper.]

3–4.] *so this ed.; as verse in Q, divided at* brothers ? / Are.   5–6. My . . .
'em] *so Dodsley 2; one line in Q.*   6. *Gives . . . letter.*] *Oliphant; not in Q.*
8.1. *Exit* Keeper.] *Dodsley 2; not in Q.*   9.1. *He . . . letter.*] *Symonds;*
Letter. *Q.*   10–17. Brother . . . mad!] *so Oliphant (subs.); divided in Q at*
cheere, / Slud . . . cheere, / *Thou . . . prisoner.* / Not . . . so, / *We . . . tricke !* /
By . . . playing. / *And . . . suddaynely !* / Be . . . mad!   12. five] *Q;* six
Collins.   20–1. prisoner. How] *Dodsley 1;* prisoner, how *Q.*   20.1.
Enter Keeper.] *so Dodsley 2 (after* news ?); *not in Q.*

---

  10. *'slud*] a variant of *'sblood*, or *God's blood*, a common oath: cf. I. iii.
165.
  11. *good cheer*] quibbling on the idea of making merry, as the phrase can
mean 'good entertainment'.
  14. *trick . . . a-playing*] suggesting a game of cards; cf. ll. 67–8 below.
  15. *suddenly*] without delay.
  17. *lie in*] be confined, quibbling on the common sense as it applies to
women (in the current use of 'confined'), to be brought to bed of a child.
  19. *still*] continually.

How now, what news?

Keeper. Bad news, my lord; I am discharg'd of you.

Junior Bro. Slave, call'st thou that bad news? I thank you,
    brothers.

Keeper. My lord, 'twill prove so; here come the officers
    Into whose hands I must commit you.

Junior Bro.   Ha?   25
    Officers? What, why?

            [*Enter three* Officers.]

1. Offic.   You must pardon us, my lord;
    Our office must be sound. Here is our warrant,
    The signet from the duke. You must straight suffer.

Junior Bro. Suffer?
    I'll suffer you to be gone, I'll suffer you   30
    To come no more; what would you have me suffer?

2. Offic. My lord, those words were better chang'd to prayers;
    The time's but brief with you; prepare to die.

Junior Bro. Sure, 'tis not so!

3. Offic.   It is too true, my lord.

Junior Bro. I tell you, 'tis not, for the duke, my father,   35
    Deferr'd me till next sitting; and I look
    E'en every minute, threescore times an hour,
    For a release, a trick wrought by my brothers.

1. Offic. A trick, my lord? If you expect such comfort,
    Your hope's as fruitless as a barren woman.   40
    Your brothers were the unhappy messengers
    That brought this powerful token for your death.

Junior Bro. My brothers? No, no.

2. Offic.   'Tis most true, my lord.

Junior Bro. My brothers to bring a warrant for my death?

25–6. Ha? . . . why] *so this ed.; one line in Q.*   26.1. *Enter* . . . Officers.]
This ed.; Enter officers. Dodsley 2.   29–30.] *so this ed.; one line in Q.*

---

    27. *sound*] Cf. III. iii. 17 and n.; the meaning here could be merely 'valid',
but the weight put on the word earlier suggests the stronger sense, 'properly carried out'.

    36. *sitting*] i.e., of the courts of law.

How strange this shows!

3. Offic.   There's no delaying time.   45

Junior Bro. Desire 'em hither, call 'em up; my brothers?
    They shall deny it to your faces.

1. Offic.   My lord,
    They're far enough by this, at least at court,
    And this most strict command they left behind 'em;
    When grief swum in their eyes, they show'd like brothers, 50
    Brimfull of heavy sorrow; but the duke
    Must have his pleasure.

Junior Bro. His pleasure?

1. Offic. These were their last words which my memory bears:
    'Commend us to the scaffold in our tears.'   55

Junior Bro. Pox dry their tears; what should I do with tears?
    I hate 'em worse than any citizen's son
    Can hate salt water. Here came a letter now,
    New-bleeding from their pens, scarce stinted yet—
    Would I'd been torn in pieces when I tore it—   60
    Look, you officious whoresons, words of comfort:
    'Not long a prisoner'.

1. Offic. It says true in that, sir, for you must suffer presently.

Junior Bro. A villainous duns upon the letter, knavish exposi-
    tion! Look you then here, sir: 'We'll get thee out by a   65
    trick', says he.

63–5. It . . . exposition] *so Q; as verse Oliphant, divided at* sir; / For . . .
Duns / Upon.   64–6.] *so this ed.; as two lines of verse in Q, divided at*
exposition, / Looke.

---

45. *delaying time*] putting off the time of execution.

58. *salt water*] the sea. The allusion is to the dangers and privations of
sea-travel, illustrated in the proverb, 'Praise the sea but keep on land'
(Tilley, S177), and perhaps to the custom of pressing men to serve in the
navy.

59. *stinted*] stopped from flowing, a word used especially of staunching
blood.

64. *duns*] a subtle or sophistical interpretation. The allusion is to the
scholastic theologian Duns Scotus, famous for the fine distinctions of his
reasoning (the modern 'dunce' is the same word; the overthrow of scholastic argument by the new learning in the 16th century made defenders of
Scotus appear blockheads or 'dunces').

2. Offic. That may hold too, sir, for you know a trick is com-
monly four cards, which was meant by us four officers.
Junior Bro. Worse and worse dealing.
1. Offic.   The hour beckons us;
The headsman waits, lift up your eyes to heaven.   70
Junior Bro. I thank you, faith; good, pretty, wholesome counsel;
I should look up to heaven as you said,
Whilst he behind cozens me of my head.
Ay, that's the trick.
3. Offic.   You delay too long, my lord.
Junior Bro. Stay, good authority's bastards; since I must   75
Through brothers' perjury die, O let me venom
Their souls with curses.
1. Offic.   Come, 'tis no time to curse.
Junior Bro. Must I bleed then, without respect of sign?
Well—
My fault was sweet sport, which the world approves;   80
I die for that which every woman loves.   *Exeunt.*

[III. v]

Enter VINDICE [*in disguise*] *with* HIPPOLITO, *his brother.*

Vind. O sweet, delectable, rare, happy, ravishing!
Hipp. Why, what's the matter, brother?
Vind.   O, 'tis able

71. pretty, wholesome] *Q* (pritty-holsome).   72. said] *Q* (sedd).   78–9.
Must . . . Well—] *so* Oliphant; *one line in* Q.

III. v. o.1. in disguise] *so* Symonds; *not in* Q.   2–3. O . . . forehead] *so*
Collins; *one line in* Q.

---

68. *four cards . . . officers*] possibly, as Collins suggested, an allusion to
the popular game of primero, in which each player held four cards, and the
best winning hand was four of the same suit; cf. *Sh. England*, II. 472–3.
A 'trick' at this time meant a hand of cards; cf. Thomas Heywood, *A
Woman Killed with Kindness*, viii. 177.
69. *dealing*] continuing the word-play in relation to a game of cards.
75. *authority's bastards*] i.e., the basest servants of the law.
76. *perjury*] violation of their promise.
78. *respect of sign*] the honour of some sign to mark the occasion.

    To make a man spring up, and knock his forehead
    Against yon silver ceiling.
Hipp.   Prithee, tell me,
    Why may not I partake with you ? You vow'd once   5
    To give me share to every tragic thought.
Vind. By th' mass, I think I did too.
    Then I'll divide it to thee: the old duke,
    Thinking my outward shape and inward heart
    Are cut out of one piece (for he that prates   10
    His secrets, his heart stands o' th' outside),
    Hires me by price to greet him with a lady
    In some fit place, veil'd from the eyes o' th' court,
    Some darken'd, blushless angle, that is guilty
    Of his forefathers' lusts, and great folks' riots;   15
    To which I easily (to maintain my shape)
    Consented, and did wish his impudent grace
    To meet her here in this unsunned lodge,
    Wherein 'tis night at noon; and here the rather,
    Because unto the torturing of his soul,   20
    The bastard and the duchess have appointed
    Their meeting too in this luxurious circle,
    Which most afflicting sight will kill his eyes
    Before we kill the rest of him.

10–12.] *so this ed.; divided in Q at* secrets, / His . . . price: / To.   16. I . . .
shape] *so Dodsley 1;* (I . . . shape) *Q.*   21. appointed] *Q^b* (appoynted)*;*
appoynted: *Q^a.*

---

   4. *silver ceiling*] perhaps alluding to the canopy over the stage at the
Globe, the underside of which was probably painted to represent the sky,
with the sun, moon, and stars represented in gold and silver (hence it was
known as 'the heavens'). See Chambers, *E.S.*, II. 544–5.
   6. *to*] i.e., in; an odd usage, perhaps an error ?
   8. *divide*] share; usually 'with' rather than 'to'.
   11. *heart . . . outside*] Cf. *Oth.*, I. i. 65–6, 'I will wear my heart upon my
sleeve For daws to peck at'; the phrase recalls the proverb, 'Who tells a
secret makes himself a slave' (Tilley, S192).
   14. *angle*] nook or corner.
   15. *riots*] wanton revels.
   16. *shape*] disguise.
   22. *luxurious*] lecherous.
   circle] perhaps embracing the whole theatre and audience at the Globe ?

Hipp. 'Twill, i'faith; most dreadfully digested.   25
    I see not how you could have miss'd me, brother.
Vind. True, but the violence of my joy forgot it.
Hipp. Ay, but where's that lady now?
Vind.   O, at that word
    I'm lost again, you cannot find me yet;
    I'm in a throng of happy apprehensions.   30
    He's suited for a lady; I have took care
    For a delicious lip, a sparkling eye.
    You shall be witness, brother.
    Be ready, stand with your hat off.   *Exit.*
Hipp.   Troth, I wonder
    What lady it should be; yet 'tis no wonder,   35
    Now I think again, to have a lady
    Stoop to a duke, that stoops unto his men.
    'Tis common to be common through the world;
    And there's more private-common shadowing vices
    Than those who are known both by their names and prices.
    'Tis part of my allegiance to stand bare   41
    To the duke's concubine,—and here she comes.

34–7. Troth . . . men] *so Oliphant; three lines in Q, divided at* be? / Yet
. . . againe, / To.   39. private-common] *This ed.;* priuate common
Q.

---

25. *dreadfully*] so as to cause fear.
   digested] worked out, or reduced to order, by him: cf. *R3*, III. i. 200,
'We may digest our complots in some form'.
   26. *miss'd me*] left me out.
   29. *find me*] i.e., catch up with me.
   30. *apprehensions*] anticipations, normally of what is fearful or adverse
(the lingering death of the duke), but paradoxically 'happy' for Vindice:
see George Chapman, *Bussy D'Ambois*, edited N. S. Brooke (Revels Plays,
1964), III. i. 22 and n.
   34. *hat off*] as in the presence of a lady of high rank: cf. l. 41.
   37. *stoops*] degrades himself to the level of.
   38. *to be common*] i.e., to be a prostitute (a 'common woman').
   39. *private-common*] enforcing a paradox, in the opposition of 'private'
and 'common' = 'public'; but also describing vices that are at once per-
sonal, as practised in private, and prevalent, as being in common use.
   shadowing] secretive, concealing themselves; a usage related to that at
Mac., v. iv. 5–6, 'thereby shall we shadow The numbers of our host'.

Enter VINDICE, *with the skull of his love dressed up in*
tires [and masked].

Vind. Madam, his grace will not be absent long.
    Secret? Ne'er doubt us, madam; 'twill be worth
    Three velvet gowns to your ladyship. Known?   45
    Few ladies respect that! Disgrace? a poor thin shell;
    'Tis the best grace you have to do it well.
    I'll save your hand that labour; I'll unmask you.
Hipp. Why, brother, brother!
Vind. Art thou beguil'd now? Tut, a lady can,   50
    At such, all hid, beguile a wiser man.
    Have I not fitted the old surfeiter
    With a quaint piece of beauty? Age and bare bone
    Are e'er ally'd in action. Here's an eye
    Able to tempt a great man—to serve God;   55
    A pretty hanging lip, that has forgot now to dissemble:
    Methinks this mouth should make a swearer tremble,
    A drunkard clasp his teeth, and not undo 'em
    To suffer wet damnation to run through 'em.
    Here's a cheek keeps her colour, let the wind   60
    Go whistle;
    Spout rain, we fear thee not; be hot or cold,
    All's one with us; and is not she absurd,

42.2. *and masked*] *This ed.; not in* Q.   46. that! Disgrace?] *so Fluchère;*
that? disgrace, *Q.;* that disgrace *Dodsley 1.*   60–1.] *so this ed.; one line*
in Q.   63. she] *This ed.;* he Q.

    42.2. tires] probably a wig (cf. l. 113), a mask (cf. l. 48) or veil (cf. l. 13),
and a head-dress; the word could signify a covering (attire), adornment,
or wig for the head: cf. *Sh. England,* II. 96–7.
    46. *shell*] an empty thing, mere externality without substance; cf. I. i. 15
and IV. iv. 10. This seems to be the necessary sense here, though not recorded in *O.E.D.,* sb. 1, 25, earlier than 1781.
    51. *At such*] at such a game; in business of this kind.
    all hid] a quibble on the signal cry in the game of hide-and-seek, and a
name for the game itself: cf. *LLL.,* IV. iii. 74.
    53. *quaint*] dainty, fine.
    53–98.] With this meditation on the skull, compare *Ham.,* V. i. 75 ff.
    60–2.] Cf. *Lr.,* III. ii. 1 and 14–15.
    63–5. *is . . . wet?*] alluding to the practice among women of painting the

Whose fortunes are upon their faces set,
That fear no other god but wind and wet?   65
Hipp. Brother, y' have spoke that right.
Is this the form that living shone so bright?
Vind. The very same.
And now methinks I could e'en chide myself
For doting on her beauty, though her death   70
Shall be reveng'd after no common action.
Does the silk-worm expend her yellow labours
For thee? for thee does she undo herself?
Are lordships sold to maintain ladyships
For the poor benefit of a bewitching minute?   75
Why does yon fellow falsify high-ways,
And put his life between the judge's lips,
To refine such a thing? keeps horse and men

75. bewitching] *Q;* bewildering *Symonds.*

---

face, and caring for the skin with cosmetics: cf. *Ham.*, v. i. 187–90, and
Tw. N., I. v. 222–3, where Olivia boasts of the colours of her face, ''Tis in
grain, sir; 'twill endure wind and weather'. I have accordingly emended
he (Q, l. 63) to *she.* The jump from the singular to the plural is characteristic of the author's habit of generalizing: cf. ll. 96–7.

72. *yellow labours*] The cocoon spun by the silkworm is yellow, or
yellowish-white, in colour.

72–98.] These are the most celebrated lines in the play, and some or all
of them have been discussed at length by many critics. Among the more
important analyses are those by T. S. Eliot (1919; in *Selected Essays*, 1951,
p. 20); M. C. Bradbrook, *Themes and Conventions of Elizabethan Tragedy*
(1936), pp. 170–1; Theodore Spencer, *Death and Elizabethan Tragedy*
(1936), pp. 238–40; L. G. Salingar, *Scrutiny*, VI (1938), 419–20; F. R.
Leavis, *Scrutiny*, XIII (1945), 120–2; and John Peter, *Complaint and Satire*
(1956), pp. 262–4. I have not attempted to duplicate the rich commentary
they provide on this passage.

74. *lordships*] estates: cf. II. i. 215–18.
ladyships] i.e., in clothes and adornments.

76. *falsify high-ways*] presumably turn highwayman (in order to obtain
money to spend on women). The odd use of the word 'falsify' has puzzled
commentators, and suggests overtones which go beyond the image of robbery, implying perhaps the violation of proper courses of behaviour, turning 'high' ways into morally 'low' ways.

78. *refine . . . thing*] enjoy (by buying with his gains) more subtle and
refined pleasure with women.

To beat their valours for her?
Surely we are all mad people, and they   80
Whom we think are, are not; we mistake those:
'Tis we are mad in sense, they but in clothes.
Hipp. Faith, and in clothes too we, give us our due.
Vind. Does every proud and self-affecting dame
Camphor her face for this? and grieve her maker   85
In sinful baths of milk, when many an infant starves
For her superfluous outside—all for this?
Who now bids twenty pound a night, prepares
Music, perfumes and sweetmeats? All are hush'd;
Thou mayst lie chaste now. It were fine, methinks,   90
To have thee seen at revels, forgetful feasts,
And unclean brothels; sure, 'twould fright the sinner,
And make him a good coward, put a reveller
Out of his antic amble,
And cloy an epicure with empty dishes.   95
Here might a scornful and ambitious woman
Look through and through herself;—see, ladies, with false
    forms
You deceive men, but cannot deceive worms.
Now to my tragic business; look you, brother,
I have not fashion'd this only for show   100
And useless property; no, it shall bear a part

80. we are] *Dodsley 2;* wee're *Q.*

---

79. *beat their valours*] wear out their strengths. The common meanings of 'beat', to batter, crush, pound, are here applied to an abstract noun, 'valour', literally prowess or boldness in facing danger, which links this phrase with the idea of highway robbery: cf. l. 76 and n.

84. *self-affecting*] self-loving.

85. *Camphor*] alluding to the use of camphor to perfume soaps (as for the 'baths' of l. 86).

94. *antic amble*] grotesque motion.

97. *Look . . . herself*] study herself in all respects; see herself wholly.
forms] appearances.

101. *property*] the sense 'stage accessory' was already well established, and Vindice speaks as if he were producing his own play. See Intro., p. **xxviii** and n.

E'en in it own revenge. This very skull,
Whose mistress the duke poison'd, with this drug,
The mortal curse of the earth, shall be reveng'd
In the like strain, and kiss his lips to death.   105
As much as the dumb thing can, he shall feel:
What fails in poison, we'll supply in steel.

Hipp. Brother, I do applaud thy constant vengeance,
The quaintness of thy malice, above thought.

Vind. [*Putting poison on the lips of the skull*] So, 'tis laid on. Now
    come, and welcome, duke;   110
I have her for thee. I protest it, brother,
Methinks she makes almost as fair a sign
As some old gentlewoman in a periwig.
                    [*Puts a mask on the skull.*]
Hide thy face now, for shame, thou hadst need have a mask
    now:
'Tis vain when beauty flows, but when it fleets,   115
This would become graves better than the streets.

Hipp. You have my voice in that. Hark, the duke's come.

Vind. Peace, let's observe what company he brings,
And how he does absent 'em, for you know
He'll wish all private. Brother, fall you back   120
A little, with the bony lady.

Hipp.   That I will.

Vind. So, so—

110. *Putting . . . skull*] Symonds; not in Q.   112. sign] *This ed.;* sine *Q.*
sin *Dodsley 2;* fine *Collins.*   113.1. *Puts . . . skull.*] *Harrison; not in Q.*
120–1.] *so this ed.; divided in Q at* little, / With.   122–3.] *so Oliphant;*
one line in Q.

---

102. *it*] a normal early form of the genitive, common in Shakespeare
(Abbott, 228).

105. *strain*] manner (literally, melody).

109. *quaintness*] ingenuity.

112. *makes . . . sign*] I take it that Vindice here manipulates the skull to
make a beckoning gesture, but 'sign' could mean simply 'show' or 'figure'.

115–16.] i.e., a mask is pointless vanity when beauty exists to be dis-
played, but when beauty has passed away, 'This' (the skull) better befits
the grave than to be shown in public.

119. *absent*] send away; a usage not recorded in *O.E.D.*

Now nine years' vengeance crowd into a minute!

[*They step aside, as the* Duke *enters, with some* Gentlemen.]

Duke. You shall have leave to leave us, with this charge,
Upon your lives: if we be miss'd by th' duchess,   125
Or any of the nobles, to give out
We're privately rid forth.
Vind. [*Aside*]   O happiness!
Duke. With some few honourable gentlemen, you may say;
You may name those that are away from court.
Gentlemen. Your will and pleasure shall be done, my lord.   130
                              [*Exeunt* Gentlemen.]
Vind. [*Aside*] 'Privately rid forth';
He strives to make sure work on 't! [*To the Duke*] Your good
grace.
Duke. Piato, well done, hast brought her? what lady is 't?
Vind. Faith, my lord, a country lady, a little bashful at first,
as most of them are; but after the first kiss, my lord, the   135
worst is past with them. Your grace knows now what
you have to do; sh' has somewhat a grave look with her,
but—
Duke. I love that best; conduct her.
Vind. [*Aside*]   Have at all!
Duke. In gravest looks the greatest faults seem less.   140
Give me that sin that's rob'd in holiness.
Vind. Back with the torch; brother, raise the perfumes.
Duke. How sweet can a duke breathe? Age has no fault.

123.1. *They . . .* Gentlemen.] *This ed., after* Symonds; *not in* Q.   127.
Aside] Oliphant; *not in* Q.   130.1. *Exeunt* Gentlemen.] Dodsley 2; *not
in* Q.   131. *Aside*] Oliphant; *not in* Q.   132. *To the Duke*] *This ed.;
not in* Q.   139. *Aside*] Dodsley 4; *not in* Q.

137. *grave*] The pun on 'grave' as place of burial is obvious, but not
obvious enough for the duke, who misses Vindice's mockery.
139. *Have at all!*] On with the business!; properly, announcing the
opening of a fight, as at *Troil.*, v. vi. 11.
140–1.] varying the proverbs 'Successful sin passes for virtue' (Tilley,
S473) and 'Rich men have no faults' (M579, first citation 1639).
143. *no fault*] He means, I suppose, 'no physical inadequacy' (that dark-

  Pleasure should meet in a perfumed mist.
  Lady, sweetly encounter'd; I came from court,   145
  I must be bold with you. [*Kisses the skull.*] O, what's this ? O!
Vind. Royal villain, white devil!
Duke.   O!
Vind.   Brother—
  Place the torch here, that his affrighted eyeballs
  May start into those hollows. Duke, dost know
  Yon dreadful vizard ? View it well; 'tis the skull 150
  Of Gloriana, whom thou poisonedst last.
Duke. O, 't has poisoned me.
Vind. Didst not know that till now ?
Duke.   What are you two ?
Vind. Villains all three! The very ragged bone
  Has been sufficiently reveng'd.   155
Duke. O, Hippolito! call treason.
Hipp. Yes, my good lord; treason, treason, treason!
           Stamping on him.
Duke. Then I'm betray'd.
Vind. Alas, poor lecher, in the hands of knaves,
  A slavish duke is baser than his slaves.   160
Duke. My teeth are eaten out.

145–6.] *so Collins; as prose in* Q. 146. *Kisses the skull.*] *Harrier; not in*
Q. 147–8. Brother . . . eyeballs] *so this ed.; one line in* Q. 149. hollows.
Duke] *Dodsley 1;* hollowes, Duke; Q.

---

ness and perfume cannot hide), but the sense 'moral defect' comes ironically into play as well.
 146. *bold*] by kissing her.
 147. *white devil*] 'white' here means 'plausible', 'fair-seeming' (and is
opposed to the common idea of the devil as black); hence the phrase could
mean 'hypocrite', but was used in a stronger sense: cf. the proverb, 'The
white devil is worse than the black' (Tilley, D310). See John Webster, *The
White Devil*, edited J. R. Brown (Revels Plays, 1960), p. 7.
 151. *whom . . . last*] She was the latest of his victims: cf. II. iii. 129, where
he says, 'Many a beauty have I turn'd to poison'.
 154. *ragged*] rough, jagged.
 160. *slavish*] vile; but quibbling too on the sense of slaves = servants,
for the duke is forced into submission, and so becomes 'slavish' in this
sense too.

Vind.   Hadst any left ?

Hipp. I think but few.

Vind. Then those that did eat are eaten.

Duke.   O, my tongue!

Vind. Your tongue ? 'twill teach you to kiss closer,

    Not like a slobbering Dutchman. You have eyes still,   165

    Look, monster, what a lady hast thou made me

    My once betrothed wife.   [*Throwing off his disguise.*]

Duke.   Is it thou, villain ?

    Nay then—

Vind.   'Tis I, 'tis Vindice, 'tis I.

Hipp. And let this comfort thee: our lord and father

    Fell sick upon the infection of thy frowns,   170

    And died in sadness; be that thy hope of life.

Duke. O!

Vind. He had his tongue, yet grief made him die speechless.

    Puh, 'tis but early yet, now I'll begin

    To stick thy soul with ulcers; I will make   175

    Thy spirit grievous sore, it shall not rest,

    But, like some pestilent man, toss in thy breast—

    Mark me, duke:

165. slobbering] *Dodsley 4; Flobbering Q.*   167. *Throwing . . . disguise.*]
Oliphant, after Dodsley 3; not in Q.   167–8. Is . . . then] *so Oliphant; one
line in Q.*   169. father] *Q^b; Father, Q^a.*   176. not] *Q^b; nor Q^a.*
177–8. But . . . duke] *so Oliphant; one line in Q.*

165. *slobbering*] dribbling. The word 'flober' (= to befoul) occurs in *Piers
Plowman* (cited in *O.E.D.*), and the form 'slobber' did not become common
before the 18th century; 'slabber' seems to have been the usual 16th–17th-
century word. Here the printer may have misread 'f' for 's' in a word that
was unfamiliar to him, for these letters were alike in the common handwriting of the time. He corrected other errors on this page (see collation to
ll. 169, 176), but did not alter this.

    Dutchman] The Dutchman slobbers as proverbially given to drink. For
the gross associations of this image, compare the phrase 'Dutch lust', I. iii.
56 and n.

    166. *made me*] made for me. It seems that Vindice should here hold the
skull by him, as if he were with his 'lady'.

    177. *pestilent*] perhaps 'infected with the plague', though this sense is not
recorded in *O.E.D.*; the common meanings, 'annoying', 'pernicious',
hardly apply here.

    Thou'rt a renowned, high and mighty cuckold.

Duke. O!   180

Vind. Thy bastard,

    Thy bastard rides a-hunting in thy brow.

Duke. Millions of deaths!

Vind.   Nay, to afflict thee more,

    Here in this lodge they meet for damned clips;

    Those eyes shall see the incest of their lips.   185

Duke. Is there a hell besides this, villains?

Vind.   Villain!

    Nay, Heaven is just, scorns are the hire of scorns;

    I ne'er knew yet adulterer without horns.

Hipp. Once e'er they die 'tis quitted.

Vind.   Hark, the music;

    Their banquet is prepar'd, they're coming—   190

Duke. O, kill me not with that sight!

Vind. Thou shalt not lose that sight for all thy dukedom.

Duke. Traitors, murderers!

Vind. What? is not thy tongue eaten out yet? Then

    We'll invent a silence. Brother, stifle the torch.   195

Duke. Treason, murder!

Vind. Nay, faith, we'll have you hush'd; now with thy dagger

    Nail down his tongue, and mine shall keep possession

    About his heart. If he but gasp, he dies.

    We dread not death to quittance injuries.   200

    Brother,

181–2.] *so this ed.; one line in* Q.   187. hire] *Scott;* hires Q.   194–5.]
so this ed.; divided in Q *at* yet? / Then.   197. hush'd; now ... dagger]
Dodsley 1; husht now ... dagger Q*;* husht now ... dagger. *Nicoll.*   200–1.]
so this ed.; one line in Q.

---

    182. rides ... brow] quibbling on the sexual implications of 'ride', and
on 'brow' as the edge of a hill; the general allusion is to setting up cuckold's
horns on the duke's brow: cf. l. 188.

    184. *clips*] embraces.

    187. *hire*] reward.

    189. *Once*] at some time.

    'tis quitted] i.e., adultery is requited (by cuckolding).

    195. *invent*] establish.

    200. *quittance*] repay.

If he but wink, not brooking the foul object,
Let our two other hands tear up his lids,
And make his eyes, like comets, shine through blood;
When the bad bleeds, then is the tragedy good.   205
Hipp. Whist, brother, music's at our ear; they come.

Enter the Bastard [SPURIO] *meeting the* Duchess. [*They kiss.
Attendants* with lights stand apart.]

Spurio. Had not that kiss a taste of sin, 'twere sweet.
Duchess. Why, there's no pleasure sweet but it is sinful.
Spurio. True, such a bitter sweetness fate hath given,
Best side to us is the worst side to heaven.   210
Duchess. Push, come; 'tis the old duke thy doubtful father,
The thought of him rubs heaven in thy way.
But I protest, by yonder waxen fire,
Forget him, or I'll poison him.
Spurio. Madam, you urge a thought which ne'er had life.   215
So deadly do I loathe him for my birth
That if he took me hasp'd within his bed,
I would add murder to adultery,
And with my sword give up his years to death.
Duchess. Why, now thou 'rt sociable; let's in, and feast.   220
Loud'st music sound; pleasure is banquet's guest.
                    Exeunt [Duchess, SPURIO *and* Attendants].

206.1–2. *They . . . apart.*] *This ed.; not in Q.*   221.1. Duchess . . . Attendants] *This ed.; not in Q;* Duchess *and* Spurio *Symonds.*

---

202. *object*] what is placed before the eyes; that is, Spurio and the duchess embracing.

204. *comets*] Cf. the 'blazing star' that appears at v. iii. 15 as an omen of disaster. Comets were generally regarded as ominous, and this couplet carries an irony in its possible reference to Spurio and to Vindice himself.

blood] the blood flowing from his torn eyelids.

206.2. *Attendants . . . apart*] See l. 213 and n.

207.] The parallel is exact between their entry kissing, and the duke's kissing of the skull, l. 146 above.

212. *rubs*] stirs up, recalls to mind.

213. *waxen fire*] Presumably the musicians or other attendants, some holding torches or candles, stand to one side, apart from Spurio and the duchess.

217. *hasp'd*] i.e., in an embrace with her.

Duke. I cannot brook—   [*Dies.*]
Vind.   The brook is turn'd to blood.
Hipp. Thanks to loud music.
Vind.   'Twas our friend indeed.
       'Tis state in music for a duke to bleed:
       The dukedom wants a head, though yet unknown;   225
       As fast as they peep up, let's cut 'em down.   *Exeunt.*

[III. vi]

       Enter the Duchess's two sons, AMBITIOSO *and* SUPERVACUO.

Ambit. Was not his execution rarely plotted?
       We are the duke's sons now.
Super.   Ay, you may thank
       My policy for that.
Ambit.   Your policy?
       For what?
Super.   Why, was 't not my invention, brother,
       To slip the judges? and, in lesser compass,   5
       Did I not draw the model of his death,
       Advising you to sudden officers,
       And e'en extemporal execution?
Ambit. Heart, 'twas a thing I thought on too.

---

222. *Dies.*] Symonds; *not in* Q.

III. vi. 2–3. Ay . . . that] *so this ed.; one line in* Q.   3–4. Your . . . what]
so this ed.; one line in Q.

---

   222. *cannot brook*] cannot put up with: cf. II. i. 234. Vindice character-
istically picks up the word as a noun and quibbles on it.
   225. *though yet unknown*] i.e., the fact that the dukedom lacks a head is
as yet not generally known.

   III. vi. 3. *policy*] stratagem.
   5. *slip*] give the slip to, circumvent.
   in . . . compass] as a lesser piece of contriving; but 'compass' here also
passes into the sense 'limits, scope', linking with the next line.
   6. *model*] plan; in early use, the word commonly meant an architect's
drawing for a building; cf. *2H4*, I. iii. 58.
   7. *sudden*] unlooked for, and swift in action.
   8. *extemporal*] immediate.

Super. You thought on 't too ? 'Sfoot, slander not your thoughts
    With glorious untruth; I know 'twas from you.   11
Ambit. Sir,
    I say 'twas in my head.
Super.   Ay, like your brains then;
    Ne'er to come out as long as you liv'd.
Ambit. You'd have the honour on 't, forsooth, that your wit   15
    Led him to the scaffold.
Super.   Since it is my due,
    I'll publish 't, but I'll ha 't in spite of you.
Ambit. Methinks y' are much too bold; you should a little
    Remember us, brother, next to be honest duke.
Super. Ay, it shall be as easy for you to be duke   20
    As to be honest; and that's never, i'faith.
Ambit. Well, cold he is by this time; and because
    We're both ambitious, be it our amity,
    And let the glory be shar'd equally.
Super. I am content to that.   25
Ambit. This night our younger brother shall out of prison;
    I have a trick.
Super.   A trick, prithee what is 't ?
Ambit. We'll get him out by a wile.
Super.   Prithee what wile ?
Ambit. No, sir, you shall not know it till 't be done,
    For then you'd swear 'twere yours.   30

[*Enter an* Officer.]

Super. How now, what's he ?
Ambit.   One of the officers.

12–13. Sir . . . head] *so this ed.; one line in* Q.   16. Led] Q (Lead).
26. our] *Dodsley 1;* out Q.   30.1. *Enter* . . . Officer.] *Dodsley 1; not in* Q.

    10. '*Sfoot*] short for 'God's foot'; an ejaculation Marston was fond of
using.
    11. *from*] alien to.
    17. *but*] only.
    19. *honest*] held in honour; the quibble on the sense 'virtuous' is brought
out in l. 21.

Super. Desired news.

Ambit.   How now, my friend?

Offic.   My lords,
  Under your pardon, I am allotted
  To that desertless office, to present you
  With the yet bleeding head—

Super. [*Aside*]   Ha, ha, excellent!   35

Ambit. [*Aside*] All's sure our own. Brother, canst weep, think'st
  thou?
  'Twould grace our flattery much; think of some dame,
  'Twill teach thee to dissemble.

Super. [*Aside*]   I have thought;
  Now for yourself.

Ambit.   Our sorrows are so fluent,
  Our eyes o'erflow our tongues. Words spoke in tears 40
  Are like the murmurs of the waters, the sound
  Is loudly heard, but cannot be distinguish'd.

Super. How died he, pray?

Offic.   O, full of rage and spleen.

Super. He died most valiantly then; we're glad
  To hear it.

Offic.   We could not woo him once to pray. 45

Ambit. He show'd himself a gentleman in that,
  Give him his due.

Offic.   But in the stead of prayer,
  He drew forth oaths.

Super.   Then did he pray, dear heart,
  Although you understood him not.

Offic.   My lords,
  E'en at his last, with pardon be it spoke, 50
  He curs'd you both.

Super.   He curs'd us? 'las, good soul!

32–3. My lords . . . allotted] *so this ed.; one line in Q.* 35, 36, 38. *Aside*]
Oliphant; not in Q. 38–9. I . . . yourself] *so Oliphant; one line in Q.*
44–5. He . . . it] *so this ed.; one line in Q.* 45. woo] *Q* (woe). 46–7.
He . . . due] *so Dodsley 3; one line in Q.* 47–8. But . . . oaths] *so Dodsley 3;
one line in Q.*

Ambit. It was not in our powers, but the duke's pleasure.
    [*Aside*] Finely dissembled o' both sides. Sweet fate!
    O, happy opportunity!

Enter LUSSURIOSO.

Luss.   Now, my lords.
Both. O!—
Luss.   Why do you shun me, brothers? You may   55
    Come nearer now;
    The savour of the prison has forsook me.
    I thank such kind lords as yourselves, I'm free.
Ambit. Alive!
Super. In health!   60
Ambit. Releas'd?
    We were both e'en amaz'd with joy to see it.
Luss. I am much to thank you.
Super. Faith,
    We spar'd no tongue unto my lord the duke.   65
Ambit. I know your delivery, brother,
    Had not been half so sudden but for us.
Super. O, how we pleaded!
Luss.   Most deserving brothers!
    In my best studies I will think of it.   *Exit.*
Ambit. O death and vengeance!
Super.   Hell and torments!   70
Ambit. Slave, cam'st thou to delude us?
Offic.   Delude you, my lords?
Super. Ay, villain, where's this head now?
Offic.   Why, here, my lord;
    Just after his delivery, you both came
    With warrant from the duke to behead your brother.
Ambit. Ay, our brother, the duke's son.

---

53. *Aside*] *Dodsley 3; not in* Q.   sides. Sweet] *Collins;* sides, sweete Q.
55–6. You may . . . now] *so this ed.; one line in* Q.   64–5. Faith . . . duke]
so this ed.; one line in Q.

---

57. *savour*] scent.

Offic.   The duke's son,   75
    My lord, had his release before you came.
Ambit. Whose head's that, then?
Offic.   His whom you left command for,
    Your own brother's.
Ambit.   Our brother's? O furies!
Super. Plagues!
Ambit.   Confusions!
Super.   Darkness!
Ambit.   Devils!
Super. Fell it out so accursedly?
Ambit.   So damnedly?   80
Super. Villain, I'll brain thee with it.
Offic.   O, my good lord.   [*Exit.*]
Super. The devil overtake thee!
Ambit.   O, fatal!
Super. O, prodigious to our bloods!
Ambit.   Did we dissemble?
Super. Did we make our tears women for thee?
Ambit. Laugh and rejoice for thee?   85
Super. Bring warrant for thy death?
Ambit.   Mock off thy head?
Super. You had a trick, you had a wile, forsooth!
Ambit. A murrain meet 'em, there's none of these wiles that
    ever come to good. I see now, there is nothing sure in
    mortality, but mortality.   90
    Well, no more words, 'shalt be reveng'd i'faith.
    Come, throw off clouds now, brother, think of vengeance,

75–6. The . . . came] *so Oliphant; one line in Q.*   77–8. His . . . own
brother's] *so this ed.; one line in Q.*   81. *Exit*] *Oliphant (after* thee!, *l. 82);
not in Q.*   91.] *so Scott; as prose in Q.*

---

83. *prodigious*] ominous.
84. *make . . . women*] a conceit based on the proverbial proneness of
women to weep, and their ability to deceive. As their tears were made
women, they merely appeared to spring from real grief; cf. Tilley, W638,
'Trust not a woman when she weeps', and W713, 716.
88. *murrain*] plague.
90. *mortality*] quibbling on the senses 'mortal existence' and 'death'.

And deeper settled hate; sirrah, sit fast,
We'll pull down all, but thou shalt down at last. *Exeunt.*

---

93. *sirrah*] a contemptuous address to the absent Lussurioso.

Act IV

Enter LUSSURIOSO, *with* HIPPOLITO.

Luss. Hippolito.
Hipp.   My lord, has your good lordship aught
    To command me in ?
Luss.   I prithee leave us.
Hipp.   How's this ?
    Come, and leave us ?
Luss.   Hippolito.
Hipp.   Your honour,
    I stand ready for any duteous employment.
Luss. Heart, what mak'st thou here ?
Hipp. [*Aside*]   A pretty lordly humour;   5
    He bids me to be present, to depart.
    Something has stung his honour.
Luss.   Be nearer, draw nearer;
    Y' are not so good, methinks; I'm angry with you.
Hipp. With me, my lord ? I'm angry with myself for 't.
Luss. You did prefer a goodly fellow to me;   10
    'Twas wittily elected, 'twas. I thought
    'Had been a villain, and he proves a knave,
    To me a knave.
Hipp.   I chose him for the best, my lord;

ACT IV, SCENE i] *Q* (*ACT. 4. SCEN. 1.*).   1–2. My . . . in] *so this ed.;
divided in Q at* Lord: / Has.   2–3. How's . . . us] *so this ed.; one line in Q.*
3–4. Your . . . employment] *so Oliphant; one line in Q.*   5. Aside] *Oliphant; not in Q.*   6–7. He . . . honour] *so Oliphant; one line in Q.*

   IV. i. 8. *not so good*] Cf. II. ii. 1–2.
   11. *wittily*] wisely.
   12. *villain . . . knave*] The joke lies in the rough equivalence of the terms.

'Tis much my sorrow, if neglect in him
Breed discontent in you.
Luss.   Neglect ? 'twas will;   15
Judge of it:
Firmly to tell of an incredible act,
Not to be thought, less to be spoken of,
'Twixt my stepmother and the bastard, O,
Incestuous sweets between 'em.
Hipp.   Fie, my lord.   20
Luss. I, in kind loyalty to my father's forehead,
Made this a desperate arm, and in that fury
Committed treason on the lawful bed,
And with my sword e'en ras'd my father's bosom;
For which I was within a stroke of death.   25
Hipp. Alack, I'm sorry. [*Aside*] 'Sfoot, just upon the stroke
Jars in my brother; 'twill be villainous music.

Enter VINDICE.

Vind. My honoured lord.
Luss. Away, prithee forsake us; hereafter we'll not know thee.
Vind. Not know me, my lord ? Your lordship cannot choose.   30
Luss. Be gone, I say; thou art a false knave.
Vind. Why, the easier to be known, my lord.
Luss. Push, I shall prove too bitter, with a word
Make thee a perpetual prisoner,
And lay this iron-age upon thee.

14–15. 'Tis . . . you] *so Dodsley 2; one line in Q.*   15–16. Neglect ? . . . it]
so Oliphant; one line in Q.   26. *Aside*] *Collins; not in Q.*

---

15. *will*] intent.
21. *forehead*] Cf. II. ii. 162–3; the thought is of cuckold's horns sprouting
there.
24. *ras'd*] scratched.
27. *Jars in*] comes in making a discord.
villainous music] atrocious music, disharmony, but also the 'music' or
harmony of villains.
35. *this iron-age*] Perhaps Lussurioso indicates his sword, threatening
violence, though the phrase also suggests iron fetters. There is also an
allusion to the Iron Age, the last of the four ages (Gold, Silver, Brazen

Vind. [*Aside*]   Mum!   35
>   For there's a doom would make a woman dumb.
>   Missing the bastard, next him, the wind's come about;
>   Now 'tis my brother's turn to stay, mine to go out.   *Exit.*

Luss. 'Has greatly mov'd me.

Hipp.   Much to blame, i'faith.

Luss. But I'll recover, to his ruin. 'Twas told me lately,   40
>   I know not whether falsely, that you'd a brother.

Hipp. Who, I ? Yes, my good lord, I have a brother.

Luss. How chance the court ne'er saw him ? Of what nature ?
>   How does he apply his hours ?

Hipp.   Faith, to curse fates,
>   Who, as he thinks, ordain'd him to be poor;   45
>   Keeps at home, full of want and discontent.

Luss. There's hope in him, for discontent and want
>   Is the best clay to mould a villain of.
>   Hippolito, wish him repair to us.
>   If there be aught in him to please our blood,   50
>   For thy sake we'll advance him, and build fair
>   His meanest fortunes; for it is in us
>   To rear up towers from cottages.

Hipp.   It is so, my lord.

---

35. *Aside*] *Dodsley 4; not in* Q.   35–6. Mum! . . . dumb] *so Dodsley 4;*
one line in Q.   37. him,] *Dodsley 1;* him Q.   come] *Dodsley 1;* comes
Q.   53–6. It . . . court] *so Oliphant; divided in* Q *at* honour, / But . . .
dwels. / Why.

---

were the others) of the world in classical mythology, and the worst; an age
of cruelty and evil.

36. *doom . . . dumb*] The words were more nearly homonymic in sound
than they are now: see Kökeritz, pp. 431–2. The phrase as a whole alludes
to the proverbial inability of women to stop talking: see Tilley, W686, 701.

37. *Missing . . . about*] Vindice has 'missed', or failed to engineer the
deaths of Spurio, who was not in bed with the duchess when Lussurioso
rushed in (II. ii), and of Lussurioso, who has escaped death through the
duke's clemency; now the wind has come about, and Lussurioso no longer
trusts him.

44. *apply*] employ.

47–8. *discontent . . . Is*] such false concords were common; see Abbott,
333, and IV. iv. 47–8 below.

50. *blood*] temper.

He will attend your honour; but he's a man
In whom much melancholy dwells.

Luss.   Why, the better.   55
Bring him to court.

Hipp.   With willingness, and speed.
[*Aside*] Whom he cast off e'en now, must now succeed.
Brother, disguise must off;
In thine own shape now I'll prefer thee to him:
How strangely does himself work to undo him.   *Exit.* 60

Luss. This fellow will come fitly; he shall kill
That other slave, that did abuse my spleen,
And made it swell to treason. I have put
Much of my heart into him, he must die.
He that knows great men's secrets and proves slight,   65
That man ne'er lives to see his beard turn white.
Ay, he shall speed him; I'll employ the brother.
Slaves are but nails, to drive out one another.
He being of black condition, suitable
To want and ill content, hope of preferment   70
Will grind him to an edge.

Enter [*two*] Nobles.

1. Noble. Good days unto your honour.

57. *Aside*] *Symonds; not in Q.*   67. the] *Dodsley 1;* thee *Q.*   71.1. *Enter two* Nobles.] *This ed., after Oliphant;* The Nobles enter. *Q* (*as part of l. 71*).   72, 74, 80. *1. Noble, 2. Noble, 3. Noble.*] I, 2, 3. *Q* (*so throughout scene*).

---

57. *succeed*] a quibble: both take his place as successor, and be successful in dealing with Lussurioso.

62. *spleen*] high spirit.

64. *heart*] inmost thoughts and feelings.

65. *slight*] unworthy of trust.

67. *speed*] i.e., kill.

68.] alluding to the common proverb, 'One nail drives out another' (Tilley, N17).

69. *of . . . condition*] of a melancholy or evil disposition. The 'black bile', one of the four humours, or fluids thought to be secreted in the spleen, and to determine a man's temperament, was regarded as the source of melancholy, which was called the 'black humour', as at *LLL.*, I. i. 227.

Luss. My kind lords, I do return the like.

2. Noble. Saw you my lord the duke?

Luss. My lord and father? is he from court?   75

1. Noble. He's sure from court; but where, which way his
    pleasure took, we know not, nor can we hear on 't.

Luss. Here come those should tell.

[*Enter two more* Nobles.]

Saw you my lord and father?

3. Noble. Not since two hours before noon, my lord; and then   80
    he privately rid forth.

Luss. O, he's rode forth.

1. Noble.   'Twas wondrous privately.

2. Noble. There's none i' th' court had any knowledge on 't.

Luss. His grace is old, and sudden; 'tis no treason
    To say, the duke my father has a humour,   85
    Or such a toy about him. What in us
    Would appear light, in him seems virtuous.

3. Noble. 'Tis oracle, my lord.   *Exeunt.*

[IV. ii]

Enter VINDICE *and* HIPPOLITO, *Vindice out of his disguise.*

Hipp. So, so, all's as it should be, y' are yourself.

Vind. How that great villain puts me to my shifts.

Hipp. He that did lately in disguise reject thee,
    Shall, now thou art thyself, as much respect thee.

76–7.] *so this ed.; as verse in Q, divided at* Court, / But . . . not, / Nor.
78.1. *Enter . . .* Nobles.] *This ed., after Oliphant; not in Q.*   80–1.] *so this
ed.; as verse in Q, divided at* Lord, / And.   82. rode] *Q* (rod).

_____

82. *rode*] once a common form of the past participle: see *2H4*, V. iii. 93,
and Abbott, 343.
84. *sudden*] rash; given to acting on a whim.
85. *humour*] caprice.
86. *toy*] whim, odd conceit.
87. *light*] frivolous or wanton.
88. *oracle*] absolute truth.

IV. ii. 2. *shifts*] meaning both 'disguises' and 'tricks' or 'devices'.

Vind. 'Twill be the quainter fallacy. But, brother,   5
    'Sfoot, what use will he put me to now, think'st thou?
Hipp. Nay, you must pardon me in that; I know not.
    'Has some employment for you, but what 'tis,
    He and his secretary the devil knows best.
Vind. Well, I must suit my tongue to his desires,   10
    What colour soe'er they be; hoping at last
    To pile up all my wishes on his breast.
Hipp. Faith, brother, he himself shows the way.
Vind. Now the duke is dead, the realm is clad in clay;
    His death being not yet known, under his name   15
    The people still are govern'd. Well, thou his son
    Art not long-liv'd; thou shalt not joy his death.
    To kill thee, then, I should most honour thee,
    For 'twould stand firm in every man's belief,
    Thou'st a kind child, and only died'st with grief.   20
Hipp. You fetch about well, but let's talk in present;
    How will you appear in fashion different,
    As well as in apparel, to make all things possible?
    If you be but once tripp'd, we fall for ever.
    It is not the least policy to be doubtful;   25

6. 'Sfoot, what] *so Q;* 'Sfoot, / What *Oliphant.*

---

5. *quainter*] more ingenious.
fallacy] deception.
9. *secretary*] confidant.
12. *pile . . . breast*] as he does finally by killing him in v. iii.
14. *clad in clay*] literally, buried: cf. Spenser, *Shepherd's Calendar*, October, l. 61, 'But O, Maecenas is yclad in clay / And great Augustus long ago is dead' (cited by Harrison). Vindice means, I take it, that the old regime is dead, and, as he goes on to indicate, he does not intend to allow Lussurioso to revive it.
17. *joy*] enjoy.
20. *Thou'st*] i.e., thou wast.
21. *You . . . present*] i.e., you speculate well (literally, take a circuitous course), but let's discuss what's to be done now. 'In present' means 'at the present time'.
22. *fashion*] manner.
25. *not . . . doubtful*] no policy to be uncertain; or, perhaps, more literally, not the least policy, and so a good one, to be apprehensive.

You must change tongue—familiar was your first.

Vind. Why,

I'll bear me in some strain of melancholy,

And string myself with heavy-sounding wire,

Like such an instrument that speaks   30

Merry things sadly.

Hipp.   Then 'tis as I meant;

I gave you out at first in discontent.

Vind. I'll turn myself, and then—

Hipp.   'Sfoot, here he comes;

Hast thought upon 't?

Vind.   Salute him; fear not me.

[*Enter* LUSSURIOSO.]

Luss. Hippolito.

Hipp.   Your lordship?

Luss.   What's he yonder?   35

Hipp. 'Tis Vindice, my discontented brother,

Whom, 'cording to your will, I've brought to court.

Luss. Is that thy brother? beshrew me, a good presence;

I wonder 'has been from the court so long.

Come nearer.   40

Hipp. Brother, Lord Lussurioso, the duke's son.

[*Vindice*] *snatches off his hat, and makes legs to him.*

[*Hippolito stands apart.*]

Luss. Be more near to us. Welcome; nearer yet.

27–8. Why . . . melancholy] *so this ed.; one line in Q.*   30–1. Like . . .
sadly] *so this ed.; one line in Q.*   33–4. 'Sfoot . . . upon 't] *so Oliphant;
one line in Q.*   34.1. Enter Lussurioso.] *Dodsley 1; not in Q.*   41. duke's]
Dodsley 1; Duke *Q.*   41.1. *Vindice*] *This ed.; not in Q.*   41.2. *Hippolito . . . apart*] *This ed.; not in Q.*

---

33. *turn*] transform.

38. *beshrew me*] a common imprecation, often used casually, but also
seriously with the sense 'may evil befall me', which registers here with
ironic effect.

41.1. *makes legs*] i.e., 'scrapes', or bows made by drawing back one leg
and bending the other.

Vind. How don you? God you god den.

Luss.   We thank thee.

How strangely such a coarse, homely salute
Shows in the palace, where we greet in fire;   45
Nimble and desperate tongues, should we name God
In a salutation, 'twould ne'er be stood on 't; Heaven!
Tell me, what has made thee so melancholy?

Vind. Why, going to law.

Luss. Why, will that make a man melancholy?   50

Vind. Yes, to look long upon ink and black buckram. I went
me to law in *anno quadragesimo secundo*, and I waded out
of it in *anno sexagesimo tertio*.

Luss. What, three and twenty years in law?

Vind. I have known those that have been five and fifty, and   55
all about pullen and pigs.

Luss. May it be possible such men should breathe, to vex the
terms so much?

Vind. 'Tis food to some, my lord. There are old men at the
present, that are so poisoned with the affectation of law-   60
words (having had many suits canvassed), that their common talk is nothing but Barbary Latin. They cannot so

---

45-7. fire; / ... tongues, ... name] *This ed., after Oliphant;* fire: / ... tongues,
... name, *Q;* fire / ... tongues! ... name *Collins.*   46-7.] *so Oliphant;
divided in Q at* name, / God.   57-9. May ... lord] *so this ed.; as verse in
Q, divided at* breath, / To.

---

43. *don ... den*] a common way of representing rustic speech.
God ... den] a form of 'God give you good even'; cf. *LLL.*, IV. i. 42.
46. *desperate*] reckless.
46-7.] The jest is that Vindice did name God in his salutation.
47. *'twould ... on 't*] No one would be scrupulous about it.
51. *black buckram*] alluding to the buckram bags carried by lawyers.
52-3. *anno ... tertio*] Such dates would normally refer to the year of a
sovereign's reign, but these (42nd and 63rd) are invented for the occasion.
54. *three*] Lussurioso's arithmetic is poor; 'one' would be more accurate.
56. *pullen*] poultry.
58. *terms*] the four terms of law-court sittings, Hilary, Easter, Trinity,
and Michaelmas.
61. *canvassed*] brought for investigation.
62. *Barbary*] outlandish, barbarous.

    much as pray but in law, that their sins may be removed
    with a writ of error, and their souls fetched up to heaven
    with a sasarara.   65

Luss. It seems most strange to me,
    Yet all the world meets round in the same bent;
    Where the heart's set, there goes the tongue's consent.
    How dost apply thy studies, fellow?

Vind. Study? Why, to think how a great rich man lies a-dying,   70
    and a poor cobbler tolls the bell for him; how he cannot
    depart the world, and sees the great chest stand before
    him when he lies speechless; how he will point you readily
    to all the boxes, and when he is past all memory, as the
    gossips guess, then thinks he of forfeitures and obliga-   75
    tions; nay, when to all men's hearings he whurls and
    rattles in the throat, he's busy threatening his poor ten-
    ants: and this would last me now some seven years' think-
    ing, or thereabouts. But I have a conceit a-coming in
    picture upon this, I draw it myself; which, i'faith la, I'll   80
    present to your honour. You shall not choose but like it,
    for your lordship shall give me nothing for it.

Luss. Nay, you mistake me then,

66. *Luss.*] *Symonds; Hip. Q.*   72. sees] *This ed.; see Q.*   77. rattles]
Q (rotles).   81–3. You . . . then] *so Q; as verse Collins, lines ending* Lordship / . . . then.

---

   64. *writ of error*] a writ brought to obtain the reversal of a judgment, on
grounds of error.

   65. *sasarara*] a variant of 'siserary', which is in turn an anglicization of
the Latin 'certiorari'. A writ of certiorari (= to be certified, or apprized)
is a writ issued by a superior court, on the complaint of someone that he
has not received justice in an inferior court. Here the superior court is that
of God.

   67. *bent*] tendency, but catching, too, the older sense of 'curve'.

   68.] a version of the proverb 'What the heart thinks the tongue speaks'
(Tilley, H334).

   75–6. *forfeitures and obligations*] legal terms meaning loss of estate or
goods, and bonds for the payment of money, in which a penalty is incurred
in case of non-payment. The rich man thinks of his lands and rents, but
the words also suggest perhaps what he owes to heaven.

   76. *whurls*] rumbles.

   79. *conceit*] witty device.

For I am publish'd bountiful enough.
Let's taste of your conceit.   85
Vind. In picture, my lord—
Luss. Ay, in picture.
Vind. Marry, this it is—A usuring father to be boiling in hell,
    and his son and heir with a whore dancing over him.
Hipp. [*Aside*] 'Has pared him to the quick.   90
Luss. The conceit's pretty, i'faith; but, take 't upon my life,
    'twill ne'er be liked.
Vind. No? Why, I'm sure the whore will be liked well enough.
Hipp. [*Aside*] Ay, if she were out o' th' picture, he'd like her
    then himself.   95
Vind. And as for the son and heir, he shall be an eyesore to no
    young revellers, for he shall be drawn in cloth of gold
    breeches.
Luss. And thou hast put my meaning in the pockets,
    And canst not draw that out. My thought was this: 100
    To see the picture of a usuring father
    Boiling in hell, our rich men would ne'er like it.
Vind. O true, I cry you heartily mercy; I know the reason, for
    some of 'em had rather be damned indeed than damned
    in colours.   105
Luss. [*Aside*] A parlous melancholy! 'Has wit enough
    To murder any man, and I'll give him means:—
    [*To him*] I think thou art ill-monied.
Vind.   Money? Ho, ho,

90. *Aside*] Dodsley *1; not in* Q.   91–2.] *so this ed.; as verse in* Q, *divided
at* ifaith, / But.   94. *Aside*] Dodsley *1; not in* Q.   103. heartily] Q
(heartly).   103–5.] *so* Q; *as verse* Symonds, *lines ending* mercy, / ... rather /
... colours.   106, 111. *Aside*] Symonds; *not in* Q.   108. *To him*] *This
ed.; not in* Q.

84. *publish'd*] well known to be.
90. *pared ... quick*] Hippolito thinks Vindice's words are sharp enough
to hurt, but Lussurioso is not sensitive enough to notice how horribly true
the image is of himself.
105. *in colours*] i.e., by being represented in a painting; but 'colours' also
means 'appearances'.
106. *parlous*] shrewd, biting.

'T has been my want so long, 'tis now my scoff.
I've e'en forgot what colour silver's of.   110
Luss. [*Aside*] It hits as I could wish.
Vind.   I get good clothes
    Of those that dread my humour, and for table-room,
    I feed on those that cannot be rid of me.
Luss. Somewhat to set thee up withal.   [*Gives him money.*]
Vind. O, mine eyes!
Luss.   How now, man?
Vind.   Almost struck blind;   115
    This bright unusual shine to me seems proud;
    I dare not look till the sun be in a cloud.
Luss. I think I shall affect his melancholy.
    How are they now?
Vind.   The better for your asking.
Luss. You shall be better yet, if you but fasten   120
    Truly on my intent. [*Beckons to Hippolito.*] Now y' are both
        present,
    I will unbrace such a close, private villain
    Unto your vengeful swords, the like ne'er heard of,
    Who hath disgrac'd you much, and injur'd us.
Hipp. Disgrac'd us, my lord?
Luss.   Ay, Hippolito.   125
    I kept it here till now that both your angers
    Might meet him at once.
Vind.   I'm covetous
    To know the villain.
Luss.   You know him, that slave-pander,
    Piato, whom we threatened last

114. *Gives . . . money.*] *Symonds; not in Q.*   121. *Beckons . . . Hippolito.*]
This ed.; not in Q   127. covetous] *Q (couetuous).*

---

118. *affect*] take a fancy to.
119. *they*] i.e., Vindice's eyes (l. 115).
122. *unbrace*] lay open.
126. *here*] in his mind. Perhaps he points to his head or heart.
128–9.] The flow of regular pentameters is jarred here by the combina-
tion 'slave-pander'; to preserve the metre, the line should end at 'slave-',
but the speech-rhythm hardly allows this.

With irons in perpetual prisonment.   130
Vind. [*Aside*] All this is I.
Hipp.   Is 't he, my lord?
Luss.   I'll tell you,
   You first preferr'd him to me.
Vind.   Did you, brother?
Hipp. I did indeed.
Luss.   And the ingrateful villain,
   To quit that kindness, strongly wrought with me,
   Being, as you see, a likely man for pleasure,   135
   With jewels to corrupt your virgin sister.
Hipp. O, villain!
Vind.   He shall surely die that did it.
Luss. I, far from thinking any virgin harm,
   Especially knowing her to be as chaste
   As that part which scarce suffers to be touch'd,   140
   Th' eye, would not endure him.
Vind.   Would you not,
   My lord? 'Twas wondrous honourably done.
Luss. But with some fine frowns kept him out.
Vind.   Out, slave!
Luss. What did me he, but, in revenge of that,
   Went of his own free will to make infirm   145
   Your sister's honour, whom I honour with my soul,
   For chaste respect; and not prevailing there
   (As 'twas but desperate folly to attempt it),
   In mere spleen, by the way, waylays your mother,

---

131. *Aside*] Dodsley 1; not in Q.   131-2. I'll ... me] *Oliphant; one line in Q.*   133. ingrateful] Q (ingreatfull).   141-2.] *so this ed.; divided in Q at* Lord, / 'Twas.   143. fine] *Collins;* fiue *Q.*

---

134. *quit*] repay.
wrought with] in modern usage, worked upon.
137. *He ... it*] doubly ironical, looking forward ultimately to the punishment that falls on Vindice himself.
144. *did me he*] Abbott, 220, says of such phrases, 'the *me* seems to appropriate the narrative of the action to the speaker, and to be equivalent to "mark *me*", "*I* tell you"'.
147. *For ... respect*] out of regard for chastity.

Whose honour being a coward, as it seems,   150
    Yielded by little force.

Vind.   Coward indeed!

Luss. He, proud of this advantage (as he thought),
    Brought me these news for happy; but I, Heaven
    Forgive me for 't—

Vind. What did your honour?

Luss.   In rage push'd him from me;   155
    Trampled beneath his throat, spurn'd him, and bruis'd;
    Indeed, I was too cruel, to say troth.

Hipp. Most nobly manag'd.

Vind. [*Aside*]   Has not Heaven an ear?
    Is all the lightning wasted?

Luss.   If I now
    Were so impatient in a modest cause,   160
    What should you be?

Vind.   Full mad; he shall not live
    To see the moon change.

Luss.   He's about the palace.
    Hippolito, entice him this way, that thy brother may
    take full mark of him.

Hipp. Heart, that shall not need, my lord. I can direct him   165
    so far.

Luss. Yet, for my hate's sake, go, wind him this way; I'll see
    him bleed myself.

---

152. this] *Dodsley 1;* their *Q.*   153–4. Brought . . . for 't] *so Collins; one
line in Q.*   158. Aside] *Dodsley 3; not in Q.*   158–9. Has . . . wasted]
so Oliphant; one line in Q.   159–60. If . . . cause] *so Oliphant; one line
in Q.*   163–71.] *so this ed.; divided in Q at* brother / May . . . him. /
Heart? . . . Lord, / I . . . sake, / Go, . . . selfe. / What . . . brother? / Nay . . .
brother? / An . . . sweare; *divided in Oliphant at* take / Full . . . lord: /
I . . . sake, / Go . . . myself. / What . . . will. / You're . . . swear.

---

153. *for happy*] as indicating success or good fortune.
   156. *Trampled . . . spurn'd him*] trampled on his body and kicked him.
Lussurioso's boasting exaggerations swell into absurdity here.
   160. *modest*] limited, small; cf. 'with modest paces', *H8,* IV. i. 82.
   164. *take . . . him*] observe him well.
   167. *wind*] entice.

Hipp. [*Aside*] What now, brother?

Vind. [*Aside*] Nay, e'en what you will; y' are put to 't, brother.   170

Hipp. [*Aside*] An impossible task, I'll swear,
    To bring him hither that's already here.   *Exit.*

Luss. Thy name, I have forgot it.

Vind.   Vindice, my lord.

Luss. 'Tis a good name, that.

Vind.   Ay, a revenger.

Luss. It does betoken courage; thou shouldst be valiant,   175
    And kill thine enemies.

Vind.   That's my hope, my lord.

Luss. This slave is one.

Vind.   I'll doom him.

Luss.   Then I'll praise thee;
    Do thou observe me best, and I'll best raise thee.

Enter HIPPOLITO.

Vind. Indeed, I thank you.

Luss.   Now, Hippolito,
    Where's the slave-pander?

Hipp.   Your good lordship would have
    A loathsome sight of him, much offensive.   181
    He's not in case now to be seen, my lord;
    The worst of all the deadly sins is in him,
    That beggarly damnation, drunkenness.

Luss. Then he's a double slave.

Vind. [*Aside*]   'Twas well convey'd,   185
    Upon a sudden wit.

Luss.   What, are you both

169, 170, 171. *Aside*] *Dodsley 1; not in* Q.   179-80. Now ... slave-pander]
Oliphant; one line in Q.   180-1. lordship ... have / A] *This ed.;* Lordship, / ... haue a Q.   185. *Aside*] *Collins; not in* Q.   185-6. 'Twas ...
wit] *so Oliphant; one line in* Q.

---

174. *revenger*] literally translating the Italian name; see above, p. 2.
178. *observe*] humour; cf. *Caes.*, IV. iii. 45.
182. *in case*] in a condition.
185. *convey'd*] carried off, managed.
186. *wit*] device.

Firmly resolv'd ? I'll see him dead myself.

Vind. Or else let not us live.

Luss.   You may direct

Your brother to take note of him.

Vind.   I shall.

Luss. Rise but in this, and you shall never fall.   190

Vind. Your honour's vassals.

Luss. [*Aside*]   This was wisely carried;

Deep policy in us makes fools of such:

Then must a slave die, when he knows too much.   *Exit.*

Vind. O, thou almighty patience! 'Tis my wonder

That such a fellow, impudent and wicked,   195

Should not be cloven as he stood, or with

A secret wind burst open.

Is there no thunder left, or is 't kept up

In stock for heavier vengeance ? There it goes !

[*Thunder sounds.*]

Hipp. Brother, we lose ourselves.

Vind.   But I have found it;   200

'Twill hold, 'tis sure; thanks, thanks to any spirit

That mingled it 'mongst my inventions.

Hipp. What is 't ?

Vind.   'Tis sound, and good; thou shalt partake it;

I'm hir'd to kill myself.

Hipp.   True.

Vind.   Prithee mark it:

And the old duke being dead, but not convey'd;   205

For he's already miss'd, too, and you know,

188–9. You . . . him] *so Oliphant; one line in Q.*   191. *Aside*] *Collins; not in Q.*   196–7. stood, or with / A] *Oliphant;* stood: / Or with a *Q.*   199.1. *Thunder sounds.*] *Collins; not in Q.*

199.1. Thunder sounds.] as God's sign of heavenly judgment: cf. v. iii. 42–3 and n.

200. *we . . . it*] Hippolito means that they have overreached themselves by promising to show Lussurioso the dead body of Piato-Vindice; but Vindice takes up his words as if to mean they had lost their way, and now he has 'found it'.

205. *convey'd*] made away with, disposed of.

      Murder will peep out of the closest husk.

Hipp. Most true.

Vind.   What say you then to this device,
      If we dress'd up the body of the duke ?

Hipp. In that disguise of yours ?

Vind.   Y' are quick, y' have reach'd it.

Hipp. I like it wondrously.   211

Vind. And being in drink, as you have publish'd him,
      To lean him on his elbow, as if sleep had caught him,
      Which claims most interest in such sluggy men ?

Hipp. Good yet, but here's a doubt: 215
      We, thought by th' duke's son to kill that pander,
      Shall, when he is known, be thought to kill the duke.

Vind. Neither, O thanks, it is substantial;
      For that disguise being on him, which I wore,
      It will be thought I, which he calls the pander, did kill   220
      the duke, and fled away in his apparel, leaving him so
      disguised to avoid swift pursuit.

Hipp. Firmer, and firmer.

Vind.   Nay, doubt not, 'tis in grain;
      I warrant it hold colour.

Hipp.   Let's about it.

Vind. But by the way, too, now I think on 't, brother,   225
      Let's conjure that base devil out of our mother.   *Exeunt.*

---

216. We] *Dodsley 1;* Me *Q.*   217. Shall] *Q^b;* Shalt *Q^a.*   223–4. Nay . . . colour] *Oliphant; one line in Q.*

   207.] proverbial; see Tilley, M1315.

   210. *reach'd*] understood.

   212. *publish'd*] proclaimed; cf. l. 84 above.

   214. *sluggy*] sluggish.

   218. *thanks*] to heaven, or to the 'spirit' of l. 201.

   substantial] soundly conceived.

   223. *in grain*] short for 'dyed in grain', fast dyed; this is another way of saying that the scheme is a sound one.

   226. *conjure*] expel; a proper word for the process of exorcism; cf. *Err.*, IV. iv. 51 ff.

[IV. iii]

> *Enter the* Duchess, *arm in arm with the* Bastard [SPURIO];
> *he seemeth lasciviously to* [look on] *her. After them, enter*
> SUPERVACUO, *running with a rapier; his brother* [AMBITIOSO]
> *stops him.*

Spurio. Madam, unlock yourself; should it be seen,
    Your arm would be suspected.
Duchess. Who is 't that dares suspect or this or these?
    May not we deal our favours where we please?
Spurio. I'm confident you may.   *Exeunt* [Duchess *and* SPURIO].
Ambit.   'Sfoot, brother, hold.   5
Super. Wouldst let the bastard shame us?
Ambit.   Hold, hold, brother;
    There's fitter time than now.
Super.   Now, when I see it?
Ambit. 'Tis too much seen already.
Super.   Seen and known;
    The nobler she's, the baser is she grown.
Ambit. If she were bent lasciviously, the fault   10
    Of mighty women that sleep soft—O death!
    Must she needs choose such an unequal sinner
    To make all worse?
Super.   A bastard, the duke's bastard!
    Shame heap'd on shame!
Ambit.   O, our disgrace!
    Most women have small waist the world throughout,   15
    But their desires are thousand miles about.

IV. iii. 0.2. *to look on her*] *Dodsley 1; to her Q.*   5. Duchess *and Spurio*]
Symonds; not in Q.   6. Wouldst] *Q* (Woult).   6–7. Hold . . . now]
Oliphant; one line in Q.   12. sinner] *Dodsley 1;* sinner: *Q.*   13–14. A . . .
shame] *Oliphant; one line in Q.*   15. waist] *Q* (waste); waists *Dodsley 1.*

IV. iii. 0.2. seemeth . . . her] Something appears to have been omitted
from this sentence in Q, and 'look on' is a reasonable guess.

    3. *or this or these*] either her arm, twined in his, or greater favours still,
perhaps kisses, which she here bestows on him.

    10. *bent lasciviously*] determined to be wanton.

    12. *unequal*] in rank and blood.

Super. Come, stay not here; let's after, and prevent;
     Or else they'll sin faster than we'll repent.   *Exeunt.*

[IV. iv]

> *Enter* VINDICE *and* HIPPOLITO, *bringing out their mother*
> [GRATIANA], *one by one shoulder, and the other by the other,*
> *with daggers in their hands.*

Vind. O thou, for whom no name is bad enough!
Grat. What means my sons ? What, will you murder me ?
Vind. Wicked, unnatural parent!
Hipp.   Fiend of women!
Grat. O, are sons turn'd monsters ? Help!
Vind.   In vain.
Grat. Are you so barbarous to set iron nipples   5
     Upon the breast that gave you suck ?
Vind.   That breast
     Is turn'd to quarled poison.
Grat. Cut not your days for 't; am not I your mother ?
Vind. Thou dost usurp that title now by fraud,
     For in that shell of mother breeds a bawd.   10
Grat. A bawd ? O name far loathsomer than hell!
Hipp. It should be so, knew'st thou thy office well.
Grat. I hate it.
Vind. Ah, is 't possible ? Thou only ? You powers on high,

17–18.] *Q*ᵇ; *lines transposed in Q*ᵃ.   18. *Exeunt.*] *Dodsley 2; after l. 16 in*
Q.

IV. iv. 0.1. *their*] *Q* (there).   2. *means*] *Q; mean Dodsley 2.*   3. *parent*]
Dodsley 1; parents Q.   12. knew'st] *Q*ᵇ (knewst); knowst *Q*ᵃ.   14.
Thou only] *so Thorndike; italicized in Q; omitted Dodsley 1.*   You powers]
Q; you heavenly powers Nicoll; Powers Symonds.

IV. iv. 2.] Cf. *Ham.*, III. iv. 21; this whole scene is indebted to the closet
scene in Shakespeare's play; see Intro., p. lxviii.
     5. *nipples*] Clearly they have set their daggers against her breast.
     7. *quarled*] ? curdled (so *O.E.D.*, citing this as the first of two examples,
and comparing the word 'quarred' from the verb 'quar', meaning to curdle).
     8. *Cut*] cut short (by being executed for murder); another allusion to
Exodus, xx. 12, following on that at II. ii. 97–8.
     12. *office*] duty; moral obligation as a mother.

That women should dissemble when they die!   15
Grat. Dissemble?
Vind.   Did not the duke's son direct
    A fellow of the world's condition hither,
    That did corrupt all that was good in thee?
    Made thee uncivilly forget thyself,
    And work our sister to his lust?
Grat.   Who, I?   20
    That had been monstrous! I defy that man
    For any such intent. None lives so pure,
    But shall be soil'd with slander—good son, believe it not.
Vind. O, I'm in doubt whether I'm myself, or no.
    Stay, let me look again upon this face.   25
    Who shall be sav'd when mothers have no grace?
Hipp. 'Twould make one half-despair.
Vind.   I was the man;
    Defy me now! let's see, do 't modestly!
Grat. O hell unto my soul!
Vind. In that disguise, I, sent from the duke's son,   30
    Tried you, and found you base metal,
    As any villain might have done.
Grat.   O no,
    No tongue but yours could have bewitch'd me so.
Vind. O nimble in damnation, quick in tune;
    There is no devil could strike fire so soon.   35
    I am confuted in a word.
Grat.   O sons,
    Forgive me; to myself I'll prove more true;

24.] *so Oliphant; two lines in Q, divided at* doubt, / Whether.   28. now!]
Collins; now? *Q.*   32–3. O ... so] *so Thorndike; one line in Q.*   36–7.
O ... true] *Oliphant; one line in Q.*

---

17. *the world's*] i.e., worldly; concerned with material ends.
19. *uncivilly*] barbarously.
20. *work*] make her yield; cf. I. iii. 144.
26. *grace*] virtue, as being under the divine influence of God's grace; cf.
l. 53.
34. *in tune*] to respond in harmony (with evil).

You that should honour me, I kneel to you.

> [*Kneels and weeps.*]

Vind. A mother to give aim to her own daughter!

Hipp. True, brother; how far beyond nature 'tis,   40
  Though many mothers do 't.

Vind. Nay, and you draw tears once, go you to bed;
  Wet will make iron blush, and change to red.
  Brother, it rains; 'twill spoil your dagger, house it.

Hipp. 'Tis done.   45

Vind. I'faith, 'tis a sweet shower, it does much good.
  The fruitful grounds and meadows of her soul
  Has been long dry: pour down, thou blessed dew,
  Rise, mother; troth, this shower has made you higher.

Grat. O you heavens,   50
  Take this infectious spot out of my soul,
  I'll rinse it in seven waters of mine eyes!
  Make my tears salt enough to taste of grace!
  To weep is to our sex naturally given;
  But to weep truly, that's a gift from heaven.   55

Vind. Nay, I'll kiss you now; kiss her, brother.
  Let's marry her to our souls, wherein's no lust,
  And honourably love her.

Hipp.   Let it be.

Vind. For honest women are so seld and rare,

38.1. *Kneels . . . weeps.*] *Symonds; not in Q.*   40. 'tis] Q^b; to't Q^a.   43.
Wet . . . iron] Q^c; Wee . . . you Q^a; Wet . . . you Q^b.   48. Has] *Q;* Have
Dodsley 1.   50–1.] *so this ed.; one line in Q.*   52. rinse] *Q* (rence).

---

39. *give aim to*] in archery, to guide the aim of the shooter; so here the
idea is of Gratiana steering Castiza to 'aim' her charms at Lussurioso.

42. *you . . . you*] addressing his dagger.

47–8. *grounds . . . Has*] See Abbott, 335; such apparently false concords,
with the third person of the verb ending in -*s*, are common in Elizabethan
usage: cf. IV. i. 47–8 and n.

51. *infectious*] infected, diseased; a common meaning.

53. *grace*] quibbling, perhaps, on the meaning 'pleasantness of flavour'
(*O.E.D.*, sb. 1).

58. *Let it be*] i.e., let it be so, let us do as you say.

59. *seld*] infrequent; the word is the modern 'seldom', but used in a way
now obsolete, as an adjective.

'Tis good to cherish those poor few that are.   60
O you of easy wax, do but imagine,
Now the disease has left you, how leprously
That office would have cling'd unto your forehead;
All mothers that had any graceful hue
Would have worn masks to hide their face at you.   65
It would have grown to this: at your foul name,
Green-colour'd maids would have turn'd red with shame.

Hipp. And then our sister, full of hire and baseness.

Vind. There had been boiling lead again.
The duke's son's great concubine, a drab of state,   70
A cloth o' silver slut, to have her train
Borne up, and her soul trail i' th' dirt—great!

Hipp. To be miserably great; rich to be
Eternally wretched.

Vind.   O common madness!
Ask but the thriving'st harlot in cold blood,   75
She'd give the world to make her honour good.
Perhaps you'll say, but only to th' duke's son,
In private; why, she first begins with one
Who afterward to thousand proves a whore:
Break ice in one place, it will crack in more.   80

Grat. Most certainly applied.

Hipp. O brother, you forget our business.

70–4.] *so this ed.; divided in Q at* Concubine: / A . . . slut, / To . . . great. /
To . . . wretched. / O . . . madness.   70. The duke's] Q^b; Dukes Q^a.
73. To be] Q^b; Too Q^a.

---

61. *easy wax*] as opposed to 'hard wax', or sealing wax, and so meaning
pliable, as easily manipulated.

62–3. *how . . . forehead*] Cf. *Ham.*, III. iv. 42–4, 'takes off the rose / From
the fair forehead of an innocent love, / And sets a blister there'.

64. *graceful*] quibbling on 'grace' as divine influence; cf. l. 53.

67. *Green-colour'd*] i.e., 'green' as young and inexperienced.

68. *hire*] payment for services (as a whore).

74. *wretched*] close enough in sound to 'rich' for the quibble to strike
home.

80.] This line is marked as a 'sentence', and looks proverbial, but is not
listed by Tilley.

Vind. And well remember'd. Joy's a subtle elf;
    I think man's happiest when he forgets himself.
    Farewell, once dry'd, now holy-water'd mead;   85
    Our hearts wear feathers, that before wore lead.
Grat. I'll give you this, that one I never knew
    Plead better for, and 'gainst, the devil than you.
Vind. You make me proud on 't.
Hipp. Commend us in all virtue to our sister.   90
Vind. Ay, for the love of heaven, to that true maid.
Grat. With my best words.
Vind.   Why, that was motherly said.
               Exeunt [VINDICE *and* HIPPOLITO].
Grat. I wonder now what fury did transport me.
    I feel good thoughts begin to settle in me.
    O, with what forehead can I look on her,   95
    Whose honour I've so impiously beset?
    And here she comes.

             [*Enter* CASTIZA.]

Cast. Now mother, you have wrought with me so strongly,
    That what for my advancement, as to calm
    The trouble of your tongue, I am content.   100
Grat. Content, to what?
Cast.   To do as you have wish'd me;
    To prostitute my breast to the duke's son,
    And put myself to common usury.
Grat. I hope you will not so.
Cast.   Hope you I will not?

---

85. *dry'd*] *Q* (dryed); *dry Dodsley 1.*   92.1. *Vindice and Hippolito*]
Symonds; not in Q.   97.1. *Enter Castiza.*] *Dodsley 2; not in Q.*

---

   83. *subtle elf*] spirit that works imperceptibly.
   87–9.] nicely illustrating Vindice's moral ambiguity; see Intro., p. xxxi.
   95. *forehead*] Cf. II. ii. 163, and l. 63 above.
   99. *what for . . . as*] an elliptical usage; 'what for' (= on account of) is
here extended to mean 'as much for'.
   103. *usury*] gain made by lending out her body; but cf. II. ii. 99 ('use'
could mean employment for sexual purposes).

That's not the hope you look to be sav'd in.   105
Grat. Truth, but it is.
Cast.   Do not deceive yourself;
 I am as you e'en out of marble wrought.
 What would you now? Are ye not pleas'd yet with me?
 You shall not wish me to be more lascivious
 Than I intend to be.
Grat.   Strike not me cold.   110
Cast. How often have you charg'd me, on your blessing,
 To be a cursed woman? When you knew
 Your blessing had no force to make me lewd,
 You laid your curse upon me: that did more;
 The mother's curse is heavy; where that fights,   115
 Suns set in storm, and daughters lose their lights.
Grat. Good child, dear maid, if there be any spark
 Of heavenly intellectual fire within thee,
 O, let my breath revive it to a flame;
 Put not all out, with woman's wilful follies.   120
 I am recover'd of that foul disease
 That haunts too many mothers; kind, forgive me,
 Make me not sick in health. If then

116. Suns] *Symonas;* Sonnes *Q.* 118–19.] *so Dodsley 2; divided in Q at* breath, / Reuiue. 122. kind, forgive] *Dodsley 1;* kinde forgiue *Q.*

107.] Castiza seems to mean, 'I am now in such a state as you wrought out of my former marble', or 'I am now as pliable as you would wish'.

116. *Suns . . . lights*] As the word 'daughters' enforces the play on 'sons', so 'suns' enforces the play on 'lights' as meaning heavenly bodies, the sun, moon, and stars (see *Genesis*, i. 16).

118. *intellectual*] spiritual; what is apprehended by the intellect, as distinct from the senses.

121–2. *disease . . . mothers*] playing on 'mother' meaning hysteria, then thought of as a disease: cf. II. i. 126, 243.

122. *kind*] perhaps used absolutely to mean 'kind one' (as one might say 'dear'), and suggesting too the sense 'of my own kind or kin', for she is addressing a close relative. Alternatively, if the punctuation of Q is correct, Gratiana may be turning from Castiza to speak generally, saying 'let kind, i.e., Nature, forgive me', so reflecting on the 'unnatural task' (II. i. 85) she had performed in tempting her daughter. For 'kind' in this sense, *O.E.D.* cites N. Fairfax, *Treatise* (1674), 'Those bounds that Dame Kind before had pitcht upon'.

My words prevail'd when they were wickedness,
How much more now when they are just and good!   125
Cast. I wonder what you mean; are not you she
For whose infect persuasions I could scarce
Kneel out my prayers, and had much ado,
In three hours' reading, to untwist so much
Of the black serpent as you wound about me?   130
Grat. 'Tis unfruitful, held tedious to repeat
What's past; I'm now your present mother.
Cast. Push, now 'tis too late.
Grat.   Bethink again,
Thou know'st not what thou say'st.
Cast.   No? Deny
Advancement, treasure, the duke's son?
Grat.   O see,   135
I spoke those words, and now they poison me.
What will the deed do then?
Advancement, true: as high as shame can pitch!
For treasure: who e'er knew a harlot rich?
Or could build by the purchase of her sin   140
An hospital to keep their bastards in?
The duke's son? O, when women are young courtiers,
They are sure to be old beggars:
To know the miseries most harlots taste,
Thou'dst wish thyself unborn, when thou art unchaste.   145

---

131. held] *Q;* child, *Collins.*   131-2. repeat / ... past; I'm] *Symonds;*
repeate ... past, / Ime *Q.*   133-5.] *so this ed.; divided in Q at* late, /
Bethinke ... sayst. / No ... sonne. / O.   135-6. O ... me] *so this ed.; one
line in Q.*   141. their] *Q;* her *Symonds.*   141-3.] *so Symonds; two lines
in Q, divided at* sonne, / Oh.

---

127. *infect*] tainted.
132. *I'm ... mother*] i.e., I really am your mother now. The word 'present'
can also mean 'ready (to help)'.
133. *Bethink*] consider.
136. *spoke ... words*] at II. i. 160.
140. *purchase*] profit.
141. *hospital*] orphanage, or institution for children to be brought up in,
as in the surviving name of the school, 'Christ's Hospital', founded in 1552.

Cast. O mother, let me twine about your neck,
  And kiss you till my soul melt on your lips;
  I did but this to try you.
Grat.   O, speak truth!
Cast. Indeed, I did but,
  For no tongue has force to alter me from honest.   150
  If maidens would, men's words could have no power;
  A virgin honour is a crystal tower,
  Which, being weak, is guarded with good spirits;
  Until she basely yields, no ill inherits.
Grat. O happy child! Faith, and thy birth hath sav'd me. 155
  'Mongst thousand daughters, happiest of all others,
  Be thou a glass for maids, and I for mothers.   *Exeunt.*

149–50.] *so this ed.; one line in* Q. 149. but] *Symonds;* not Q. 157. Be]
Dodsley 2; Buy Q.

---

 150. *honest*] virtuous.
 151. *would*] should choose or desire (to be honest).
 154. *inherits*] takes possession, dwells there. *O.E.D.* first records this
sense in Tourneur's *Transformed Metamorphosis* (1600), l. 6, 'O where can
life celestial inherit / If it remain not in a heav'nly spirit'; but see also
Middleton, *Blurt Master Constable* (1602), I. ii. 39.
 155. *happy*] blessed.
 157. *glass*] mirror.

Act V

Enter VINDICE *and* HIPPOLITO [*with the body of the Duke dressed in
Vindice's disguise; they arrange the body to look like a sleeping man*].

Vind. So, so, he leans well; take heed you wake him not,
    brother.

Hipp. I warrant you, my life for yours.

Vind. That's a good lay, for I must kill myself. Brother, that's
    I; that sits for me; do you mark it? And I must stand   5
    ready here to make away myself yonder—I must sit to
    be killed, and stand to kill myself. I could vary it not so
    little as thrice over again; 't has some eight returns, like
    Michaelmas term.

Hipp. That's enow, o' conscience.   10

Vind. But sirrah, does the duke's son come single?

Hipp. No, there's the hell on 't; his faith's too feeble to go
    alone. He brings flesh-flies after him, that will buzz
    against supper-time, and hum for his coming out.

Vind. Ah, the fly-flap of vengeance beat 'em to pieces! Here   15
    was the sweetest occasion, the fittest hour, to have made

ACT V, SCENE i] *Collins; not in Q.*   0.1–2. *with . . . man*] *This ed., after
Symonds; not in Q.*   4–5.] *so Oliphant; as verse in Q, lines ending* my
selfe? / . . . it.   5. sits] *Q;* fits *Collins.*   12. faith's] *Q^b;* faith *Q^a.*

---

   v. i. 4. *lay*] bet.

   4–5. *that's I*] referring to the duke's body.

   8. *returns*] i.e., ways of describing the same situation. Properly 'returns'
were the reports of a sheriff on writs directed to him by a court of law;
hence the word came to mean the days on which such reports were to be
made. In Michaelmas Term there were eight such days.

   13. *flesh-flies*] properly blow-flies, that eat and lay eggs in dead flesh; a
gruesome image for Lussurioso's followers, suggesting a linkage with the
dead body of the duke.

   my revenge familiar with him; shown him the body of
the duke his father, and how quaintly he died, like a politician in hugger-mugger, made no man acquainted with
it; and in catastrophe, slain him over his father's breast;   20
and O, I'm mad to lose such a sweet opportunity.

Hipp. Nay, push, prithee be content; there's no remedy present. May not hereafter times open in as fair faces as this?

Vind. They may, if they can paint so well.

Hipp. Come, now to avoid all suspicion, let's forsake this   25
room, and be going to meet the duke's son.

Vind. Content; I'm for any weather. Heart! step close, here
he comes.

Enter LUSSURIOSO.

Hipp. My honoured lord!

Luss. O me! you both present?   30

Vind. E'en newly, my lord, just as your lordship entered now.
About this place we had notice given he should be, but in
some loathsome plight or other.

Hipp. Came your honour private?

Luss. Private enough for this; only a few   35
Attend my coming out.

Hipp. [*Aside*] Death rot those few!

Luss.   Stay, yonder's the slave.

Vind. Mass, there's the slave indeed, my lord.

---

17. shown] *This ed.;* show *Q.*   18. died] *Q*^b*;* did *Q*^a*.*   20. slain] *Q*
(slaine)*;* slay *Collins.*   37. *Aside*] *Scott; not in Q.*

---

18. *quaintly*] ingeniously.

18–20. *died . . . it*] Cf. Middleton, *Phoenix* (printed 1607), I. vi. 71,
'Would he die so like a politician, and not once write his mind to me?'
'Politician' here is used in its earliest, rather sinister, sense of 'crafty in-
triguer', a kind of man who would do things 'in hugger-mugger', i.e., in
secret.

20. *in catastrophe*] in conclusion, or at the end of a tragedy; Vindice is
dramatizing the situation to himself; see Intro., p. xxviii and n.

24. *paint*] as with cosmetics: cf. III. v. 63–5 and n.

27. *I'm . . . weather*] proverbial; Tilley, C421.

step close] keep out of sight: cf. *Mac.*, V. i. 19.

[*Aside*] 'Tis a good child; he calls his father slave.

Luss. Ay, that's the villain, the damn'd villain. Softly,   40
    Tread easy.

Vind.   Puh, I warrant you, my lord,
    We'll stifle in our breaths.

Luss.   That will do well.
    Base rogue, thou sleep'st thy last. [*Aside*] 'Tis policy
    To have him kill'd in 's sleep, for if he wak'd
    He would betray all to them.

Vind.   But my lord—   45

Luss. Ha? what say'st?

Vind.   Shall we kill him now he's drunk?

Luss. Ay, best of all.

Vind. Why, then he will ne'er live to be sober.

Luss. No matter, let him reel to hell.

Vind. But being so full of liquor, I fear he will put out all the   50
    fire.

Luss. Thou art a mad beast.

Vind. [*Aside*] And leave none to warm your lordship's golls
    withal,—for he that dies drunk falls into hellfire like a
    bucket o' water, qush, qush.   55

Luss. Come, be ready, nake your swords, think of your
    wrongs. This slave has injured you.

Vind. Troth, so he has: [*Aside*] and he has paid well for 't.

Luss. Meet with him now.

---

39. *Aside*] Dodsley *1; not in* Q.   41–2. Puh . . . breaths] *so* Oliphant; *one
line in* Q.   43. *Aside*] Oliphant; *not in* Q.   52. beast] Q^a; brest Q^b.
53, 58. *Aside*] *This ed.; not in* Q.   56. nake] Q^b; make Q^a.

---

52. *beast*] The corrector of Q seems to have introduced an error in alter-
ing to 'breast' here, for although this word can be defended as equivalent
to the heart, meaning the repository of feelings and thought, it does not
fit the context at all well, and I have therefore preferred the uncorrected
reading.

53. *golls*] hands.

55. *qush*] presumably a form of 'quash', meaning 'to make a splashing
noise' (*O.E.D., v.* 5).

56. *nake*] unsheathe (make naked).

59. *Meet . . . him*] encounter him (as an enemy); cf. *1H4*, IV. iv. 13.

Vind. You'll bear us out, my lord?   60

Luss. Puh, am I a lord for nothing, think you? Quickly now.

              [*Vindice and Hippolito stab the Duke's body.*]

Vind. Sa, sa, sa; thump. There he lies.

Luss. Nimbly done. Ha! O, villains, murderers,

    'Tis the old duke my father!

Vind.   That's a jest.

Luss. What, stiff and cold already?   65

    O, pardon me to call you from your names;

    'Tis none of your deed:—that villain Piato,

    Whom you thought now to kill, has murder'd him,

    And left him thus disguis'd.

Hipp.   And not unlikely.

Vind. O rascal! Was he not asham'd   70

    To put the duke into a greasy doublet?

Luss. He has been cold and stiff, who knows how long?

Vind. [*Aside*] Marry, that do I!

Luss. No words, I pray, of anything intended.

Vind. O, my lord.   75

Hipp. I would fain have your lordship think that we have
    small reason to prate.

Luss. Faith, thou say'st true. I'll forthwith send to court

    For all the nobles, bastard, duchess, all;

    How here, by miracle, we found him dead,   80

    And in his raiment that foul villain fled.

Vind. That will be the best way, my lord, to clear us all; let's
    cast about to be clear.

Luss. Ho, Nencio, Sordido, and the rest.

    Enter all [*his followers, among them* SORDIDO *and* NENCIO].

61.1. *Vindice . . . body.*] *This ed.; not in Q.*   73. *Aside*] *Dodsley 1; not in*
Q.   79. duchess, all;] *Q; Duchess; tell Dodsley 1.*   82–3.] *so Q; as*
verse Symonds, divided at Lord, / To.   84.1. *his . . . Nencio*] *This ed.; not*
in Q.

---

   60. *bear us out*] support us.
   62. *Sa, sa, sa*] said to represent the French exclamation 'ça, ça, ça', once
used by fencers when delivering a thrust; cf. *Lr.*, IV. vi. 205.
   66. *from your names*] i.e., by names remote from those you deserve.

Sord. My lord.   85
Nencio. My lord.
Luss. Be witnesses of a strange spectacle:
    Choosing for private conference that sad room,
    We found the duke my father geal'd in blood.
Sord. My lord the duke?—run, hie thee, Nencio,   90
    Startle the court by signifying so much.   [*Exit* NENCIO.]
Vind. [*Aside*] Thus much by wit a deep revenger can,
    When murder's known, to be the clearest man.
    We're furthest off, and with as bold an eye
    Survey his body as the standers-by.   95
Luss. My royal father, too basely let blood
    By a malevolent slave.
Hipp. [*Aside*]   Hark,
    He calls thee slave again.
Vind. [*Aside*]   'Has lost, he may.
Luss. O sight! Look hither, see, his lips are gnawn
    With poison.
Vind.   How, his lips? By th' mass, they be.   100
Luss. O villain! O rogue! O slave! O rascal!
Hipp. [*Aside*] O good deceit; he quits him with like terms!

    [*Enter* Nobles, *preceding* AMBITIOSO *and* SUPERVACUO.]

1. Noble. Where?
2. Noble. Which way?

85, 90. *Sord.*] *This ed.;* 1. *Q.*   86. *Nencio.*] *This ed.;* 2. *Q.*   91. *Exit*
Nencio.] *Harrier; not in Q.*   92. *Aside*] *Symonds; not in Q.*   97, 98.
Aside] *Dodsley 1; not in Q.*   97–8. Hark . . . again] *so this ed.; one line in*
Q.   99–100. O . . . poison] *so Symonds; one line in Q.*   102. *Aside*]
Symonds; not in Q.   102.1. Enter . . . Supervacuo.] *Symonds; not in Q.*
103, 104. *1. Noble, 2. Noble.*] 1., 2. *Q (so throughout scene).*

---

  89. *geal'd*] congealed.
  92. *can*] can do, as commonly; cf. *Troil.*, II. ii. 135, and Abbott, 307.
  93. *clearest*] most innocent; or, here, free from suspicion.
  102. *quits*] pays him back. Hippolito thinks of him as addressing not the
murderer of the duke, but the duke himself, who once called Lussurioso
'villain, traitor' (II. iii. 15).

Ambit. Over what roof hangs this prodigious comet   105
    In deadly fire ?
Luss.   Behold, behold, my lords,
    The duke my father's murder'd by a vassal,
    That owes this habit, and here left disguis'd.

        [*Enter* Duchess *and* SPURIO.]

Duchess. My lord and husband!
2. Noble. Reverend majesty!
1. Noble.   I have seen these clothes,   110
    Often attending on him.
Vind. [*Aside*]   That nobleman
    Has been i' th' country, for he does not lie.
Super. [*To Ambitioso*] Learn of our mother, let's dissemble too;
    I am glad he's vanish'd—so, I hope, are you ?
Ambit. [*To Supervacuo*] Ay, you may take my word for 't.
Spurio. [*Aside*]   Old dad dead ?
    I, one of his cast sins, will send the fates   116
    Most hearty commendations by his own son;
    I'll tug in the new stream, till strength be done.

106–8. Behold . . . disguis'd] *so Oliphant; as prose in Q.*   108.1. *Enter . . .*
Spurio.] *Dodsley 2; not in Q.*   110–11. I . . . him] *so this ed.; one line in Q.*
110. clothes] *Q* (cloths).   111. *Aside*] *Symonds; not in Q.*   111–12.
That . . . lie] *so this ed.; one line in Q.*   113. *To Ambitioso*] *This ed.; not*
in Q.   115. *To Supervacuo*] *This ed.; not in Q.*   *Aside*] *Oliphant; not*
in Q.

---

105. *prodigious*] ominous.

comet] This looks forward to the actual appearance of a comet in v. iii,
but I take it that Ambitioso here speaks in metaphor, in general reference
to the calamity.

106. *deadly*] fatal, as boding death.

108. *owes*] owns.

111–12. *That . . . lie*] Alluding to the proverbial associations of the court
with deceit (cf. Tilley, C718, 724), and of truth with simplicity, which is
found in the country (cf. Tilley, T575, 571).

116–17.] Spurio here seems to point forward to v. iii. 54, where he kills
Ambitioso.

118. *tug . . . stream*] tug as at an oar, i.e., contend or strive, in the new
movement of events.

Luss. Where be those two that did affirm to us
    My lord the duke was privately rid forth ?   120
1. Noble. O, pardon us, my lords; he gave that charge
    Upon our lives, if he were miss'd at court,
    To answer so. He rode not anywhere;
    We left him private with that fellow here.
Vind. [*Aside*] Confirm'd.
Luss.   O heavens, that false charge was his death!
    Impudent beggars! durst you to our face   126
    Maintain such a false answer ? bear him straight
    To execution.
1. Noble.   My lord!
Luss.   Urge me no more.
    In this, the excuse may be call'd half the murder.
Vind. You've sentenc'd well.
Luss.   Away, see it be done.   130
                [*Exit* First Noble, *guarded.*]
Vind. [*Aside*] Could you not stick ? see what confession doth!
    Who would not lie, when men are hang'd for truth ?
Hipp. [*To Vindice*] Brother, how happy is our vengeance!
Vind. [*To Hippolito*]   Why, it hits
    Past the apprehension of indifferent wits.
Luss. My lord, let post-horse be sent into all places to entrap 135
    the villain.
Vind. [*Aside*] Post-horse, ha, ha!
2. Noble. My lord, we're something bold to know our duty.

---

125. *Aside*] Symonds; not in Q.   127-8. Maintain . . . execution] *so Thorn-dike; one line in Q.*   130.1. *Exit . . . guarded.*] *This ed.; not in Q.*   131. *Aside*] Symonds; not in Q.   133. To Vindice, To Hippolito] *This ed.; not in Q.*   133-4. Why . . . wits] *so Collins; one line in Q.*   135-6.] *so this ed.; as verse in Q, divided at* sent, / Into.   137. *Aside*] Dodsley 1; not in Q.   138. 2. Noble.] *This ed.; Nob. Q; 1st Noble. Symonds.*

---

125. *Confirm'd*] Vindice is congratulating himself on the success of his plot to make others appear guilty of the duke's murder, and the word carries two meanings, both 'True enough' (i.e., I can corroborate that) and 'My innocence is confirmed'.
    131. *stick*] stop talking.
    134. *wits*] intellects.
    135. *post-horse*] speedy couriers on horseback.

Your father's accidentally departed;
The titles that were due to him meet you.   140
Luss. Meet me ? I'm not at leisure, my good lord.
I've many griefs to despatch out o' th' way :—
[*Aside*] Welcome, sweet titles! [*To them*] Talk to me, my lords,
Of sepulchres, and mighty emperors' bones;
That's thought for me.
Vind. [*Aside*]   So one may see by this   145
How foreign markets go:
Courtiers have feet o' th' nines, and tongues o' th' twelves;
They flatter dukes, and dukes flatter themselves.
2. Noble. [*To Lussurioso*] My lord, it is your shine must comfort us.
Luss. Alas, I shine in tears, like the sun in April.   150
Sord. You're now my lord's grace.
Luss. My lord's grace ? I perceive you'll have it so.
Sord. 'Tis but your own.
Luss. Then heavens give me grace to be so.
Vind. [*Aside*] He prays well for himself.
3. Noble. [*To the Duchess*]   Madam, all sorrows   155
Must run their circles into joys. No doubt but time
Will make the murderer bring forth himself.
Vind. [*Aside*] He were an ass then, i'faith.
3. Noble.   In the mean season,

---

143. *Aside*] Dodsley 1; *not in* Q.   *To them*] *This ed.; not in* Q.   145.
Aside] Symonds; *not in* Q.   149. *2. Noble.*] Symonds; *Nob.* Q.   *To
Lussurioso*] *This ed.; not in* Q.   151, 153. *Sord.*] *This ed.; Nobl.* Q.   151.
You're] Q (*Your*).   155, 158. *Aside*] Dodsley; *not in* Q.   155, 158, 164.
3. Noble.] *This ed.; Nob(l).* Q; *1st Noble.* Symonds.   155. *To the Duchess*]
This ed.; not in Q.

---

139. *accidentally*] by a chance event, and not as a result of a plot against
him.

145–6. *one . . . go*] The proverb 'You may know by the market men how
the markets go' (Tilley, M676) perhaps helps to explain Vindice's point,
that as the new duke behaves, so his courtiers will follow suit. I cannot
explain 'foreign', except as a jest for, and a means of distancing the action
from, a London audience.

147. *feet . . . twelves*] Nicoll explains this as referring to sizes of shoes:
their feet take size nine shoes, but their flattering tongues are three sizes
larger.

Let us bethink the latest funeral honours
Due to the duke's cold body—and, withal,   160
Calling to memory our new happiness
Spread in his royal son. Lords, gentlemen,
Prepare for revels.
Vind. [*Aside*] Revels?
3. Noble.   Time hath several falls;
Griefs lift up joys, feasts put down funerals.   165
Luss. Come then, my lords; my favours to you all.
    [*Aside*] The duchess is suspected foully bent;
    I'll begin dukedom with her banishment!
                      Exeunt LUSSURIOSO, Nobles, *and* Duchess.
Hipp. [*To Vindice*] Revels!
Vind. [*To Hippolito*]   Ay, that's the word; we are firm yet.
    Strike one strain more, and then we crown our wit.   170
                      Exeunt VINDICE *and* HIPPOLITO.
Spurio. [*Aside*] Well, have at the fairest mark!—so said the
    duke when he begot me—
    And if I miss his heart, or near about,
    Then have at any; a bastard scorns to be out.   [*Exit.*]

162. Spread] *Q;* Speed *Symonds.*   164, 167. Aside] *Symonds; not in Q.*
168.1. Lussurioso] *Thorndike;* Duke *Q.*   169. To Vindice, To Hippolito]
This ed.; not in Q.   170.1. Exeunt . . . Hippolito.] *Thorndike;* Exeu. Bro.
Q.   171. Aside] *Oliphant; not in Q.*   have at] *Dodsley 1;* haue *Q.*
174. Exit.] *Symonds; not in Q.*

---

159. *bethink*] consider; cf. IV. iv. 133.
    latest] last.
164. *falls*] The point is clear—cf. the proverb 'Times change' (Tilley,
T343, 340)—although the meaning of this word is uncertain: perhaps
fashions, or changes, by metaphor from the article of clothing, the veil or
collar known as a 'fall' (so Nicoll); or moments of being thrown down,
suggested by 'falls' in wrestling; or hinting of autumns, seasons of decline
and decay.
165. *Griefs . . . funerals*] i.e., griefs make joy the greater, and feasts dispel
the sadness of funerals: cf. *Ham.,* I. ii. 12.
169. *firm*] secure, unsuspected.
170. *Strike . . . strain*] sound one tune, or theme; cf. V. ii. 1.
171. *mark*] target; i.e., Lussurioso, the new duke.
174. *out*] out of office or sway: cf. *Lr.,* V. iii. 15.

Super. Note'st thou that Spurio, brother ?   175
Ambit. Yes, I note him to our shame.
Super. He shall not live, his hair shall not grow much longer;
    in this time of revels, tricks may be set afoot. See'st thou
    yon new moon ? It shall outlive the new duke by much;
    this hand shall dispossess him, then we're mighty.   180
    A masque is treason's licence, that build upon;
    'Tis murder's best face when a vizard's on.   *Exit.*
Ambit. Is 't so ? 'Tis very good.
    And do you think to be duke then, kind brother ?
    I'll see fair play; drop one, and there lies t'other.   *Exit.*   185

[v. ii]

    Enter VINDICE *and* HIPPOLITO *with* PIERO *and other* Nobles.

Vind. My lords, be all of music; strike old griefs
    Into other countries,
    That flow in too much milk, and have faint livers,
    Not daring to stab home their discontents.
    Let our hid flames break out, as fire, as lightning,   5
    To blast this villainous dukedom, vex'd with sin;
    Wind up your souls to their full height again.

175, 177. *Super.*] *Q; Amb. Nicoll.*   175. Note'st] *Q* (Not'st).   176,
183. *Ambit.*] *Q* (*And., l. 183*); *Sup. Nicoll.*   183. 'Tis] *Dodsley 1;* 'ts *Q.*

v. ii. 0.1. Nobles] *This ed.; Lords Q.*   1–2. My . . . countries] *so Oliphant;
one line in Q.*

---

181. *masque*] a dance by men disguised and masked or vizarded, a common form of entertainment at great feasts. For the idea of using a masque
to engineer the climax of his play, the author is probably indebted to
Marston's *Antonio's Revenge*; see Intro., p. xxi.

    v. ii. 1. *strike*] quibbling on the sense 'play (a tune)': cf. v. i. 170.
    3. *flow . . . milk*] are not manly enough: cf. *Lr.*, I. iv. 342.
    livers] The liver was commonly imaged as the seat of passion, and hence
of courage (as 'white-livered' means 'cowardly').
    7. *Wind . . . again*] The idea is of becoming braced for action; perhaps
echoing Marston, *Antonio's Revenge*, IV. iii (M.S.R., l. 1672), 'wind up
invention / Unto his highest bent'. Cf. I. iii. 142 above.

Piero. How?

1. Noble.   Which way?

2. Noble.   Any way; our wrongs are such,
    We cannot justly be reveng'd too much.

Vind. You shall have all enough;—revels are toward,   10
    And those few nobles that have long suppress'd you
    Are busy'd to the furnishing of a masque,
    And do affect to make a pleasant tale on 't;
    The masquing suits are fashioning; now comes in
    That which must glad us all—we to take pattern   15
    Of all those suits, the colour, trimming, fashion,
    E'en to an undistinguish'd hair almost;
    Then, ent'ring first, observing the true form,
    Within a strain or two we shall find leisure
    To steal our swords out handsomely,   20
    And when they think their pleasure sweet and good,
    In midst of all their joys, they shall sigh blood.

Piero. Weightily, effectually.

3. Noble. Before the t'other maskers come—

Vind. We're gone, all done and past.   25

Piero. But how for the duke's guard?

Vind.   Let that alone;
    By one and one their strengths shall be drunk down.

Hipp. There are five hundred gentlemen in the action,
    That will apply themselves, and not stand idle.

Piero. O, let us hug your bosoms!

8. *2. Noble.*] Symonds (*2nd Lord.*); *3.* Q.

---

13. *affect*] pretend.
    tale] the fiction or allegory of the masque.
    17. *undistinguish'd hair*] a hair which cannot be separated out and observed by itself. The phrase 'to a hair', meaning 'to a nicety', 'with the utmost exactness', occurs in *Troil.*, III. i. 137 (the first example listed in *O.E.D.*).
    18. *form*] order of the dance.
    19. *strain*] i.e., of music.
    24. *t'other*] a common form, still in dialectal use: cf. *Ham.*, II. i. 56.
    27. *drunk down*] quenched or overcome by drinking.

Vind.   Come, my lords,   30
   Prepare for deeds, let other times have words.   *Exeunt.*

[v. iii]

In a dumb show, the possessing of the young Duke [LUSSURIOSO] *with
all his* Nobles; *then sounding music. A furnished table is brought forth;
then enters the* Duke *and his* Nobles *to the banquet. A blazing star
appeareth.*

1. Noble. Many harmonious hours, and choicest pleasures,
   Fill up the royal numbers of your years.
Luss. My lords, we're pleas'd to thank you,—though we know
   'Tis but your duty now to wish it so.
1. Noble. That shine makes us all happy.
3. Noble.   His grace frowns.   5
2. Noble. Yet we must say he smiles.
1. Noble.   I think we must.
Luss. [*Aside*] That foul, incontinent duchess we have banish'd;
   The bastard shall not live. After these revels,
   I'll begin strange ones; he and the stepsons
   Shall pay their lives for the first subsidies.   10
   We must not frown so soon, else 't had been now.

v. iii. 1, 5. *1. Noble.*] Dodsley 1; Nob(le). Q.   7. *Aside*] Symonds; not in Q.

31.] proverbial: cf. Tilley, W797, 820, 'Not words, but deeds'.

v. iii. 0.1–4.] There are two entries here, first the dumb-show of the
installation of Lussurioso, who then enters a second time with his nobles
to the banquet.

0.1. *possessing*] establishment in authority; presumably the new duke
is formally throned, and the nobles do homage.

0.3. *blazing star*] This could be an anticipatory direction, for the star is
not noticed until l. 15. How the flare (l. 19) was managed we do not know,
but a blazing star seems to have been a traditional effect at the open-air
theatres of the time; see Chambers, *E.S.*, III. 76, 110.

5. *shine*] smiling aspect. The image of the ruler as the sun is commonplace: cf. *Cym.*, v. v. 474.

10. *subsidies*] i.e., instalments of the retribution I mean to exact; properly
sums of money granted by parliament to the sovereign for special needs,
usually, in the reign of James I, taking the form of a tax on lands or goods.

11. *else . . . now*] i.e., otherwise I would have to arrange their deaths now.

1. Noble. My gracious lord, please you prepare for pleasure;
   The masque is not far off.
Luss.   We are for pleasure.
   Beshrew thee, what art thou? thou made'st me start!
   Thou hast committed treason:—a blazing star!   15
1. Noble. A blazing star? O, where, my lord?
Luss.   Spy out.
2. Noble. See, see, my lords, a wondrous dreadful one.
Luss. I am not pleas'd at that ill-knotted fire,
   That bushing, flaring star,—am not I duke?
   It should not quake me now. Had it appear'd   20
   Before, it I might then have justly fear'd;
   But yet they say, whom art and learning weds,
   When stars wear locks, they threaten great men's heads.
   Is it so? you are read, my lords.
1. Noble.   May it please your grace,
   It shows great anger.
Luss.   That does not please our grace.   25
2. Noble. Yet here's the comfort, my lord; many times,
   When it seems most, it threatens farthest off.
Luss. Faith, and I think so, too.

14. thou made'st . . . start!] *Thorndike;* madst . . . start? *Q.*   19. bushing]
Q; blushing *Scott.*   flaring] *Q;* staring *Collins.*   20–1. appear'd / Before, it I] *Collins;* appeard, / Before it, I *Q.*   21. it] *Q;* omitted *Dodsley 1.*
23. wear] *Q* (were).   27. most] *Q;* most near *Dodsley 1.*

---

14. *thou*] i.e., the blazing star.
   15. *treason . . . star*] A comet was thought to bode death: see v. i. 105–6,
and *Caes.,* II. ii. 30.
   16. *Spy out*] In what direction they look we cannot tell, but as they are
at a banquet, they presumably pretend to look out of an imaginary window
at a real firework.
   19. *bushing*] describing the comet's 'tail': *O.E.D.* cites Fleming's con-
tinuation of Holinshed's *Chronicles* (1587), III. 1314, 'There appeared a
blazing star in the south, bushing toward the east'.
   20. *quake*] cause to tremble.
   22. *art . . . weds*] i.e., who combine practical skill and learning.
   23.] It was a common superstition that comets, or stars with a trail of
'hair' ('crystal tresses' in Shakespeare's phrase, *1H6,* I. i. 3), boded death
to princes: see *Sh. England,* I. 452.
   24. *read*] well-read, learned.

1. Noble.   Beside, my lord,
    You're gracefully establish'd, with the loves
    Of all your subjects; and for natural death,   30
    I hope it will be threescore years a-coming.
Luss. True? no more but threescore years?
1. Noble. Fourscore I hope, my lord.
2. Noble.   And fivescore, I.
3. Noble. But 'tis my hope, my lord, you shall ne'er die.
Luss. Give me thy hand, these others I rebuke;   35
    He that hopes so, is fittest for a duke;
    Thou shalt sit next me. Take your places, lords;
    We're ready now for sports, let 'em set on.
    You thing, we shall forget you quite anon!
3. Noble. I hear 'em coming, my lord.

> *Enter the masque of revengers, the two brothers* [VINDICE
>   *and* HIPPOLITO], *and two* Lords *more.*

Luss. [*Aside*]   Ah, 'tis well;   40
    Brothers, and bastard, you dance next in hell.

> *The revengers dance;*
> *at the end, steal out their swords, and these four kill the four*
>   *at the table in their chairs. It thunders.*

Vind. Mark, thunder! Dost know thy cue, thou big-voic'd cryer?
    Dukes' groans are thunder's watchwords.
Hipp.   So, my lords,
    You have enough.
Vind.   Come, let's away; no ling'ring.
Hipp. Follow. Go!   *Exeunt* [*all the maskers but* VINDICE].   45

40. *Aside*] *Symonds; not in Q.*   42.] *so Oliphant; two lines in Q, divided at*
Thunder? / Dost.   43–4. So ... enough] *so Oliphant; one line in Q.*   45.
Exeunt] *so Dodsley 2; after l. 44 in Q.*   *all ... Vindice*] *Thorndike; not in Q.*

---

36. *fittest*] i.e., the fittest companion.
39. *thing*] the star, which must still be visible.
42–3. *thunder ... watchwords*] This use of thunder as, so to speak, the
voice of God, has its origin in the Bible; see *Job*, xxvi. 14. The immediate
suggestion, however, may have come from *Lr*, III. ii, etc. See also IV. ii.
199 above.

Vind. No power is angry when the lustful die;

    When thunder claps, heaven likes the tragedy.   *Exit.*

Luss. O, O!

Enter the other masque of intended murderers, stepsons [AMBITIOSO
and SUPERVACUO], *Bastard* [SPURIO], *and a* Fourth Man, *coming
in dancing. The* Duke [LUSSURIOSO] *recovers a little in voice, and
groans—calls,* 'A guard! Treason!'
*At which, they all start out of their measure, and turning towards the
table, they find them all to be murdered.*

Spurio. Whose groan was that?

Luss. Treason! A guard!

Ambit.   How now, all murder'd?

Super.   Murder'd! 50

4. Noble. And those his nobles!

Ambit.   Here's a labour sav'd,

    I thought to have sped him. 'Sblood, how came this?

Super. Then I proclaim myself; now I am duke.

51. *4. Noble.*] Q (4.); *3rd Noble.* Symonds.   53. *Super.*] *Fluchère; Spur.*
Q.

---

47. *claps*] suggesting heavenly applause.

52. *sped*] killed.

53–5.] Q is confusing here, for it lacks stage-directions, and has the
speech-heading *Spu.* at l. 53; this must be an error, for the bastard could
hardly proclaim himself duke. The obvious correction, of what looks to be
a compositor's misreading, is to alter *Spu* to *Super*, as suggested by C. S.
Napier, *T.L.S.*, 13 March 1937, and Clifford Leech, *R.E.S.*, XVII (1941),
335–6. It makes sense if Supervacuo speaks here, to be stabbed by Ambitioso, who is killed by Spurio, who is, in turn, slain by the 4th Noble.
However, Ambitioso claimed at III. i. 13 and at III. vi. 19 to be heir, and,
to make for consistency, Nicoll altered the speech-headings in the passage
v. i. 175–83 (see collation), exchanging the speeches assigned in Q to Supervacuo and Ambitioso, who says, in Q, 'do you thinke to be Duke then,
kinde brother:'. E. M. Waith, *M.L.N.*, LVII (1942), 119–21, went further
and proposed to re-assign the speeches here in v. iii, so as to give Ambitioso
the whole of 'Here's a labour . . . now I am Duke', ll. 51–3, and Supervacuo
the phrase, 'Thou Duke? Brother, thou liest.', l. 54. This seems to me to
be pressing the idea of consistency too far; Ambitioso and Supervacuo are
much alike; each is anxious to be duke, and to be rid of the other (see III.
i. 13–14; III. vi. 19–20; v. i. 184–5), and either might claim the dukedom
here, for their rivalry in villainy is what matters to the audience. I have

Ambit. Thou duke? Brother, thou liest.   [*Stabs Supervacuo.*]

Spurio.   Slave, so dost thou.

                                      [*Stabs Ambitioso.*]

4. Noble. Base villain, hast thou slain my lord and master?   55

                                      [*Stabs Spurio.*]

    Enter [VINDICE, HIPPOLITO, *and the other*] *first masquers.*

Vind. Pistols! Treason! Murder! Help, guard my lord
    The duke.

               [*Enter* ANTONIO *with a* Guard.]

Hipp.   Lay hold upon this traitor.

                [*The Guard seizes the Fourth Noble.*]

Luss.   O!

Vind. Alas, the duke is murder'd.

Hipp.   And the nobles.

Vind. Surgeons, surgeons! [*Aside*] Heart, does he breathe so long?

Ant. A piteous tragedy, able to make   60
    An old man's eyes bloodshot.

Luss. O!

Vind. Look to my lord the duke. [*Aside*] A vengeance throttle
    him!—

    Confess, thou murderous and unhallow'd man,
    Didst thou kill all these?

4. Noble.   None but the bastard, I.   65

Vind. How came the duke slain, then?

4. Noble.   We found him so.

Luss. O, villain!—

---

54. *Stabs Supervacuo.*] *Fluchère; not in* Q.   54.1. *Stabs Ambitioso.*]
Symonds; not in Q.   55.1. *Stabs Spurio.*] *Symonds; not in* Q.   55.2.
Vindice . . . other] *so Symonds; not in* Q.   masquers] *this ed.;* men Q.
56–7. Pistols . . . duke] *so this ed.; one line in* Q.   57.1. *Enter . . .* Guard.]
Symonds; not in Q.   57. this] Q; these *Dodsley.*   traitor] *Collins;*
Traytors Q.   57.2. *The . . . Noble.*] *Harrier; not in* Q.   59, 63. *Aside*]
Dodsley 1; not in Q.   60. make] *Dodsley 2;* wake Q.

---

therefore followed Fluchère in emending only the one obvious error, the
speech-heading *Spu.* at l. 53.

Vind. Hark!

Luss.   —Those in the masque did murder us.

Vind. Law you now, sir;—

O marble impudence! will you confess now ?   70

4. Noble. 'Sblood, 'tis all false.

Ant.   Away with that foul monster,

Dipp'd in a prince's blood.

4. Noble.   Heart, 'tis a lie!

Ant. Let him have bitter execution.

[*Exit the* Fourth Noble, *guarded.*]

Vind. New marrow! No, I cannot be express'd.

How fares my lord the duke ?

Luss.   Farewell to all;   75

He that climbs highest has the greatest fall.

My tongue is out of office.

Vind.   Air, gentlemen, air!

[*Whispering in his ear*] Now thou'lt not prate on 't, 'twas

Vindice murder'd thee,—

Luss. O!

Vind.   —murder'd thy father,—

Luss.   O!   [*Dies.*]

Vind.   —and I am he.

Tell nobody. [*To the others*] So, so, the duke's departed.   80

Ant. It was a deadly hand that wounded him;

The rest, ambitious who should rule and sway,

After his death were so made all away.

Vind. My lord was unlikely.

71. 'Sblood] *Dodsley 1;* Sloud *Q;* 'Slud *Collins.*   73.1. *Exit . . . guarded.*]
Harrier; not in Q.   78. *Whispering . . . ear*] *Symonds; not in Q.*   79.
Dies.] *Dodsley 2; not in Q.*   79–80. and . . . departed] *so this ed.; one line
in Q.*   80. *To the others*] *This ed.; not in Q.*

69. *Law you*] a common exclamation, like 'La you', *Tw. N.,* III. iv. 95.
74. *marrow*] figuratively, delicious food for his revenge.
be express'd] put my feelings into words.
76.] proverbial; see Tilley, C414.
84. *unlikely*] not fit (to be duke). This line is a syllable short, and it is
possible that a word has dropped out, or that 'unlikely' is a compositor's
misreading.

Hipp.　　　　　　　　　　Now the hope
　　Of Italy lies in your reverend years.　　　　　　　85
Vind.　Your hair will make the silver age again,
　　When there was fewer but more honest men.
Ant.　The burden's weighty, and will press age down;
　　May I so rule that heaven may keep the crown.
Vind.　The rape of your good lady has been quited　　90
　　With death on death.
Ant.　　　　　　　　Just is the law above!
　　But, of all things, it puts me most to wonder
　　How the old duke came murder'd.
Vind.　　　　　　　　　　　　O, my lord.
Ant.　It was the strangeliest carried, I not heard of the like.
Hipp.　'Twas all done for the best, my lord.　　　　95
Vind.　All for your grace's good. We may be bold to speak it
　　now; 'twas somewhat witty carried, though we say it.
　　'Twas we two murdered him.
Ant.　You two?
Vind.　None else, i'faith, my lord; nay, 'twas well manag'd.　100
Ant.　Lay hands upon those villains.
　　　　　　　　[*The Guard seize Vindice and Hippolito.*]
Vind.　　　　　　　　　How? on us?
Ant.　Bear 'em to speedy execution.
Vind.　Heart, was 't not for your good, my lord?
Ant.　　　　　　　　　　　My good?

89. may keep] *Dodsley 1;* nay keepe *Q.*　94. I] *Q;* I've *Dodsley 1.*　96–8.]
so Oliphant; as verse in Q, lines ending now, / . . . it. / . . . him.　101.1. *The
. . . Hippolito.*] *This ed.; not in Q.*　102. to] *Q* (two).　103–4. My . . .
he] *so Oliphant; one line in Q.*

　86. *silver age*] See IV. i. 35 and n.
　87. *honest*] virtuous.
　89. *keep*] protect.
　90. *quited*] paid for.
　94. *carried*] managed.
　　not heard] a construction more common in the present tense (Abbott)
305), but cf. *Ant.*, II. ii. 39, 'It not concern'd me'.
　97. *witty*] cleverly; the adjective used as an adverb, a common practice:
see Abbott, I.

Away with 'em! Such an old man as he;
You that would murder him would murder me.   105
Vind. Is 't come about?
Hipp.   'Sfoot, brother, you begun.
Vind. May not we set as well as the duke's son?
    Thou hast no conscience; are we not reveng'd?
    Is there one enemy left alive amongst those?
    'Tis time to die, when we are ourselves our foes.   110
    When murd'rers shut deeds close, this curse does seal 'em:
    If none disclose 'em, they themselves reveal 'em.
    This murder might have slept in tongueless brass,
    But for ourselves, and the world died an ass.
    Now I remember, too, here was Piato brought forth a   115
    knavish sentence once: no doubt, said he, but time will
    make the murderer bring forth himself. 'Tis well he
    died, he was a witch.
    And now, my lord, since we are in for ever,
    This work was ours, which else might have been slipp'd,   120
    And, if we list, we could have nobles clipp'd,
    And go for less than beggars; but we hate

---

111. murd'rers] *Dodsley 1;* murders *Q.*   115–18.] *so this ed.; as verse in*
Q, lines ending Piato / . . . time / . . . himselfe? / . . . witch; *in Oliphant,*
lines ending Piato / . . . doubt / (Said he) / . . . forth / . . . witch.

---

106. *come about*] turned out this way, happened so; but with a sense of
change or reversal; cf. IV. i. 37.
107. *set . . . son*] The quibble on 'son' enforces the idea of setting, or
dying, like the sun; cf. IV. iv. 116.
108. *conscience*] sense of what is right.
111–12.] varying the common proverb 'Murder will out', Tilley, M1315.
113. *brass*] alluding to the common use of brass for memorial tablets to
the dead in churches.
115–17. *Now . . . himself*] The 'sentence', or wise saying, is a variant of
the common proverb, 'Time brings truth to light' (Tilley, T324, 333).
118. *witch*] wizard (as foreseeing what would happen).
119. *are in*] involved in the business: cf. *LLL.,* IV. iii. 16.
120. *slipp'd*] allowed to pass unnoticed.
121. *nobles clipp'd*] presumably referring to the lords who joined with
them in the revenge-masque, l. 39.1–2; 'clipp'd' is a playful way of alluding to execution, as if it were the clipping, or mutilation, of the gold coins
called nobles, worth 6s. 8d.

To bleed so cowardly. We have enough, i'faith;
We're well, our mother turn'd, our sister true;
We die after a nest of dukes. Adieu.   125
     Exeunt [VINDICE *and* HIPPOLITO, *guarded*].
Ant. How subtilly was that murder clos'd! Bear up
  Those tragic bodies; 'tis a heavy season.
  Pray heaven their blood may wash away all treason!   *Exeunt*.

FINIS.

123–4. enough, i'faith; / We're] *Oliphant;* ynough, / Yfaith, we're *Q.*
125.1. *Vindice . . . guarded*] *so Oliphant; not in Q.* 128. *Exeunt*] *Oliphant;*
Exit Q.

---

124. *turn'd*] converted.
126. *clos'd*] kept out of sight.

APPENDIX A

William Painter's *The Palace of Pleasure*

The story reprinted here is taken from *The Palace of Pleasure* (1566–7), edited by Joseph Jacobs (1890), II. 75–80. His text, here modernized, was copied from the edition of 1575.

Painter's novel is a pretty close translation of the twelfth novel of the second day in the *Heptameron* of Marguerite of Navarre; and the story it tells is based on historical events, for it describes the assassination of Alessandro de' Medici, which took place in 1537. The tale of this duke's attempt to seduce a virtuous woman, and to make her brother help him to satisfy his lust, has links both with the attempt of Lussurioso to seduce Castiza through the agency of Vindice (*The Revenger's Tragedy*, I. iii; II. i), and with the duke's hiring of Vindice to 'greet him with a lady' (III. v). Alessandro was murdered in the bed where he expected to find the girl, and in the play the duke is murdered in the 'unsunned lodge' where he is expecting an assignation with a lady.

The incontinency of a duke, and of his impudency to attain his purpose, with the just punishment which he received for the same.

In the city of Florence (the chiefest of all the Tuscan) there was a duke that married the Lady Margaret the bastard daughter of the Emperor Charles the fifth. And because she was very young, it was not lawful for him to lie with her, but, tarrying till she was of riper years, he entertained and used her like a noble gentleman. And who, to spare his wife, was amorous of certain other gentlewomen of the city. Amongst whom he was in love with a very fair and wise gentlewoman, that was sister to a gentleman, a servant of his, whom the duke loved so well as himself, to whom he gave so much authority in his house, as his word was so well obeyed and feared as the duke's himself, and there was no secret thing in the duke's mind, but he declared the same unto him, who might full well have been called a second himself. The duke, seeing his sister to be a woman of great honesty, had no ways or means to utter unto her the love that he bare her; after he had invented all occasions possible, at length he came to this gentleman which he loved so well, and said unto him: 'My friend, if there were anything in all the world wherein I were able to pleasure thee, and would not do it at thy request, I should be afraid to say my fantasy, and much ashamed to crave your help and assistance: but the love is such which I bare thee, as, if I had a wife, mother or daughter, that were able to save thy life, I would rather employ them, than to suffer thee to die in torment: and if thou do bear unto me that affection, which am thy master, think verily that I do bear unto thee the like. Wherefore I will disclose unto thee such a secret and privy matter, as the silence thereof hath brought me into such plight as thou seest, whereof I do look for none amendment but by death, or by the service which thou mayest do me, in a certain matter which I purpose to tell thee.' The gentleman, hearing the reasons of his master, and seeing his face not fained, but all besprent with tears, took great compassion upon him and said, 'My lord, I am your humble servant: all the goods and worship that I have doth come from you. You may say unto me as to your most approved friend. Assure yourself, that all which resteth in my power and ability is already at your commandment.' Then the duke began to tell him of the love that he bare unto his sister, which was of such force as, if by his means he did not enjoy her, his life could not long continue. For he said that he knew right well that entreaty and presents were with her of no regard. Wherefore he prayed him that, if he loved his life so well as he did his, to find means for him to receive that benefit, which without him he was in despair never to recover. The brother, which loved his sister and honour of his kindred more than the duke's pleasure, made a certain reverence unto him, humbly beseeching him to use his travail and pain in all other causes saving in that, because it was a suit so slanderous and infamous, as it would purchase dishonour to his whole family, adding further, that neither his heart nor his honour could serve him to consent to do that service. The duke, inflamed with unspeakable fury, put his finger between his teeth, and, biting of the nail, said unto him in great rage, 'Well then, sith I find in thee no friendship, I know what I have to do.' The gentleman, knowing the cruelty of his master, being sore afraid, replied, 'My lord, for so much as your desire is vehement and earnest, I will speak unto her, and bring you answer of her mind.' And as he was departing, the duke said unto him, 'See that you tender my life as thou wilt that I shall do thine.' The gentleman, understanding well what that word did mean, absented himself a day or twain to advise what were best to be done. And amongst divers his cogitations, there came to his remembrance the bounden duty which he did owe to his master, and the goods and honours which he had received at his hands; on the other side, he considered the honour of his house, the good life and chastity of his sister, who (he knew well) would never consent to that wickedness, if by subtlety she were not surprised, or otherwise forced, and that it were a thing very strange and rare, that he should go about to defame himself and the whole stock of his progeny. Wherefore he concluded, that better it were for him to die, than to commit a mischief so great unto his sister, which was one of the honestest women in all Italy. And therewithal considered how he might deliver his country from such a tyrant, which by force would blemish and spot the whole race of his ancient stock and family. For he knew right well that, except the duke were taken away, the life of him and his affinity could not be in security and safeguard: wherefore, without motion made to his sister of that matter, he devised how to save his life and the reproach that should follow. Upon the second day he came unto the duke, and told him in what sort he had practised with his sister and that, although the same in the beginning was hard and difficult, yet in the end he made her to consent, upon condition that he would keep the same so secret as none but himself and he might know of it. The duke, desirous and glad of those news, did soon believe him, and embracing the messenger, promised to give him whatsoever he would demand, praying him with all speed that he might enjoy his desired purpose. Whereupon they appointed a time; and to demand whether the duke were glad and joyful of the same, it were superfluous. And when the desired night was come, wherein he hoped to have the victory of her whom he thought invincible, he and the gentleman alone withdrew themselves together, not forgetting his perfumed coif and sweet shirt wrought and trimmed after the best manner. And when each wight was gone to bed, both they repaired to the appointed lodging of his lady, where, being arrived, they found a chamber in decent and comely order. The gentleman, taking off the duke's night-gown, placed him in the bed, and said unto him, 'My lord, I will now go seek her, which cannot enter into this chamber without blushing, howbeit I trust before to-morrow morning she will be very glad of you.' Which done, he left the duke, and went into his own chamber, where he found one of his servants alone, to whom he said, 'Hast thou the heart to follow me into a place where I shall be revenged upon the greatest enemy that I have in the world?' 'Yea, sir,' answered his man. Whereupon the gentleman took him with him so suddenly, as he had no leisure to arm himself with other weapon but with his only dagger. And when the duke heard him come again, thinking he had brought her with him that he loved so dearly, he drew the curtain, and opened his eyes to behold and receive that joy which he had so long looked for, but in place of seeing her which he hoped should be the conversation of his life, he saw the acceleration of his death, which was a naked sword that the gentleman had drawn, who therewithal did strike the duke, which was in his shirt void of weapon, although well armed with courage, and sitting up in his bed, grasped the gentleman about the body, and said, 'Is this thy promise which thou hast kept ?' And seeing that he had no other weapon but his teeth and nails, he bit the gentleman in the arm, and by force of his own strength he so defended himself, as they both fell down into the floor. The gentleman, fearing the match, called for his man, who, finding the duke and his master fast together, drew them both by the feet into the midst of the chamber, and with his dagger assayed to cut the duke's throat. The duke defended himself till such time as the loss of his blood made him so weak and feeble that he was not able to contend any longer. Then the gentleman and his man laid him again into his bed, where they accomplished the effect of that murder. Afterwards, drawing the curtain, they departed and locked the dead body in the chamber. And when he saw that he had gotten the victory of his enemy, by whose death he thought to set at liberty the common-wealth, he supposed his fact to be unperfect if he did not the like to five or six of them which were nearest to the duke, and best beloved of him. And to attain the perfection of that enterprise, he bade his man to do the like unto them one after another, that he had done to the duke. But the servant, being nothing hardy or courageous, said unto his master, 'Methinks, sir, that for this time ye have done enough, and that it were better for you now to devise way how to save your life, than to seek means to murder any more. For if we do consume so long space of time to kill every of them, as we have done in murdering of the duke, the daylight will discover our enterprise before we have made an end, yea, although we find them naked and without defence.' The gentleman, whose evil conscience made him fearful, did believe his servant, and, taking him alone with him, went to the bishop that had in charge the gates of the city, and the use of the posts, to whom he said, 'This evening (my lord) news came unto me that mine own brother lieth at the point of death, and craving licence of the duke to go see him, he hath given me leave. Wherefore I beseech you command the posts to deliver me two good horse, and that you will send word to the porter than the gates may be opened.' The bishop, which esteemed no less his request than the command-ment of the duke his master, incontinently gave him a billet, by virtue whereof both the gates were opened, and the horse made ready according to his demand. And under colour and pretence of visiting his brother, he rode to Venice, where, after he had cured himself of the duke's bitings fastened in his flesh, he travelled into Turkey. In the morning, the duke's servants, seeing the time so late before their master returned, suspected that he was gone forth in visiting of some lady, but when they saw he tarried so long, they began to seek for him in every place. The poor duchess, into whose heart the love of her husband strongly did invade, understanding that he could not be found, was very pensive and sorrowful. But when the gentleman which he so dearly loved was not likewise seen abroad, search was made in his chamber, where, finding blood at the chamber door, they entered in; but no man was there to tell them any news, and following the tract of the blood, the poor servants of the duke went to the chamber door, where he was, which door they found fast locked, who incontinently brake open the same; and seeing the place all bloody, drew the curtain, and found the wretched carcass of the duke lying in the bed, sleeping his endless sleep. The sorrow and lamentation made by the duke's servants, carrying the dead body into his palace, is easy to be conjectured. Whereof, when the bishop was advertised, he repaired thither, and told how the gentleman was gone away in the night in great haste, under pretence to go to see his brother; whereupon it was evidently known that it was he that had committed the murder. And it was proved that his poor sister was never privy to the fact, who, although she was astonished with the suddenness of the deed, yet her love towards her brother was far more increased, because he had delivered her from a prince so cruel, the enemy of her honesty; for doing whereof he did not stick to hazard his own life. Whereupon she persevered more and more in virtue, and although she was poor, by reason her house was confiscate, yet both her sister and she matched with so honest and rich husbands as were to be found in Italy; and afterwards they both lived in good and great reputation.

APPENDIX B

Heliodorus, *Æthiopica*

The episode printed here is an extract from the *Æthiopica* as translated by Thomas Underdown (1587); I have taken it from the edition by Charles Whibley (Tudor Translations, 1895), pp. 20–1. Cnemon's invasion of his father's bedchamber in the expectation of taking his stepmother in adultery closely resembles the sequence in the play where Lussurioso rushes into the duke's bedchamber, expecting to find his stepmother in bed with Spurio (II. ii. 160–II. iii. 28). In both texts the father behaves in the same way, first praying for mercy, and then, as the son stands 'amazed', calling for his arrest. The spelling of the original is modernized.

[Cnemon is telling the story of his life. He relates that his stepmother, Demeneta, fell violently in love with him, and tried to seduce him. When he repulsed her attempts, she sought to revenge herself on him, and sent her maid, Thisbe, to give him false information. Thisbe led him to believe that his stepmother was practising adultery, and that he might take her in bed with the adulterer.]

Yes (said she) if you will, I will deliver the adulterer to you, even in the deed doing. If you will so do (quoth I) you shall do me a pleasure. With all my heart (said she) not only for your own sake, who hath been injured by her tofore, but for mine also . . . wherefore, if thou be a man, apprehend him. I promised her I would so do, and she for that time went her way. About three nights after, she came, and waked me out of my sleep, and told me that an adulterer was come in, and that my father upon occasion suddenly was gone into the country, and he, according to appointment, was gone to bed to Demeneta, therefore it was expedient for me to haste to be revenged, and put on my sword, that the knave might not escape. I did so, and taking my sword in my hand, followed those which carried a candle before, and went to the bed chamber. When I came near the door, and perceived the glimmering of a candle through the slivers and the doors locked: Very angry as I was, brake up the doors, and ran in crying out, where is that same villain, the worthy lover of this chaste Dame?

Which when I had said, I came to the bed in mind to slay them both, but therewith my Father (O God) leapt out of the bed, and falling on his knees, before me, said, My son, have pity upon thy Father, spare his white hairs, that hath brought thee up. We have done thee wrong indeed, yet not so great that therefore with death thou shouldest be revenged on me. Give not so much to thy wrath, neither by thy Father's blood imbrue thy hands. This with much more spake my father, humbly upon his knees, desiring me to save his life. But I, as I had been stricken with a thunderbolt, stood still amazed, and looked round about after Thisbe, who had I know not how conveyed herself away, neither had one word to say, neither could I tell, what was best to do, and in this case my sword fell out of my hands, which Deme-neta straightway caught up, and my father, then out of danger, laid hands upon me, and commanded me to be bound.

Index to Annotations

An asterisk before a word indicates information which supplements or corrects that given in *O.E.D.* The index generally lists the form of a word that appears in the text, but the basic form is given where it makes for greater ease of reference, or for the grouping together of more than one occurrence of a word.

quit-rent, I. i. 39
quittance, *vb*, III. v. 200
*qush, V. i. 55

Ragged, III. v. 154
raise, I. iii. 123
rare, I. iii. 23, II. ii. 21
rase, IV. i. 24
ravel, II. ii. 68
ravished, II. i. 194
reach, *vb*, I. i. 82, IV. ii. 210
read, *p. ppl.*, V. iii. 24
receive, II. ii. 38
refine, III. v. 78
relation, I. iv. 40
remember, I. iii. 40
repugnant, I. iii. 98
respect, *sb.*, III. iv. 78, IV. ii. 147
returns, *sb.*, V. i. 8
revenue, II. ii. 72
rich, II. i. 173–4
ride, *vb*, III. v. 182, IV. i. 82
right, I. i. 94
—— honourable, II. i. 46
——, too much, I. ii. 80
rim, I. iii. 62
riots, III. v. 15
rod, II. i. 223
room, I. iv. 32
rough, make, I. ii. 166
rub, *vb*, III. v. 212
rushes, II. ii. 82

Sa, sa, sa, V. i. 62
salt water, III. iv. 58
sasarara, IV. ii. 65
saver, I. iv. 54
savour, III. vi. 57
scarlet, *sb.*, II. iii. 105
scrivener, I. iii. 48
sea, full, II. ii. 136
season, II. ii. 10
secretary, I. i. 129, IV. ii. 9
seem, IV. iii. 0. 2
seen (ne'er be seen in 't), II. i. 66
seld, IV. iv. 59
self-affecting, III. v. 84
'sessed, I. ii. 65
set by, III. i. 8

'sfoot, III. vi. 10
shades, II. i. 156
shadow, *vb*, II. ii. 161
*shadowing, III. v. 39
shape, III. v. 16
*shell, III. v. 46
shifts, IV. ii. 2
shine, *sb.*, V. iii. 5
short, I. ii. 184
siftings, I. iii. 22
sign, *sb.*, I. ii. 142, III. iv. 78, III. v.
112
silver age, IV. i. 35, V. iii. 86
—— ceiling, III. v. 4
simple, I. iii. 139
sirrah, III. vi. 93
sisters, II. ii. 144
sitting, *vbl sb.*, III. iv. 36
skin, III. i. 7
slavish, III. v. 160
slight, IV. i. 65
slip, III. vi. 5, V. iii. 120
slobbering, III. v. 165
'slud, I. iii. 165, III. iv. 10
sluggy, IV. ii. 214
socket, out of the, II. iii. 44
sold, bought and, III. i. 6
some, I. ii. 99, II. i. 102, II. iii. 76
son-in-law, I. ii. 24
sound, *adj.*, II. iii. 78, III. iii. 17,
III. iv. 27
speak, I. i. 91
speed, *vb*, IV. i. 67, V. iii. 52
spirit, I. iii. 92
spleen, II. iii. 93, IV. i. 62
spurn, IV. ii. 156
spy out, V. iii. 16
square out, II. i. 152
stand on 't, IV. ii. 47
star, blazing, V. iii. 0.3, 15
stars wear locks, V. iii. 23
start, *vb*, II. ii. 159
state, II. i. 95
step close, V. i. 27
stick, *vb*, V. i. 131
still, III. iv. 19
stinted, III. iv. 59
stirring, I. ii. 181, II. i. 200
stoops, III. v. 37